The Shakespearean Stage is the only authoritative book that describes all the main features of the original staging of Shakespearean drama in one volume: the acting companies and their acting styles, the playhouses, the staging and the audiences. For twenty years it has been hailed as not only the most reliable but the liveliest and most entertaining overview of Shakespearean theatre available to undergraduates.

For this third edition Professor Gurr has thoroughly revised the book, bringing it right up to date and incorporating many new discoveries, including those of the archaeologists at the sites of the Rose and the Globe theatres. The invaluable appendix, which lists all the plays performed at a particular play-house, the playing company and date of performance, has also been revised and rearranged.

The Shakespearean Stage
1574–1642

The Shakespearean Stage 1574–1642

Third Edition

ANDREW GURR
Professor of English
University of Reading

CAMBRIDGE UNIVERSITY PRESS

Cambridge
New York   Port Chester   Melbourne   Sydney

Published by the Press Syndicate of the University of Cambridge
The Pitt Building, Trumpington Street, Cambridge CB2 1RP
40 West 20th Street, New York, NY 10011-4211, USA
10 Stamford Road, Oakleigh, Victoria 3166, Australia

First published 1992

Printed in Great Britain at the University Press, Cambridge

British Library cataloguing in publication data
Gurr, Andrew
The Shakespearean stage 1574–1642 – 3rd ed.
1. England. Theatre, history 1574–1642
I. Title
792.0942

Library of Congress cataloguing in publication data
Gurr, Andrew
The Shakespearean stage, 1574–1642 / Andrew Gurr. – 3rd ed.
p. cm.
Includes bibliographical references and index.
ISBN 0-521-41005-3. – ISBN 0-521-42240-x (pbk)
1. Shakespeare, William, 1564–1616 – Stage history – To 1625.
2. Shakespeare, William, 1564–1616 – Stage history – 1625–1800.
3. Shakespeare, William, 1564–1616 – Stage history – England.
4. Theatre – England – History – 16th century.   5. Theatre – England –
History – 17th century.   I. Title.
PR3095.G87   1991
792'.0942 – dc20   91-6385 CIP

ISBN 0 521 41005 3 hardback
ISBN 0 521 42240 x paperback

Contents

𝓎𝓎𝓎

Illustrations

Preface to Second Edition

IN PREPARING the first edition of this book I felt it was important to limit the number of illustrations, on the grounds that relatively few pictures from the Shakespearean period are reliable evidence for the stages and stage practices, and also because the bulk of the evidence is in words. I think that this view is still broadly valid. None the less it does now seem right to use more illustrations, if only to enlarge the visual dimension of what will always be an impressionistic picture. I have avoided using hypothetical reconstructions, because they are the wrong kind of impressionism, but material details such as facsimiles of playhouse documents, pictures of playhouse exteriors and interiors and of players, with a few suggestive items from the London environment, have been added. The total number of illustrations has trebled.

In the preface to the first edition I emphasised my debt to the four volumes of scholarship compiled by Edmund Chambers on the Elizabethan stage and the seven volumes by Gerald Eades Bentley on the Jacobean and Caroline stage. Ten years later their work must still give any attempt to depict the Shakespearean stage its blessedly solid foundation, but to single out those eleven volumes, weighty in every sense though they are, seems ungracious to all the other scholars who have helped to sharpen the vague lines and erase the slips of pencil that even scholarly flesh is heir to. This edition adds a bibliography that attempts to list all the major contributions to this vast body of scholarship.

I use sketch-pad metaphors because my object is to put together a picture of the Shakespearean stage, to portray the local circumstances that sponsored some of the greatest literature ever written. It has to be a sketch because it is ultimately a subjective exercise. However rigorously one compiles the factual evidence, however much the hard facts are held in position and spaces left blank rather than filled with conjecture, the result will not be photographic realism. The components are too ephemeral and too fragmentary. It is therefore important both that a single, cohesive view should be established, and that it should be acknowledged as a sketch, not a photograph.

The work of revision to bring the details of this sketch up to date has been on the whole reassuring. It has been more a matter of adding to the details than altering any major emphasis. And that, I hope, will enable the book to continue serving its original purpose: to help our understanding of the Shakespearean drama by minimising misunderstandings of the plays as they were originally conceived and composed.

The term 'Shakespearean' is used to cover what are normally called the Elizabethan, Jacobean and Caroline periods – that is, the latter half of Elizabeth's reign, from the 1570s to 1603, the whole of the reign of James I, 1603–25, and the period of rule (as distinct from reign) of Charles I, 1625–42. Shakespeare's own contact with the London theatre world extended only from about 1590 to 1616, but he stands on its highest peak, and his name if anyone's has to be given to the period. The theatre conditions that supplied Shakespeare with the venue for his plays came into existence in the 1570s, and disappeared abruptly in 1642. The first official recognition of the London-based commercial acting companies was given in 1574; a total ban on playing was imposed in 1642, and was thoroughly enforced for the next eighteen years, long enough to destroy almost all traces of Shakespearean theatre conditions and traditions. The seventy years of play-acting in which Shakespeare's career was embedded needs to be seen as a whole, and the best single word for it is Shakespearean.

A number of the variables of the Shakespearean period have been regularised for convenience. The old-style system of dating, which began the calendar year in March instead of on 1 January, has been silently adjusted to the modern dating. The titles of plays and the names of players, which were spelt in various ways even by their owners, have been regularised in the forms adopted by Chambers and Bentley. On the other hand money is recorded in the old form of pounds, shillings and pence. That is, the 'penny' mentioned in this book is one two-hundred-and-fortieth part of a pound, one-twelfth of a shilling, not the one-hundredth part of a pound that is the modern value for a penny. The quotations use the old denotation of the penny as 'd.', not the modern 'p.'. In accordance with the same principle of supplying an authentic picture of the Shakespearean background, quotations are given wherever possible in the original spelling, except that the Elizabethan typographical conventions of i for j, initial v and medial u have been altered to the modern usage. And to be consistent in the same principle, actors are normally called players, theatres are playhouses, playwrights (a term which crept into favour along with 'actors' in the 1630s) are given their own name for themselves, poets. Their product is the unserious business of playing.

A Note for the Third Edition

ƔƨƔ

A DECADE is a long time in Shakespearean scholarship. In preparing this revision of a work which was originally done more than twenty years ago and first brought up to date ten years ago, I had doubts about whether it should not now be left to recede quietly into history as a record of one interpretation amongst many of the plethora of imperfect evidence which we have about the circumstances of Shakespearean playwriting and playgoing. So many new lines of investigation have been started since 1979, when the second edition of this work was prepared, that it might have been better to leave the work of making this sort of survey to other hands and minds. In the end I decided to make this one last revision because, while a lot has been done in the last ten years, most of the major discoveries are still in process, and a long way from completion. Perhaps another decade or so, once the many volumes in the *Records of Early English Drama* have all been published and the much needed new history of the playing companies is written; when the rebuilt Globe on Bankside has been in operation for some time, and its discoveries about techniques of acting at the Globe assimilated; when the foundations of the Globe and the Rose and possibly other playhouses have been thoroughly unearthed and studied by the archaeologists; when the final, culminating volume of Glynne Wickham's *Early English Stages*, dealing with staging from 1576 onwards, has at last appeared; that will be the time for someone else to draw both breath and conclusions with a truly fresh appraisal of the far-flung evidence.

In this third edition some, though small, account has been taken of the shifts in priorities which have appeared in the last decade, under the pressure of new theories about the heuristic and self-reflexive nature of this game of studying Shakespeare's working conditions. The Appendix listing the plays and their circumstances of performance, for instance, is now arranged in the alphabetical order of the plays themselves, not their dead authors. But for the most part the revision simply seeks to incorporate the new evidence that has appeared since 1980. The groundplan of the Rose playhouse and a few of its implications, the Globe's entrance lobby, a better translation of Orazio Busino's Italian, some recent conjectures about the staging of the plays, revised datings and related information about particular plays, these and other details have been inserted in the relevant chapters. There is even a small attempt in Chapter 2 at humanising the old picture of Philip Henslowe as a tight-fisted theatre impresario. Chapter 4, on the design of the different kinds of playhouse, has had the most additions. For different reasons Chapter 6, on the audiences, has had the least. Subheadings have been added to each chapter to clarify the organisation of the material.

Andrew Gurr
Reading 1990

Acknowledgements

THE AUTHOR and publisher would like to thank the following for permission to reproduce the illustrations: the Marquess of Tavistock and the Trustees of the Bedford Estates (for Nos. 1 and 38a); Glynne Wickham, *Early English Stages, 1300–1660*, Vol. II, Part 2, 1576–1660 (Routledge, London 1972; Columbia University Press) (2, 30); the British Library (3, 4b, 6, 8, 9, 12, 13, 16, 33); the University Library, Cambridge (4a); the Governors of Dulwich College (5, 7, 10, 14, 15, 17); the Master and Fellows of Magdalene College, Cambridge (11); Andrew Fulgoni Photography (18); the Bibliotheek der Rijksuniversiteit, Utrecht (22); the Guildhall Library, City of London (23, 24, 28, 34); the Museum of London (25); the Benchers of the Honorable Society of the Middle Temple (27); the Provost and Fellows of Worcester College, Oxford (29, 32); the Department of the Environment (31); the Victoria and Albert Museum (35); the Marquess of Bath (36); the Duke of Devonshire and the Trustees of the Chatsworth Settlement (37, 38b).

1. Introduction

1.   THEN AND NOW

HAMLET, like any other Shakespearean nobleman, wore his hat indoors. When the foppish and murderous Osric came flourishing his headgear with the invitation to fight Laertes, Hamlet undoubtedly doffed his bonnet in reply to Osric's flourish, and then put it back on. Osric's failure to follow suit led to Hamlet's reproof ('Put your bonnet to his right use, 'tis for the head'). The unbonneted Hamlet familiar to modern audiences is a creation of the indoor theatre and fourth-wall staging, where every scene is a room unless it is specified otherwise, and where everyone goes hatless accordingly. Hamlet in 1601 walked under the sky in an open amphitheatre, on a platform that felt out-of-doors in comparison with modern theatres but indifferently represented indoors or out to the Elizabethans. There was a wall at the back of the platform, fronting the 'tiring-house' or room where the players changed, the off-stage area. It gave access to the playing area by two or more doors and a balcony. These places of entry could equally well provide the imagination with the exterior doors and balcony of a house or the interior doors and gallery of a great hall. Hamlet's headgear was worn with equal indifference to the imagined scene.

The wearing of hats on stage is a minor matter in comparison with, say, Hamlet's use of a 'nighted colour' in his clothes, so far as the play's general concerns go. But unless we know Hamlet is himself bonneted the point of his verbal fencing with Osric may be missed. Hats are useful either to guard the wearer's face against the sun, or to keep the head warm. Hamlet's request that Osric should put his bonnet to its right use is taken by Osric to be made out of concern for the hot sun ('I thank your lordship, it is very hot'). Hamlet, having been too much 'in the "son"', denies this ('No, believe me, 'tis very cold, the wind is northerly'), an equally good reason for keeping his own hat on; and when Osric hastens to agree, catches him up on it ('But yet, methinks, it is very sultry and hot for my complexion'). He keeps his hat on with both reasons. Hamlet is not just making Osric look a fool. Hats were doffed (put off) as a gesture of respect. At the end of the gesture they went back on the head. Only a courtier in the presence of the king

1

would keep his hat in his hand. For Osric to keep his hat off in Hamlet's presence was excessively deferential, especially in a creature of the usurping King addressing that King's victim, and Hamlet ensures that the excess is made apparent. Shakespeare made stage business out of similar by-play with hats in *Love's Labour's Lost*, V.i, *A Midsummer Night's Dream*, IV.ii, and *As You Like It*, III.iii. Unless we know that Hamlet kept his hat on while Osric continued to flourish his, we miss the real point of the incident. It also helps to know that a typical Elizabethan 'bonnet' in 1600 had a high crown, a narrow brim and a round dome – a kind of elongated bowler hat – in order to visualise Horatio's image of Osric running off like a baby lapwing 'with the shell on his head'.

Hamlet makes highly sophisticated use of the theatre conditions of its time. The company of players who arrive in II.ii were real, not the caricatures of players found in *A Midsummer Night's Dream* or Marston's *Histriomastix*, and the specimen of their work that the leading player offers is a genuine, if deliberately archaic, set speech, an audition piece, not a parody. Despite Polonius's interruptions, the player delivers his 'passionate speech' about rugged Pyrrhus with such good inward accompaniment to his outward appearance of passion that he changes colour and tears come into his eyes. And all this, as Hamlet bitterly tells himself afterwards, is monstrously for a fiction, a 'dream of passion':

> what would he do,
> Had he the motive and the cue for passion
> That I have?

All that is really monstrous, of course, is that Hamlet has no more motive or cue for passion than the player; he himself is as much a fiction as the player. What Shakespeare is doing in this scene is to refine on the familiar Elizabethan paradox of 'tragedy played in jest', the view that sees murders done for entertainment, and appearances pretending to be reality. The fictitious Hamlet rails at the fiction of the player. Shakespeare's refinement is to make this paradoxical situation not a joke but an emphatic assertion of Hamlet's reality.

There are many other details of the play's staging that depend on contemporary life. The disposition of the stage for the play-within-the-play, for instance, which has exercised the ingenuity of some commentators, must have followed the pattern for plays at Court: the performers of the play at the back of the stage by the largest opening in the tiring-house wall (the so-called discovery-space), King Claudius and Queen Gertrude on the 'state' or throne at the front of the stage in the middle of the amphitheatre yard, Hamlet and Ophelia to one side with a view of both.[1] Another example is the dumb-show, the mimed plot-summary with which the play-within-the-play begins. Dumb-shows were a fairly archaic device by the time *Hamlet* was written, but not so archaic that

1. Giles Brydges, the third Lord Chandos, wearing the kind of hat that Osric flourished. Most hats made in England before 1600 were of leather, with a narrow brim and a seam across the flat crown. An example is preserved in the Museum of London. The more fashionable headgear, of the kind Osric would have worn, was most likely to have been made in France or the Netherlands. The image of him running off like a newly hatched lapwing with the shell still on his head suggests a hat like the one worn by Lord Chandos in this portrait by the Dutch painter Hieronimo Custodis, painted in 1589 and now at Woburn Abbey. See R. Strong, *The English Ikon* (London 1969), no. 148.

Shakespeare's contemporaries hesitated to use them. Nor were they such rare devices that Hamlet should not have foreseen the players using one. The mistake in prematurely revealing the mousetrap through the dumb-show is partly due to Hamlet's lack of foresight, and his failure to allow for the players' stupidity is a component in the savagery with which he greets them when they come out to start the play itself. Again, when Polonius is stabbed through, as the Second Quarto and the schoolboy joke have it, the arras, it is worth knowing that the cloth behind which Polonius hid hung in front of a 'discovery-space', an alcove or similar structure deep enough to conceal quite substantial properties. The player of Polonius could have called out from the back of the alcove, leaving room for the player of Hamlet to make a full-blooded lunge through the curtain without fear of actually running his fellow through. Polonius could then safely come forward to become a corpse, before Hamlet drew the cloth back to reveal him. The duel at the climax in V.ii must have been similarly full-blooded. Fencing displays were a feature of the entertainment the stages offered to the Elizabethan public, and at least one player (Richard Tarlton the clown) was a Master of Fence. Though Hamlet claims in his opening soliloquy to be utterly unlike Hercules (the archetypal man of action), he would certainly have been required to belie his words when it came to the duel with Laertes.

2. THE LONDON FOCUS

It would be possible to write several books clarifying such details just for the plays of Shakespeare. Explanatory notes of this kind however belong properly in editions of the plays. My purpose in writing this book is broader, concerned with the shape of the wood rather than single trees, in the hope that knowing the shape of the wood might help in understanding the trees a little. Or, to change one inexact metaphor for another, to sketch in a deeper background in order to sharpen the focus of the foreground.

The background features of the Shakespearean drama are important to our understanding of the plays for many reasons, not least because the features were at the same time thoroughly distinctive and thoroughly transient. Except for a few of the poets, nobody gave a thought to

---

2. A vignette from the title-page of *Roxana* (1632) by William Alabaster, showing hangings (an 'arras') behind the players. The rail at the stage edges and the sitting posture of the spectators around the stage suggest it depicts a hall playhouse, though whether it represents any specific London playhouse is doubtful. See John H. Astington, 'The Origins of the *Roxana* and *Messallina* Illustrations', *ShS* 43 (1991), pp. 149–69.

posterity. The companies that bought the plays were actively hostile to the idea of printing them. The players were there to give entertainment and to take money. There was no reason to make the product durable or to record it for future generations. So the plays lived in a medium as ephemeral as the sounds through which they came to life.

Even for the majority of the poets it was entertainment they were creating, not art, and the poets accordingly wrote for their age, not for all time. Their paymasters were players, not printers. In *Hamlet* the travelling players turn up because they were fetched to divert Hamlet's attention and distract him from his melancholy. They were a casual diversion from serious affairs. The poets merely supplied the raw material for such diversions, material for the most part as transient as the performances that gave it life. The publisher of Jasper Mayne's *The City Match* (1639) claimed that the poet, a clergyman amateur, held the belief 'that works of this light nature . . . be things which need an apology for being written at all, not esteeming otherwise of them, whose abilities in this kind are most passable, than of masquers who spangle and glitter for a time, but 'tis thoroughly tinsel'. Shakespeare and Jonson, in other words, are no more substantial than Christmas decorations. It follows from this attitude – a widespread orthodoxy – that plays were dependent on the conditions of performance as few written works have ever been. They were working playscripts before they became written texts. Not many objects in the foreground of literature have been so dependent on their background to give them form and identity. Plays by their nature were thoroughly occasional productions.

Another consideration shaping this book is the business motive of the players, which directed them to London. Almost the whole of Shakespearean drama was written for companies that used their play-books solely for the purpose of making their living, and by far the best living was to be made in the metropolis. Except for the occasional university student like Jasper Mayne, or the amateur satirist of *Hog Hath Lost His Pearl*, writing for a group of apprentices, no poet wrote with anything but the London companies in mind. London was where the players could perform in their own custom-built playhouses, week after week and year after year. Everywhere else they had to use town halls, market-places, or if they were lucky the great halls in the manor-houses of the nobility. Although Bristol had its own playhouse in the early years of the seventeenth century,[2] no poet wrote expressly for it, or for the companies that passed through Norwich or Newcastle or even Stratford. In London there were regular venues, regular audiences, regular incomes. Every player's ambition was to belong to a company securely resident in London. And equally, the only place where a play could be profitably marketed was with the companies working in

London. Since London was the peak of the mountain of entertainment thrown up in the seventy or so years of Shakespearean theatre, this book economises by confining itself to the conditions that existed for the performance of plays only in that one fortunate city.

Playhouses were places of impure art, and in some eyes they were not even places of legitimate entertainment. William Harrison commented when the first playhouses were built in 1576 that 'It is an evident token of a wicked time when plaiers wexe so riche that they can build such houses.'³ To Harrison the entertainment they offered was no better than that of 'houses of baudrie'. They were even built in the same neighbourhoods, as Prynne, the Puritan author of a massive attack on playing, wrote in 1633:

our Theaters if they are not Bawdy-houses, (as they may easily be, since many Players, *if reports be true, are common Panders*,) yet they are Cosin-germanes, at *leastwise neighbours to them*: Witnesse the *Cock-pit*, and *Drury–lane*: *Black-friers Play-house*, and *Duke-humfries*; the *Red-bull*, and *Turnball-street*: the *Globe*, and *Bank-side Brothel-houses*, with others of this nature.⁴

The poet and epigrammatist John Davies sketched the day of a typical playgoer, an idle gallant, in terms that also acknowledged the equivalent status of brothels and playhouses ('In Fuscum': *Epigrammes*, 39):

> *Fuscus* is free, and hath the world at will,
> Yet in the course of life that he doth leade,
> He's like a horse which turning rounde a mill,
> Doth alwaies in the selfe same circle treade:
> First he doth rise at 10. and at eleven
> He goes to *Gyls*, where he doth eate till one,
> Then sees a play til sixe, and sups at seaven,
> And after supper, straight to bed is gone,
> And there till tenne next day he doth remaine,
> And then he dines, then sees a commedy,
> And then he suppes, and goes to bed againe.
> Thus rounde he runs without variety:
> Save that sometimes he comes not to the play
> But falls into a whore-house by the way.

Such an idea of playgoing was hardly likely to sponsor a devotional attitude to their art in the players. Playing was deplored by the authorities, in 1574 when innyards were the venues, and the crowds were largely artisans and apprentices, just as it was deplored in 1633, when playhouses were in great halls in the heart of London, and the trouble was caused more by the coaches of the great than by tumultuous apprentices. In 1574 the city authorities described the scene in these words:

the inordynate hauntyinge of greate multitudes of people, speciallye youthe, to
playes, enterludes, and shewes, namelye occasyon of ffrayes and quarrelles,
eavell practizes of incontinencye in greate Innes, havinge chambers and secrete
places adjoyninge to their open stagies and gallyries, inveglynge and alleurynge
of maides, speciallye orphanes and good Cityzens Children under Age, to
previe and unmete Contractes, the publishinge of unchaste uncomelye and
unshamefaste speeches and doynges, withdrawinge of the Queenes Majesties
Subjects from dyvyne service on Sonndaies and hollydayes, at which Tymes
suche playes weare Chefelye used, unthriftye waste of the moneye of the poore
and fond persons, sondrye robberies by pyckinge and Cuttinge of purses,
utteringe of popular busye and sedycious matters, and manie other Corruptions
of youthe and other enormyties, besydes that allso soundrye slaughters and
mayheminges of the Quenes Subjectes have happened by ruines of Skaffoldes,
fframes and Stagies, and by engynes, weapons, and powder used in plaies.[5]

The inns were in the City jurisdiction, and by the turn of the century
the City Fathers managed to close them to the players. The playhouses
designed and built as playhouses were located just outside the City
jurisdiction, and in 1633 it was the Privy Council, the executive
instrument of the King's government, that had to intervene to impose
traffic regulations in the vicinity of the leading playhouse. They declared
that

Whereas ye Board hath taken consideracion of the great inconveniencs that
growe by reason of the resort to the Play house of ye Blackffryars in Coaches,
whereby the streets neare thereunto, are at the Playtime so stopped that his
Ma^{ts} Subjects going about their necessarie affayres can hardly finde passage and
are oftentymes endangered: Their lps remembring that there is an easie passage
by water unto that playhouse wthout troubling the streets, and that it is much
more fit and reasonable that those wch goe thither should goe thither by water
or else on foote rather than the necessarie businesses of all others, and the
publique Commerce should be disturbed by their pleasure, doe therefore Order,
that if anie p[er]son man or woman of what Condicion soever repaire to the
aforesayd Playhouse in Coach so soone as they are gone out of their Coaches
the Coach men shall departe thence and not retourne till the ende of the play,
nor shall stay or retourne to fetch those whome they carryed anie nearer wth
their Coaches then the farther parte of St Paules Church yarde on the one syde,
and ffleet-Conduite on the other syde, and in ye tyme betweene their departure
and returne shall either returne home or else abide in some other streets lesse
frequented with passengers and so range their Coaches in those places that the
way be not stopped, wch Order if anie Coachman disobey, the next Constable
or Officer is hereby charged to commit him p^{r}esently to Ludgate or Newgate;
And the Lo: Mayor of ye Citie of London is required to see this carefully
pfourmed by the Conestables and Officers to whom it apperteyneth and to
punish every such Conestable or officer as shall be found negligent therein.
And to the ende that none may p^{r}etende ignorance hereof, it is lastly ordered
that Copies of this Order, shallbe set up at Paules Chaine, by direction of the

Lorde Mayor as also at the west ende of St Paules Church, at Ludgate and the Blackfryers Gate and Fleete Conduite.[6]

A contemporary noted that these regulations were duly enforced, but that, human flesh being what it is, they were not effective for more than two or three weeks.

The official records of course are chiefly concerned with the troubles the players made. The other side of the story is suggested by the awed wonder with which foreign travellers described what they saw on the London stages, and the declarations of much-travelled Englishmen like Fynes Moryson, who said in his *Itinerary* (p. 476)[6], written in 1617, that

The Citty of London alone hath foure or five Companyes of players with their peculiar Theaters Capable of many thousands, wherein they all play every day in the weeke but Sunday, with most strang concourse of people, besydes many strange toyes and fances exposed by signes to be seene in private houses, to which and to many musterings and other frequent spectacles, the people flocke in great nombers, being naturally more newefangled then the Athenians to heare newes and gaze upon every toye, as there be, in my opinion, more Playes in London then in all the partes of the worlde I have seene, so doe these players or Comedians excell all other in the worlde. Whereof I have seene some stragling broken Companyes that passed into Netherland and Germany, followed by the people from one towne to another, though they understoode not their wordes, only to see theire action, yea marchants at Fayres bragged more to have seene them, then of the good marketts they made.[7]

In the sixteenth century life for the playing companies was a constant battle to keep a foot-hold in London in the teeth of the City Fathers and the Puritan preachers. According to the preachers, apprentices were seduced away into idleness by the temptations of the players, and as everyone knows the Devil finds work for idle hands. The City Fathers, most of whom employed apprentices, understandably felt themselves to be better employers than the Devil. The Court, however, lacking the personal interest in the matter that the City Fathers had, held no similar objections to playing. In 1572 and 1574 it more or less openly took the leading companies of players under its wing. Only with such protection could the players afford to invest in permanent playhouses. In 1576 and 1577 two open amphitheatres and one indoor hall started as commercial venues for playing, all of them, for safety, in the suburban spaces just outside the City's jurisdiction. This gave them an immunity the inns could not have, and with royal help they proved sound and lasting investments. Not until the political balance of power was reversed, nearly seventy years later, did the City finally get its way over the Court and the players. In the early seventeenth century, when the leading London companies all basked in the warmth of royal patronage, the City's hostility was necessarily quiescent. For nearly forty years London

3. A triumphal arch depicting London, built for King James's entry into London in
1603. This arch, designed by Ben Jonson and the first in the sequence, depicted
London. It included the City musicians, shown in the galleries on each side. In the
central niche was the 'Genius of the City', personified by the thinly clad Edward
Alleyn, shown with arm raised. When James reached the arch Alleyn made a speech
written for the occasion by Thomas Dekker. Dekker's speech was printed in an
account of James's entry published in 1604. Stephen Harrison engraved pictures of
all the arches for his *Arches of Triumph*, also published in 1604.

never had less than six playhouses, and four regular companies performing daily except on Sundays and for most of Lent, or when the
plague set every man apart from his fellows. Only in 1642, when the
King's impoverishment forced him to put himself at Parliament's mercy,
did the City and the Puritans gain the power to close the haunts of
idleness.

The players performed their own small part in the downfall. Their
aims and objects changed drastically through the period, reflecting the
shifts in the social structure that brought about the revolution in society
at large. Under Elizabeth the players might be summoned to Court to
make a contribution to the Christmas festivities, and they might more
often be called on to entertain a noble or gentleman's friends at his
private house. But the plays that were performed on such occasions
were not different from the fare the players gave to the citizenry, who
could not afford such expensive exclusiveness. The idle artisan's admission fee was a minimal penny. For this he had equally the choice of
Shakespeare or the baiting of bulls and bears, the same choice as the
Queen. The Queen sent for the players or her bear-warden, the
apprentices were enticed with hand-written playbills posted up around
the town, on which they might read where plays were available (we
don't really know whether they were told *what* plays were being
performed). One of the few handbills that have survived shows what
the rival kind of entertainment for the apprentices was. It is an undated
advertisement for an afternoon at the Beargarden, probably from early
in the reign of James. Written in a large, plain hand, it says

Tomorrowe beinge Thursdaie shalbe seen at the Beargardin on the banckside a
great Mach plaid by the gamstirs of Essex who hath chalenged all comers what
soever to plaie v dogges at the single beare for v pounds and also to wearie a
bull dead at the stake and for your better content shall have plasant sport with
the horse and ape and whiping of the blind beare   Vivat Rex[8]

This kind of show, and its theatrical equivalents, was available to high
and low alike in the sixteenth century. Except for what the intermittently
active boy companies provided, it could be said that the basic penny fee
bought the apprentice as much as Elizabeth herself could buy, and
entertainment moreover of exactly the same kind.

In the seventeenth century, under the Stuarts, the picture was
modified. The citizen amphitheatres continued to offer a pennyworth
of bear-baiting or playgoing throughout the period, but the upper end
of the market expanded and altered radically. Just before 1600 the hall
playhouses reopened inside the city walls. By 1629 there were three
halls and three open-air playhouses, and most of the new plays were
being written for the companies occupying the halls, and their wealthy
patrons. The smaller capacity of the auditoria at the hall playhouses

was more than compensated for by their higher prices. The cheapest admission fee to the Blackfriars only gained you a place on the rearmost bench in the upper gallery. The same fee would buy you the luxury of a lord's room at the Globe. With a price range between 6d. and 2s. 6d., as against the 1d. to 6d. range of the amphitheatres, the halls automatically catered for the wealthier levels of London society. Besides their roofs, and their central location close to the wealthier residential areas, the Blackfriars and its kin also catered for the wealthy with such practices as allowing a few spectators to sit on the stage itself to view the play. For a young gallant anxious to parade his newest clothes, the chance to sit in full view alongside the players must have been irresistible. It took an order from the king in person to ban sitting on the stage at the smallest of the hall playhouses in 1639. As it became acceptable for fashionable ladies to occupy the boxes alongside the stage, the social advantage of parading oneself at the Blackfriars or the Cockpit came second only to an appearance at the Court itself. By 1642, even though the open amphitheatres were still running citizen fare, the hall playhouses had become closely identified with Court circles and Court tastes. Their closure by Parliament in that year was the clearest measure of the Court's loss of power.

3.   LIFE IN LONDON

It is worth emphasising that the single penny which gained an apprentice admission to the Bel Savage or the Theatre in the 1570s was still the basic price at the Fortune, the Red Bull and the Globe in 1642. The hall playhouses expanded their price range with more costly seats and boxes, and their minimum sixpenny charge must have excluded most apprentices. This was an extension of the market, though, not a change. The basic penny lost some of its value through inflation, and while most prices rose artisan wages remained steady. And so did playhouse prices. Amphitheatres, baiting-houses, prize-fights and whorehouses were always within reach for the great majority of·the working population as well as the wealthy.

The industrious artisan throughout the period earned about 6s. a week (6s. 5¾d. for masons, 6s. 2¾d. for carpenters).[9] Apprentices earned very considerably less than that, though board and lodging were provided in the terms of their indentures. To such artisans a good food diet cost as much as half the weekly wage, in Tudor times. The Tudor soldier's daily food allowance was 24 ounces of wheat bread and two-thirds of a gallon of beer, each costing a penny; 2 pounds of beef or mutton (cod or herring on fish days), at a cost of 2d.; half a pound of butter, and a pound of cheese. The cost of this diet under Elizabeth was about 6d., but food prices never recovered from the seven successive bad harvests at the end of the century, and rose by about 25 per cent in the early seventeenth century. By the mid-century beef was as much as 5*d*. a pound. Bread and circuses went together in price throughout the period, but the quantity of bread that could be bought for the price of admission to the playhouse steadily declined.

The price of manufactured articles, as always in a predominantly subsistence economy, was markedly higher than the cost of food. It is difficult to be specific about prices, because they were likely to fluctuate more according to quality than by the type of commodity, and because prices also varied according to the social status of the purchaser. A pair of silk stockings might cost £2 or £4, depending on quality and purchaser. A woman's gown might cost anything from £ 7 to £20 or more. The Earl of Leicester paid £543 for seven doublets and two cloaks, at an average cost for each item rather higher than the price Shakespeare paid for a house in Stratford. The same Earl's funeral cost £3,000, five times what it cost to construct the second Blackfriars playhouse. The tendency of the better playing companies to cater for the higher income brackets is understandable.

It is difficult to generalise about the distribution of income through the country, and the social patterns to which it relates, and even more difficult to locate the playhouse audiences amongst those social patterns. Statistics are inadequate and potentially misleading. None the less a broad picture does appear, suggesting that while the poor, and particularly the London artisan poor, grew poorer, the number of the rich grew markedly, and especially in London. Large numbers of the seventeenth-century gentry, chiefly based in the cities, drew wealth both from the relatively few very rich noblemen of the sixteenth century and from the poor through the inflation of prices and the stability of wages. Trade was especially prosperous for the London merchant. The East India Company, floated in 1600 with a capital of £72,000, brought its investors a minimum return of 121 per cent on each voyage.[10] In that year, 1600, there were estimated to be in the country as a whole 60,000 yeomen and others with incomes of £40 to £100, well above the artisan and schoolmaster level of £15. As many as 10,000 had incomes of £300 to £500. The average income of nobles was £2,000 to £3,000, which was about what a prosperous merchant could rise to.[11] From that date a good deal of the wealth turned up in the form of money, not land, which was the traditional form that wealth took until the sixteenth century. Drake's bullion ships indirectly helped the players, because the more that wealth came to hand in the readily exchangeable form of money, the more idle gallants, hangers-on at Court and Inns-of-Court lawyers were created to seek the entertainment the players were selling. In *The Alchemist* III.iv the trickster Face urges the gullible young country gentleman Kastril to turn his land into cash, on the grounds that 'men of spirit hate to keep earth long'. Spending power was cash, not property.[12] It was inevitable that the moneyed and therefore leisured audiences came to override the penny-paying apprentices in the eyes of the players in the course of the seventeenth century.

4. SOCIAL DIVISIONS

The different kinds of repertory that were maintained at the different playhouses confirm the evidence of these economic changes. In the seventeenth century the so-called 'citizen' playhouses, the amphi-theatres in the suburbs on the eastern and northern sides of the city – chiefly the Fortune and the Red Bull – went on with a staple list of plays made up from the favourites of the end of the previous century. Marlowe's plays ran at these playhouses until the closure. Heywood became the Red Bull's leading playwright, and his lavishly staged plays, or displays, of the Four Ages mark a high point of achievement for the companies who catered for the citizen audiences. There was only one interruption to this pattern, when Christopher Beeston, the player of the early Red Bull company who ran its finances, set up a hall playhouse in Drury Lane and stocked it with players and plays from the amphi-theatre. On the two following Shrove Tuesday holidays gangs of apprentices tried to mob the new hall playhouse and destroy it, presumably in protest at having their plays taken away from the penny playhouse and transferred to a sixpenny venue.

Beeston built his new playhouse, the Cockpit, in 1616. The next apprentice holiday was Shrove Tuesday at the beginning of Lent in 1617. A contemporary gives a vivid account of what happened:

The Prentizes on Shrove Tewsday last, to the nomber of 3. or 4000 comitted extreame insolencies; part of this nomber, taking their course for Wapping, did there pull downe to the grownd 4 houses, spoiled all the goods therein, defaced many others, & a Justice of the Peace coming to appease them, while he was reading a Proclamation, had his head broken with a brick batt. Th' other part, making for Drury Lane, where lately a newe playhouse is erected, they besett the house round, broke in, wounded divers of the players, broke open their trunckes, & whatt apparrell, bookes, or other things they found, they burnt & cutt in peeces; & not content herewith, gott on the top of the house, & untiled it, & had not the Justices of Peace & Sherife levied an aide & hindred their purpose, they would have laid that house likewise even with the grownd. In this skyrmishe one prentise was slaine, being shott throughe the head with a pistoll, & many other of their fellowes were sore hurt, & such of them as are taken his Majestie hath commaunded shal be executed for example sake.[13]

In the following year the apprentices planned to try again, assembling at the Fortune to attack both the Cockpit and the Red Bull. The Privy Council had notice this time, though, and stopped them. Having rebuilt his Drury Lane playhouse (it was sometimes called the Phoenix, because of its instant rebirth from the flames of 1617), in the following years Beeston often took plays from the Red Bull's repertory for staging at his hall playhouse. It is not quite clear how far it was the apprentice patrons or how far the apprentices' favourite plays that gave the Red Bull its reputation as a 'citizen' playhouse in distinction to the hall playhouses, since the Cockpit often ran Red Bull plays for its privileged audiences.[14]

On the whole the plays performed at the 'citizen' playhouses were heroic and spectacular rather than romantic, and the comedy was broad rather than high or witty. Dekker's *Shoemaker's Holiday*, a play written for the Rose in 1599, is reasonably representative of one type of the entertainment aimed at citizens. It glorifies the 'gentle craft' of shoemaking, has a legendary master-shoemaker and his journeymen as its heroes, ending in triumph with the shoemaker's election as Lord Mayor of London when he entertains the King and the city's apprentices at his banquet. It is an enormously cheerful celebration of the citizen virtues of goodwill and good work. The romantic interest crosses social barriers, with a young nobleman disguising himself as a shoemaker to woo the citizen daughter of the Lord Mayor. With the help of his fellow-workers he overcomes the hostility both of his own aristocratic uncle and his beloved's father. This assertion of social mobility follows the tradition of such plays as *Friar Bacon and Friar Bungay*, or *Fair Em the Miller's Daughter of Manchester, with the Love of William the Conqueror*, and even *The Merry Wives of Windsor*, and was regularly imitated in plays like *The Fair Maid of Bristow*.

In Stuart times the companies performing at the amphitheatres seem to have relied on an established repertoire of plays. They bought markedly fewer new plays in Caroline times than when Shakespeare was writing. Most of the new plays went to the hall playhouses, designed to cater for changing fashion in 'wit' and for the increasingly significant proportion of women in the audience. Battles and duels with swords were popular on the open stages, but indoors where the stages were much smaller and cluttered with fashion-conscious gallants it was preferable to fence with words and to present spectacles of costume rather than fireworks.

Plays written for the indoor stages also show markedly less enthusiasm for social mobility. Merchant pretensions were ignored or deplored, in such plays as Massinger's *New Way to Pay Old Debts*, written in Caroline times and for audiences prepared to pay a minimal 6*d*. The villain of the piece, the grasping middle-class merchant Overreach, tries to persuade the noble Lord Lovell to marry his beautiful (and virtuous) daughter, Margaret. For the sake of the plot Lord Lovell seems to concur, but afterwards he says emphatically (IV.i):

> Were *Overreach*'s stat's thrice centupl'd; his daughter
> Millions of degrees, much fairer than she is,
> (Howe're I might urge presidents to excuse me)
> I would not so adulterate my blood
> By marrying *Margaret*, and so leave my issue
> Made up of several pieces, one part skarlet,
> And the other *London* blew. In my owne tombe
> I will interre my name first.

Scarlet was the colour worn by nobles and Court officials, blue the merchant's colour.

The plays available for a penny included the heroics of fantasy romances like Heywood's *Four Prentices of London*. Its heroes are four apprentices, nobles in disguise ('all high borne, / Yet of the Citty-Trades they have no scorne'), who march across Europe and Asia performing the incredible feats of knight-errantry that were the staple fare of the chivalric romances long popular with the sixteenth-century reading public.[15] The citizen taste for this kind of romantic heroics was burlesqued by Beaumont in *The Knight of the Burning Pestle*, written for the sixpenny private playhouse repertory in 1607. Beaumont's burlesque is very much in the manner of *Don Quixote*, which was almost contemporary with it. The play shows a citizen Grocer and his wife being fooled by a sophisticated boy company at the Blackfriars into exposing their taste for *Don Quixote*-like feats of improbable valour. At each pause in the play the Grocer and his wife lay new demands on the players for feats of arms from their apprentice, whom they have thrust on the players to take the leading part. At the beginning of Act IV, for instance, they confer on what they would like to follow:

CITIZEN. What shall we have *Rafe* do now boy?

BOY. You shall have what you will sir.

CITIZEN. Why so sir, go and fetch me him then, and let the Sophy of *Persia* come and christen him a childe.

BOY. Beleeve me sir, that will not doe so well, 'tis stale, it has beene had before at the red Bull.

WIFE. *George* let *Rafe* travell over great hils, and let him be very weary, and come to the King of *Cracovia*'s house, covered with blacke velvet, and there let the Kings daughter stand in her window all in beaten gold, combing her golden locks with a combe of Ivory, and let her spy *Rafe*, and fall in love with him, and come downe to him, and carry him into her fathers house, and then let *Rafe* talke with her.

CITIZEN. Well said *Nell*, it shal be so: boy let's ha't done quickly.

BOY. Sir, if you will imagine all this to be done already, you shall heare them talke together: but wee cannot present a house covered with blacke velvet, and a Lady in beaten gold.

CITIZEN. Sir boy, lets ha't as you can then.

BOY. Besides it will shew ill-favouredly to have a Grocers prentice to court a kings daughter.

CITIZEN. Will it so sir? you are well read in Histories: I pray you what was sir *Dagonet*? was not he prentice to a Grocer in London? read the play of the *Foure Prentices of London*, where they tosse their pikes so: I pray you fetch him in sir, fetch him in.

So the boy goes off to prepare Rafe, apologising on the way to the 'gentlemen' in the audience for this fresh affront to their tastes. The incident with the Sophy of Persia was in *The Travels of the Three English Brothers*, by Day and Wilkins, performed at the Red Bull in 1607. Sir Dagonet was actually King Arthur's jester.

In the first decade of the century several of the hall playhouse plays had what Beaumont called 'girds at citizens'. Two or three years after Beaumont's play Nathan Field, who probably acted in it, wrote a play of his own for the company, *A Woman is a Weathercock*, in which one player says to another (II.i):

> Ile thinke
> As abjectly of thee, as any Mongrill
> Bred in the Citty; Such a Cittizen
> As the Playes flout still.

The boy company at the Blackfriars provided witty and satirical comedies for their 'gentlemen' audiences. When they disappeared from the forefront of the scene after 1609 there seems to have followed a period of uncertainty in which girds at citizens were muted. Shakespeare's company had taken over the leading hall playhouse, and their repertory had never been anti-citizen (*The Merry Wives of Windsor* is a beautiful example of a citizen play, ending as it does with a gentleman marrying a wealthy merchant's daughter). In fact even the audience at the Blackfriars in 1607 for the boy company's performance of Beaumont's play seem not to have appreciated his satire on the Red Bull's citizen repertoire, since the play was not a success at its first appearance. Beaumont was premature in thinking that the sixpenny-payers in 1607 would be anti-citizen.

Later on, however, the taste of the indoor playhouse audiences for wit and satire reasserted itself, and by Caroline times the distance between the repertories favoured by the citizens at the northern public playhouses, and the gallants and Inns-of-Court men at the private playhouses in the city was fairly distinct. The wealthier taste was for wit, salacity ('sallets'), a closer fidelity to the unities of time and place, and more complex emotional patterns in romance and tragedy alike. Art, in playwriting as in the visual forms, became more self-conscious and Mannerist.[16] In tragedy the world frequently appears as pervasively corrupt and corrupting, where all motives are expedient and evil brings about the downfall of everyone, as in Middleton's *Women Beware Women*, or Massinger's *The Roman Actor*. In romances the milieu has a pastoral element, the golden world of Sidney's *Arcadia*, especially in the Beaumont and Fletcher plays. Fashions changed in the more aristocratic repertories, however, and it is the changeability more than the principles embodied in the plays that marks the difference from citizen repertories.[17]

In looking at the repertories and the social divisions they may reflect, as everywhere else in the picture, we must beware of oversimplification. The representation of contemporary life in thoroughly prejudicial forms was not a feature only of the more gentlemanly plays. A letter of 1601 from the Privy Council condemned a company performing at the Curtain for doing just that. 'We do understand', they wrote,

that certaine players that use to recyte their playes at the Curtaine in Moore-feildes do represent upon the stage in their interludes the persons of some gentlemen of good desert and quality that are yet alive under obscure manner, but yet in such sorte as all the hearers may take notice both of the matter and the persons that are meant thereby.[18]

The Curtain players shortly after this became the Red Bull players. It was not only gentlemen of good desert that became their targets either. In 1638 the Red Bull company found itself in trouble for a play that lampooned one of the most notorious of the monopolist merchants, Sir William Abell, a City Alderman.[19] The identification of 'citizen' playhouses does not indicate their identity with the interests of the City's magnates.

5 . THE POETS

In describing the general outlines of a picture of the period, it remains now to take some notice of the suppliers to the playing companies, the poets themselves. Much the largest body of playwriting in the Shakespearean period was hack-work. In the commercial conditions of the time, when all that was asked of the playwrights was to supply an entertainment industry, it could hardly have been anything else. What has survived into this century is probably not a large proportion of the total output, though it is likely to include most of the cream. Certainly what is read today is only the cream, and being so it can mislead us about the rest.

The grammar schools set up in the sixteenth century were producing scholars for whom there was no work. The theatre's appetite for plays was the most obvious source of income for such men, talented dramatists or not. And although the demand for plays was great, the number of hack-writers able to supply them was greater still. So it was a buyer's market for plays. Poets were the servants of the players, in economic servitude to them. The Cambridge scholars who wrote the Parnassus plays said so from the safety of their university (2 *Return from Parnassus*):

> And must the basest trade yeeld us reliefe?
> Must we be practis'd to those leaden spouts,
> That nought downe vent but what they do receive?   (IV.iv)

There was more money in playing than in playwriting:

> With mouthing words that better wits have framed,
> They purchase lands, and now Esquiers are made.   (V.i)

That Shakespeare died better off than many of his fellow-dramatists is probably more due to his share in his company of players and in their property than to his pen alone.

Of Shakespeare we really know almost nothing substantial, except that besides being a poet faithful to his company he was an exceptionally good businessman. In his early years, before 1594 when he joined the Chamberlain's Men and made his fortune with them, he dallied with aristocratic patronage as well as playing, and no doubt received good money for it. But the survival of his plays dating from 1594 and earlier is significant. When they were incorporated in the First Folio in 1623 they were the property of the Chamberlain's Men's successors, the King's Men. Plays were then the property of the company that bought them from the playwright. That the King's Men should own the pre-1594 plays suggests that Shakespeare somehow kept in his own possession the ownership of the early plays and that he did not sell them to the companies that first performed them. Through the early years when fortune's wheel was spinning with uncomfortable speed for the companies it was obviously wise to keep playbooks as financial assets, and take them from company to company. Presumably this is how they ended up with the Chamberlain's Men. They may well have been the capital with which Shakespeare bought himself a share in the company. The profit that brought him, and his investments as a Stratford property-owner, are well known.

Shakespeare became in effect the Chamberlain's Men's resident poet. The plays surviving in the First Folio and such accurate dating as can be made for them suggest that he wrote one serious play and one light play a year, more or less, throughout his active writing career. Another player–poet, Heywood, worked with Queen Anne's Men, the Red Bull company of 1605–19. In 1633 he claimed to have had 'either an entire hand, or at the least a maine finger' in the writing of 220 plays.[20]

The appetite for plays and the evident commercial incentive to produce in quantity led to a good deal of collaborative writing. As many as four or five authors might contribute to the text of a single play.

Philip Henslowe, one of the best-known and most prosperous theatre impresarios, kept in close touch with several hack-writers. He frequently employed them to patch on additions or alterations to plays he had bought for his companies, or to old plays that needed freshening up. He paid Ben Jonson to write additions to Thomas Kyd's *Spanish Tragedy* (*Henslowe's Diary*, pp. 182, 203). Some authors shopped around with their services, others stayed more or less literally indebted to one impresario. Jonson was incapable of maintaining good relations with any one employer for long. He moved from Henslowe to the Chamberlain's Men, from them to the boys of Blackfriars, then to and fro between Shakespeare's Men and the boys for a decade, and to other companies thereafter.

Of the twenty-five or more poets who made a living or part of a living by writing for the playing companies, probably not more than eight had regular contracts.[21] Shakespeare seems to have led the way in this as in so many other of his activities. His liaison with the Chamberlain's Men from 1594 was copied by Heywood, who was also a player and signed a two-year contract with Henslowe in 1598. They were followed by Dekker, William Rowley, also a player (a 'fat foole'), Fletcher, Massinger, Shirley and Brome. To judge from a comparison of what Henslowe was paying at the turn of the century (about £5) with what Brome commanded in the 1630s (at least £20, or £54 per annum on the promise of three plays a year), it increasingly became a lucrative business.

As the number of plays in the repertory increased, of course, the demand for new plays dropped off. New fashions became increasingly a self-conscious development out of the familiar and popular species of established plays. The King's Men, outstandingly the leading company in the 1630s, with the most socially reputable playhouse at Blackfriars, commissioned only four new plays a year. Under Charles sixty-four out of eighty-eight known plays distinguished by being staged at Court were old, some of them by twenty years or more. This lowering of the priority for novelty coincided with a rise in the status of plays to the level of poetic 'works', worthy of publication in folio along with graver matter. Charles himself read plays, and marked his copies with appreciative comments. Courtiers and gallants began to figure amongst the writers of plays. There was less collaborative writing, with its aura of hack-work, and a greater readiness to publish plays for reasons of pride instead of money. John Ford was a gentleman resident at the Middle Temple, an Inn of Court which prided itself on its literary talents. He spent nearly twenty years writing laborious poems on the one hand, but on the other collaborating with Dekker and other hacks in writing plays for the citizen repertories. Only under Charles did he start writing plays on his own. He wrote now for the new and privileged market,

first the Blackfriars and later Beeston's Cockpit. Some of his late plays
he published under an anagram of his name, 'Fide Honor'.

Only one contract between a poet and a playing company has
survived in any detail, and then only because it was broken and as a
result came into the lawcourts.[22] In July 1635 Richard Brome, who was
once Jonson's assistant and who started playwriting for the Kings' Men
at the Globe, signed a contract with Queen Henrietta's Men, who were
then playing at the Salisbury Court hall playhouse. He was to write
three plays a year for them for the next three years. This was a higher
level of production than the two plays annually that most poets
managed, and part of the dispute became a question whether Brome
had firmly promised nine plays in all over the three years, or simply
said he would do his best. He actually completed five. In return he was
to receive 15s. a week throughout the term of the contract, plus one
day's profit from each play. The practice of giving poets a day's takings
seems to have operated since before 1611.[23] We do not know how
standard was the weekly wage.

What basically caused the trouble between Brome and his employers
was the plague. It interrupted playing drastically in 1636, and altogether
prevented the players from gaining their London income for a good half
of the three years of Brome's contract. The weekly wage therefore
became intermittent, though by the end of the period the company
claimed they were only £5 behind in their payments. In that time Brome
had supplied only five plays, and moreover had sold one of them to a
rival impresario, William Beeston, when he was short of ready cash.

Despite these shortfalls on both sides of the contract, Brome and the
company entered on a new contract in 1638. The terms offered Brome
were more generous – £1 weekly, plus the profits for one day of each
new play – but the demands were still for three plays yearly, and for
the poet's exclusive services for seven years. Also the plays still owing
from the previous contract were not forgotten. Two were to be delivered
in the first year, and a third at any time during the contract. If Brome
fell behind again half of his wage would be forfeit.

Predictably Brome did not manage such a rate of production. After
less than a year he was seduced away once again by Beeston, who now
had a new company at the Cockpit to find plays for. The contract itself
could not be found, and the affair sank into the arms of the law, where
the depositions of both parties in the dispute are preserved. From the
depositions it is clear that whether or not a contracted poet received a
weekly wage from the company employing him, he was expected to
write only for his employers, to provide a fixed number of plays each
year, and not to publish any of them for at least the term of his contract.
The players do not seem to have held copyright in the modern sense –
Shirley published all the plays he wrote for Queen Henrietta's Men

after he left them, although they still used his plays in their repertory.[24] Occasionally the players may have given permission for a play to appear in print while the poet was still under contract.

It seems likely that the practice of benefit days, when the poet took the profits of his new play, was the standard method of payment for all poets, whether they were contracted to the players or not. The eight or so poets who had a steady working relationship with a single company presumably had not only this specific reward but also the security of a written contract and a steady wage. They were all evidently happy enough with this system. Some freelanced, like Jonson. Others must have signed long-term contracts, like Shakespeare, Fletcher and Shirley. The fundamental principle they all held, which underlies all consideration of the body of literature they produced, is that their works were written for the stage, for the playing companies, and that the durability of print was a secondary consideration, the sort of bonus that would normally only come in the wake of a successful presentation in the company repertoire.

6.   THE CITY AND THE COURT

Most of the other matters relating to the poets are too near the foreground to be dealt with in a study of the background. Two questions, though, or rather one question with two aspects, does have to be given some consideration. That is, first, the social allegiances of the poets and their engagement with their audiences, and secondly their engagement with the Court.

There were social tensions latent amongst all the playhouse audiences, and the record of the players exploiting those tensions with satire is considerable. Censorship held down comments on foreign policy, except for the spectacular eruption of anti-Spanish feeling in Middleton's *A Game at Chess* in 1624, and the censor also reacted to satire on living personages. But there was the Marprelate uproar of the late 1580s, mockery of Scotsmen by the boy companies in the early years under James, attacks on the Lord Mayor in *Hog hath Lost his Pearl* (1613), on Mompesson in *A New Way to Pay Old Debts*, and on Abell at the Red Bull in 1638, and attacks on royal policy by Massinger and others under Charles – the examples of satire that drew the censor's attention are only the peaks of a mountain of contemporary allusions. They were a very marketable commodity.

Social tensions showed up in different forms at different kinds of venue. At the citizen amphitheatres under the Stuarts the union of City Fathers and Puritans against playing was offset by the continuing patronage of the northern playhouses, the Fortune and Red Bull, by citizens and apprentices. On the Bankside, and especially in the hall playhouses, both poets and audiences had the Court much more in their minds. The reasons for this are complex, and the evidence open to a wide range of interpretation. Throughout the period the best companies might expect to be summoned to perform at Court. Every Christmas as many as a dozen plays would entertain the monarch and the assembled courtiers and ambassadors. To be summoned was an acknowledgement of status. Only the best of the companies performing in London were ever called for. So in a sense it was the ultimate goal of all the players, the final accolade for their success. What is not clear is whether the existence of this goal had any influence on the players' professional habits.

The records of the Revels Office and the Works accounts show how much time and money went into the preparation of the Court festivities, and the Court would in any case have been the top of the market so far as the players were concerned. The difficulty is in ascertaining how much they deliberately catered for that end of their market, and therefore how much influence the Court venues might have had on the day-to-day presentations around the city. Richard Hosley has gone so far as to suggest that the tiring-house façades, such as the Swan with its two broad entry doors and gallery above, were modelled on the screens in the halls of great houses.[25] Whenever players performed in a great hall, whether at Court or on their travels, they might expect to use the floor of the hall as their stage and the screen at one end as their means of entry and exit. Hall screens might therefore have provided a model for the tiring-house fronts in the commercial playhouses, though we should not forget that the street theatres of the sixteenth century, where travelling players erected a platform with a curtained booth at the back for their tiring-house, provided a broadly similar set of facilities.[26] Two kinds of venue, two traditions, came together in the course of the Shakespearean period. One was the popular theatre of the street and the market-place, the home of the nomadic travelling mummers, tumblers and players. The other was the great hall where the lord's retainers were occasionally summoned to entertain their employer. Both traditions, I suspect, merged in the permanent London playhouses where the stability of a good income and audiences consistent in both attendance and taste created a kind of central, normative venue different from either the street booth or the great hall.

The Court did of course provide one potentially very powerful influence in the form of the masques by which most of the major events, especially royal marriages, were celebrated. Players probably took speaking parts in these lavishly presented shows of verse, music and dance, and at the very least must have seen evidence in the shows of what the Court liked. The principle of masquing was a banquet of all the senses. Hence not only did orchestras play, choristers sing and courtiers dance, ladies as well as gentlemen donning the most colourful costumes for the occasion, but the eye was dazzled by the *trompe l'oeil* effects of Inigo Jones's perspective scenery. The stories of the masques were entirely allegorical, whereas the great majority of plays based themselves on realism. But music, dancing and the speaking of verse did also feature in the plays, especially those staged at the hall playhouses, and the temptation to imitate the feast of the other senses, especially the eye, must have gripped the players when they saw what the Court was able to do. Costume (apparel) was a major feature on the commercial stage, and the masquers' dress was both enviable and capable of being copied in the playhouses.

Beyond that, however, the players' resources were limited in both time and money. It took days to set up a Court venue for a masque, to fix the perspective scenery and the sort of machines that could fly boys in on an angle or, as in Campion's masque for Lord Hay's wedding in 1607, to contrive a House of Darkness through which bats and owls could flit on wires. It was dazzlingly clever, but it was costly in time and money, and none of the professional players ever used changeable scenery on their stages. Throughout the whole period the audiences they confronted daily on their home ground went away feasted with much less, or with a markedly different fare, than the Court enjoyed when it banqueted on its masques. Only with the Restoration did the visual feast of perspective scenery arrive to transform English staging.

There is room for disagreement over how much Court fashions might have influenced what the players and their poets offered on the common stages, and disagreement there is. The advantage to the players of pleasing the Court was straightforward. Financially they gained little. The fee for taking a play to Court was £10, comparable to the income they would get from a good day in their common playhouse. What they did gain from royal patronage was prestige, and more tangibly some protection against the wolves of Guildhall, who prowled round the London folds throughout the sixteenth century. When James gave his name to Shakespeare's company and his wife's and son's names to the two other leading groups of London-based players, he gave them security as well as prestige. How far in return they consciously shaped their stage presentations to match what they understood to be the Court fashion remains an open question.

It is hard to see how Court preferences would have had a really radical effect on common staging. Appearances at Court were infrequent, at best not more than half-a-dozen a year, compared with the daily appearances in the common playhouses. The Court's love of masques involved big spending on stage effects, which the common players could never dream of imitating in their plays. The two forms of spectacle were entirely different from each other. It was not the players so much as the poets who seem to have responded to the pressures of Court fashions, and even then much more in their masques than in their plays.

The poets clearly saw their work in plays and in masques as distinct. Both forms, according to Jonson, who wrote a good many of both, should combine instruction with the pleasure they gave. As he declared in the prefatory note to his masque *Love's Triumph*,

all Repraesentations, especially those of this nature in court, publique Spectacles, eyther have bene, or ought to be the mirrors of mans life, whose ends, for the excellence of their exhibiters (as being the donatives, of great Princes, to their people) ought always to carry a mixture of profit, with them, no lesse then delight.[27]

But the audience at Court, the home of the ruler, was different from the audience at the Blackfriars. So the masques written for the Court defined virtue in the abstract instead of evoking pity or laughter over a simulacrum of reality. Muriel Bradbrook has pointed out that Jonson's masque *Hymenaei*, which launched the great era of Jacobean masques with its vision of the ideals of courtly conduct, should be set against his play *Sejanus*, which heralded James's reign by an account of the disastrous vices of a Roman court ruled by a homosexual.[28] Charles on at least one occasion looked over his censor's shoulder and ordered a passage from one of Massinger's plays to be struck out because it was 'insolent'. The distance of what was written for the Court from what appeared on the popular stages makes it clear that poets and players alike led their own lives, and saw no need to imitate Court fashions in the process of earning their daily bread.

Jonson was a more markedly opinionated poet than most of his fellow-writers. Quite apart from *Sejanus*, his *Catiline* of 1611 is almost certainly a fictitious presentation of the Gunpowder Plot, and a defence of his own dubious part in it (like Marlowe before him, he seems to have found one source of finance in spying for the government). He was a violent controversialist against several of his fellow-poets in his contributions to the so-called Poetomachia, or War of the Theatres, in 1601–2.[29] With all this, however, he was also and always a passionate moralist, a running commentary on the follies of his times. Whatever the players made out of what he sold them, his masques were also statements of opinion, moral and political. The man who could write under a Stuart that 'A *good King* is a publike Servant'[30] was brave as well as outspoken, and no acquiescent royalist. Jonson was imprisoned in 1597 for a seditious play, in 1598 for killing a man (a player) in a duel, and in 1605 for another play, *Eastward Ho!*, which he wrote along with Chapman and Marston for the boys of Blackfriars, and in which they satirised the King and his Scottish entourage.

Other playwrights were less loudly opinionated than Jonson, but not much less forthright. Phillip Massinger, who wrote for several companies, including the King's Men, between 1613 and 1639, on the whole wrote plays like his *The City Madam* (for the King's Men at Blackfriars in about 1632). This play (the title is an antonym for 'Court lady') has a curiously ambivalent attitude to its citizen characters. It begins with a situation like those of the satires, showing up citizen greed and folly, but it ends with citizen values triumphant. The same author's *The Roman Actor*, however, written in 1625–6 at the beginning of the second Stuart's reign, is a veritable mirror for magistrates, a trenchant sermon to the new ruler and a playwright's manifesto.[31] On the political front it sets out the dangers of wrong rule, displayed in the conveniently distant setting of ancient Rome, where the chronic question of the divine right of kings was irrelevant. And defending its author's own interests it puts up a spirited case for players and playing. Players are necessary members of the commonwealth, says the title character at the beginning of the play,

> That with delight joyne profit and endeavour
> To build their mindes up faire, and on the Stage
> Decipher to the life what honours waite
> On good, and glorious actions, and the shame
> That treads upon the heeles of vice.

The profit of course was moral and educational, not financial.

The chapters that follow in this book present the background to the plays in the fullest practicable detail. First, the history of the playing companies provides the essential story of what happened through the seventy years between the granting of the first royal patent in 1574 and the closure in 1642. The next chapter describes the players themselves, their social backgrounds and their playing. The playhouses that they built for themselves once they had royal protection, and the staging of plays in the playhouses are described next; and finally a look at the audiences for the plays fills in some details of the general picture set out in the Introduction.

2. The Companies

1. THE LAWS OF PLAYING

THE 'Acte for the punishment of Vacabondes' of 1572 served the companies of players much as it was designed to serve the commonwealth of England as a whole. It authorised the better members of the profession to pursue their trade and turned the idle and poor members to higher things. It was an early step in the progress of the professional players from strolling entertainers, who never performed in the same place twice running, to permanently established repertory companies, with enormous financial investments backing them and a position in London guaranteed by the King himself. The statute of 1572 required each company to be authorised by one noble or two judicial dignitaries of the realm:

All and everye persone and persones beynge whole and mightye in Body and able to labour, havinge not Land or Maister, nor using any lawfull Marchaundize Crafte or Mysterye whereby hee or shee might get his or her Lyvinge, and can gyve no reckninge howe he or she dothe lawfully get his or her Lyvinge; & all Fencers Bearewardes Common Players in Enterludes & Minstrels, not belonging to any Baron of this Realme or towardes any other honorable Personage of greater Degree; all Juglers Pedlars Tynkers and Petye Chapmen; whiche seid Fencers Bearewardes Comon Players in Enterludes Mynstrels Juglers Pedlers Tynkers & Petye Chapmen, shall wander abroade and have not Lycense of two Justices of the Peace at the leaste, whereof one to be of the Quorum, when and in what Shier they shall happen to wander . . . shalbee taken adjudged and deemed Roges Vacaboundes and Sturdy Beggers.[1]

Ordinary gentlemen who wished to support a company of entertainers now ran the risk of losing them as vagabonds. A further statute of 1598 took away the licensing power from the magistrates too, leaving only great nobles with the authority to lend their names to the players. And when James came to the throne in 1603 he took the patronage of the chief London companies into his own family – one for himself, one for the Queen, one for the heir apparent, Prince Henry.[2]

    Players were a royal pleasure, and to please royalty was a major aim of the companies. The story of the companies between 1572 and 1642 is one of increasing royal favour and protection, from the first 1572 statute,

27

which gave warrant to their quality, through the accolade of direct royal patronage after 1603, to the final period when the royal protection ceased to be meaningful. There is, none the less, despite the royal favours and the various origins of the companies in employment as entertainers – adult mummers or boy choristers[3] – no question but that the profit motive was totally predominant. The companies were independent commercial organisations, not doing what pleasure-bent lord or royalty commanded, but going where and doing what brought most money and best audiences.

The relations of the various acting companies to the great, and to the specific patrons who gave them their names, is a complex question. Relations changed radically as the companies became an established feature of London life. In 1583, when Elizabeth gave orders to form a company under her own name, there were probably two powerful reasons dictating her decision. One was the way great lords such as Leicester and Oxford were using their playing companies in the Christmas festivities at Court as emblems of their own power. The other was the sustained attack on playing in London fostered by the Lord Mayor and Corporation. Elizabeth's formation of the leading players from every company into the Queen's Men checked the rivalry among the great nobles and at the same time gave powerful backing to the continued presence of the players in London. When James took over the patronage of the Chamberlain's Men in 1603 and later made his son and his wife patrons of the other leading companies he was renewing and systematising Elizabeth's tactic. Under Charles, the first monarch to take a personal interest in plays, royal patronage continued, but the players now divided themselves between the theatres performing for the privileged and the Court, and the 'citizen' playhouses catering for London's masses. By then the early use by great nobles of their playing companies to strengthen their political influence had been replaced, for players, poets and patrons alike, by a broader pattern of social allegiances which came to reflect the sharp divisions inside London society that split open and engulfed the players in the wars of the 1640s.

Whatever the social allegiances, all the playing companies were driven by the need to make a living. Company organisation was commercial, a core of shareholders and decision-makers, and a periphery of hired hands, backed in many cases by a theatre- and property-owning impresario who supplied ready cash in return for a share of the takings. Success meant working in London where the biggest audiences were, and where there might be the accolade of performing in the Christmas season of festivities at Court. For the players London meant living in one place instead of travelling and, more important, enjoying a steady income. For the company as a whole it meant a much larger membership than the travelling companies could afford, and therefore less doubling of parts and backstage work. A London company might have as many as twelve sharers compared with the six of a travelling company. The impresario with his playhouse would also have a store of properties and plays to expand the repertoire. London offered the two essentials for success, financial backing and a permanent playing place. The honey was in London, and the bees proved tenacious in clinging to it. Usually what dislodged them was a total prohibition on London playing because of the plague, when they had to resume travelling. In the later years it might be the impresario who broke them up to form new combinations of players more amenable to his financial terms. There were always new combinations ready to swarm in.

As the quality of the common players grew in the course of the sixteenth century, and as they developed from mumming and tumbling to acting, so their recognition by the government increased, and so likewise the hostility to them in London from the City Fathers. Their status was a matter for hostilities between the Crown and the Lord Mayor and aldermen for nearly a whole century before 1642. The threat to the common players from the statute of 1572 was a very real one, since the City Fathers had long before given notice of their willingness to enforce it. Primarily it was a renewal of the old series of statutes against retainers, which restricted the number of liveried servants that a noble might employ to those of his immediate household. Technically therefore the companies, if they were to protect themselves against the municipalities, had to enroll themselves in such a household, and carry their patron's livery as his personal retainers; though of course they would not, except for specific services in entertaining him, receive any wage for their position. James Burbage, writing on behalf of his company to the Earl of Leicester in 1572, made this very clear:

To the right honorable Earle of Lecester, their good lord and master.
Maye yt please your honour to understande that forasmuche as there is a certayne Proclamation out for the revivinge of a Statute as touchinge retayners, as youre Lordshippe knoweth better than we can enforme you thereof: We therfore, your humble Servaunts and daylye Oratours your players, for avoydinge all inconvenients that maye growe by reason of the saide Statute, are bold to trouble your Lordshippe with this our Suite, humblie desiringe your honor that (as you have bene alwayes our good Lord and Master) you will now vouchsaffe to reteyne us at this present as your houshold Servaunts and daylie wayters, not that we meane to crave any further stipend or benefite at your Lordshippes hands but our lyveries as we have had, and also your honors License to certifye that we are your houshold Servaunts when we shall have occasion to travayle amongst our frendes as we do usuallye once a yere, and as other noble-mens Players do and have done in tyme past, Wherebie we maye enjoye our facultie in your Lordshippes name as we have done heretofore.[4]

The protection of a patron, especially one so powerful, accommodating, and ready to get them opportunities to play at Court as Leicester was, clearly had enormous value. Still more so was the explicit royal protection that the same company was offered, unprecedentedly, two years later, in a patent of 10 May 1574. This was the first royal patent for a company of adult players. It specified the permissible scope of the company in unambiguous terms, and came to serve as a model for all patents granted subsequently:

Elizabeth by the grace of God quene of England, &c. To all Justices, Mayors, Sheriffes, Baylyffes, head Constables, under Constables, and all other our officers and mynisters gretinge. Knowe ye that we of oure especiall grace, certen knowledge, and mere mocion have licenced and auctorised, and by these presentes do licence and auctorise, oure lovinge Subjectes, James Burbage, John Perkyn, John Lanham, William Johnson, and Roberte Wilson, servauntes to oure trustie and welbeloved Cosen and Counseyllor the Earle of Leycester, to use, exercise, and occupie the arte and facultye of playenge Commedies, Tragedies, Enterludes, stage playes, and such other like as they have alredie used and studied, or hereafter shall use and studie, aswell for the recreacion of oure loving subjectes, as for oure solace and pleasure when we shall thincke good to see them, as also to use and occupie all such Instrumentes as they have alreadie practised, or hereafter shall practise, for and during our pleasure. And the said Commedies, Tragedies, Enterludes, and stage playes, to gether with their musicke, to shewe, publishe, exercise, and occupie to their best commoditie during all the terme aforesaide, aswell within oure Citie of London and liberties of the same, as also within the liberties and fredomes of anye oure Cities, townes, Bouroughes &c whatsoever as without the same, thoroughte oure Realme of England. Willynge and commaundinge yow and everie of yowe, as ye tender our pleasure, to permytte and suffer them herein withoute anye yowre lettes, hynderaunce, or molestacion duringe the terme aforesaid, anye acte, statute, proclamacion, or commaundement heretofore made, or hereafter to be made, to the contrarie notwithstandinge. Provyded that the said Commedies, Tragedies, enterludes, and stage playes be by the master of oure Revells for the tyme beynge before sene & allowed, and that the same be not published or shewen in the tyme of common prayer, or in the tyme of great and common plague in oure said Citye of London. In wytnes whereof &c. wytnes oure selfe at Westminster the xth daye of Maye.[5]

The players in all probability gave their thanks to Elizabeth when Leicester laid on his famous entertainment at Kenilworth in the following year, and they performed at Court over Christmas in both 1574 and 1575.

They had other business in London too. Through family links Burbage had already established contact with an early playhouse in Stepney. His brother-in-law, John Brayne, built an amphitheatre consisting of a scaffold of galleries and a large stage in a yard called the Red Lion in 1567.[6] It does not seem to have been a great success, and may have been constructed too soon to be securely profitable as a regular venue for a playing company. By 1576, though, the new legislation and his 1574 warrant prompted Burbage to take another step towards real security, the establishment of his own permanent playing headquarters in London. With his brother-in-law as co-financier, in 1576 he used his qualifications as a member of the carpenters' company and built the Theatre. On land leased for twenty-one years, and with a special proviso in the lease that he could dismantle and remove the construction if need be, he set up the framework that was later to be reused for the Globe, and gave it a grand Roman name as the first of its kind in London. He was probably still sceptical about the security of playing in London, because the proviso he tried to build into the lease was partly an attempt to preserve his investment in building materials from the usual fate of structures put up on leasehold land, which reverted to the owner when the lease expired.

He need not have worried, at least for the duration of his lease. The Theatre was in regular use by early in 1577, and a neighbour, the Curtain, was set up soon after. Both were located in the suburb of Shoreditch outside the jurisdiction of the City Fathers, whose opposition was soon in evidence. It intensified with the launching of a pamphlet campaign against playing and playhouses once the Theatre was in use. This campaign did not stop until the Queen gave playing her patronage in 1583. Outside the city limits and inside the royal patronage, from 1583 the London foot-hold and the corollary London profits were secure.

For the next few years Leicester's Men and the other companies able to reach London, Sussex's, Warwick's, Essex's and Oxford's, continued the pattern of playing in London while they could, and travelling each summer. They played at first only once or twice a week, but the Puritans were soon complaining of a greater frequency.[7] The Puritan preachers and City Fathers alike renewed their attacks in 1582–3, and were given ammunition by an Act of God on 13 January 1583, a Sunday, at Paris Garden when some scaffolding collapsed, killing eight spectators and injuring many more.[8] This was at a bear-baiting, but all forms of entertainment were branded alike in City eyes. It may have been this event and the outcry it caused as much as the scramble of players around London that led Sir Francis Walsingham on behalf of the government to depute the Master of the Revels to cream off the current acting talent and form one predominant company with the Queen's own name and patronage. As Edmond Howes later described it,

Comedians and stage-players of former time were very poor and ignorant in respect of these of this time: but being now grown very skilful and exquisite actors for all matters, they were entertained into the service of divers great lords: out of which companies there were twelve of the best chosen, and, at the request of Sir Francis Walsingham, they were sworn the queens servants and were allowed wages and liveries as grooms of the chamber: and until this yeare 1583, the queene had no players. Among these twelve players were two rare men, viz. Thomas [i.e. Robert] Wilson, for a quicke, delicate, refined, extemporall witt, and Richard Tarleton, for a wondrous plentifull pleasant extemporall wit, he was the wonder of his time.[9]

The Queen's Company, possessing as it then did all the most famous players – Wilson, John Laneham, and probably Tarlton from Leicester's, John Dutton from Oxford's, John Bentley and John Singer – held its predominance for the next five years. Its existence under the royal protection may well have helped the City Fathers to mollify their attitude to the players. Granting access to the one royally supported company gave them the right to refuse access to all the lesser stars in the circuit. In 1585 they produced a relatively modest list of requirements for the 'toleration' of players, including restrictions on playing during time of plague and restrictions in the authorisation of companies. They summed up their requests as follows:

That they hold them content with playeing in private houses at weddings etc without publike assemblies.

If more be thought good to be tolerated: that then they be restrained to the orders in the act of common Counsell tempore Hawes.

That they play not openly till the whole [plague] death in London have been by xx daies under 50 a weke, nor longer than it shal so continue.

That no playes be on the sabbat.

That no playeing be on holydaies but after evening prayer: nor any received into the auditorie till after evening prayer.

That no playeing be in the dark, nor continue any such time but as any of the auditorie may returne to their dwellings in London before sonne set, or at least before it be dark.

That the Quenes players only be tolerated, and of them their number and certaine names to be notified in your Lordships lettres to the L. Maior and to the Justices of Middlesex and Surrey. And those her players not to divide themselves into several companies.

That for breaking any of the orders, their toleration cesse.[10]

With this on paper, the Queen's Men ruled in the City and the relations of City and Court government remained unaltered for a few years.

The Puritan attacks on the stage were aimed fairly precisely at the purveyors of entertainment such as bull- and bear-baiting, tumbling, fencing displays and plays ('Theaters, Curtines, Heaving houses, Rifling boothes, Bowling alleyes, and such places').[11] They saw no difference between bear-baiting, fencing matches, playing and prostitution. Nor did they entirely exclude the boy players attached to the singing schools of St Paul's and the Chapel Royal at Windsor, and at such schools as the Merchant Taylors'. There are records of Puritan attacks specifically aimed at them. Even in the academic exercise of playing the profit motive was rearing its head, and in 1573 plays were banned at Merchant Taylors' because of the rowdyism of the audience. They were commercial shows open to the public. Therefore they were on a par with and in competition with the adult companies, not only at Court, where they had traditionally entertained the Crown with plays, but also in London.[12]

2. THE EARLY BOY COMPANIES

The Chapel Children moved into the City to a playhouse in the Blackfriars precinct, which was at that time still free of the City's jurisdiction, in 1576, the year that the first adult players' theatre was built. This 'first' Blackfriars playhouse was owned by Richard Farrant, deputy to William Hunnis as Master of the Chapel Children. He appears to have taken over Hunnis's duties in 1576 largely in order to run the Children at the playhouse as a commercial enterprise. He can have taken up the lease of the Blackfriars property in that year for no other reason. His company was listed along with the adults in 1578 in a Privy Council protection order.[13] In 1580 he died, and his company was eventually taken in hand by Henry Evans, a scrivener, and John Lyly, the playwright, presumably for similarly commercial purposes. The Paul's Children at about the same time, 1582, lost their Master, Sebastian Westcott, under whom the commercial aspects of their playing had not been predominant. After Westcott's death the boys seem to have joined forces with the Blackfriars company, as they had done for Court performances on occasions in the past.

In the course of 1584 the company was deprived of the Blackfriars playhouse, and consequently disappeared from the commercial stage. The Paul's Children resumed activities under their own identity in the same year, under a new Master, Thomas Giles, with the services of Lyly as their poet. They performed regularly at Court up to 1590. In that year Lyly's part in the Martin Marprelate religious controversies, and his company, who had helped to publicise his contributions, were officially disowned and all the playing companies for a time were suppressed. The adult companies, also involved in the Marprelate mudslinging, were considerably dampened by the experience, and the boy companies did not resurface for several years.

3. THE EARLY ADULT COMPANIES

The adult companies were still rising and falling with some regularity. The Queen's Men were depressed after the death of their famous clown in 1588, and suffered a number of desertions. Worcester's were their closest rivals through the five years they were on top, and it was from Worcester's rather than the Queen's that the leading actors of the next decade, and in particular one, Edward Alleyn, emerged. From 1588 two years of rapidly changing fortunes reshuffled the company membership until in 1590 two companies amalgamated to take the predominant position on the London scene. This was the joint enterprise of the Admiral's and Strange's Men. It lasted until the last of the major reshuffles in 1594, out of which emerged the most successful company of all, Shakespeare's.

The membership of Shakespeare's company and of the company that shared a monopoly of London playing with it after 1594 seems largely to have been drawn from the amalgamated company of 1590–4. The years up to 1594 were strained and frenetic. Marlowe and his university fellows were producing radically new and hugely popular plays. The Queen's Men had lost their predominance. There was a massive new appetite to cater for. And yet times were hard again – the plague was inhibiting London performances, and as a result companies were breaking and their members having to travel; the turnover of company membership was faster between 1588 and 1594 than it ever was before or after. Just how precarious and changeable an existence it was we can see if we trace what is known of the chief players through these years.

We can pick up the trail at Elsinore, of all places, in June 1586, where three players, Will Kemp the clown, George Bryan and Thomas Pope, are recorded as playing for Danish royalty, probably after serving the Earl of Leicester in the Netherlands. In September Kemp returned to England while Bryan and Pope went to play for the Elector of Saxony. In 1590 the latter two reappear in the records of the Strange's–Admiral's amalgamation at the Theatre, probably under the leadership of Edward Alleyn. Their names are among the actors named in the plot of the second part of *The Seven Deadly Sins*, which survives among the Alleyn papers at Dulwich College and has been attributed to the amalgamation in this year.[14] Of Bryan and Pope's fellow-actors in this play, two (Richard Cowley and Augustine Phillips) stayed with them in the Strange's part of the amalgamated company until the four of them went to form the Chamberlain's Men, Shakespeare's company, in 1594. Will Kemp rejoined his former fellows while the amalgamation still lasted, some time before 1593, since he is recorded on the title-page of *A Knack to Know a Knave* (of 1593 or earlier) as having performed his 'merrimentes' in it along with Alleyn. A warrant from the Privy Council of 6 May 1593 permitting the amalgamated company to travel names Alleyn as the Lord Admiral's Man, with Bryan, Pope, Kemp, Phillips and John Heminges as the leading Strange's Men.[15] Nothing of Heminges's earlier

4. (a) A possible portrait of Alleyn as Tamburlaine. Most of the engravings in Richard Knolles, *A Generall Historie of the Turkes* (1603), are copies of portraits in Boissard's *Vitae et Icones Sultanorum Turcicorum*, published in Frankfurt in 1596. One exception is the portrait of Tamburlaine shown here. Martin Holmes (*ThN* 5, 1950, 11–13) suggested that Knolles's engraver, Laurence Johnson, used the figure of Alleyn in his most famous stage role. It is true that Johnson's Tamburlaine wears what looks like a Cadiz beard, popular in London after Essex's expedition to Cadiz in 1596. His dress might be an Elizabethan doublet and jerkin, topped by a long brocade or damask coat. A coat described as copper-laced is listed among Henslowe's inventories as belonging to the part of Tamburlaine. John Astington has, however, questioned whether this portrait can have been taken from the stage, on the grounds that it is not so unique a type of engraving in Knolles as Holmes claimed, and that it has distinct resemblances to earlier presentations of Turkish costume.

(b) A detail from the arch (Illustration 3, page 10), showing Edward Alleyn as the 'Genius of the City' making his speech of welcome to King James.

history is known except that he might have been a Queen's Man; he could have been a long-term member of the amalgamation, his name not appearing in the *Seven Deadly Sins* plot because he played one of the roles for which no player is named. A letter of Alleyn's written from Bristol to his wife in London during the tour mentions Richard Cowley as another member. All of these except Alleyn moved into Shakespeare's company, the Chamberlain's Men, when it was formed in 1594.

The amalgamation was a curious kind of company organisation even in a period of such sharply fluctuating fortunes as the companies suffered over these years. Alleyn had been a Worcester's man for six or more years up to 1589, when he seems to have joined a new grouping calling itself the Admiral's. The group was suppressed in 1590, possibly because of the players' involvement in the Marprelate troubles, and yet Alleyn retained his personal status as the Lord Admiral's servant, and some of his fellows seem to have retained their separate identity as Admiral's Men with him in the amalgamation. A Strange's company had performed at Court in the winter of 1588–9, and may have suffered with the Admiral's in the cold official winds of the Marprelate displeasure. A combined company would strengthen numbers for London playing while retaining the two patrons' warrants for separate touring with smaller numbers.

The amalgamated group played at James Burbage's playhouse, the Theatre, in 1590–1. The plot of 2 *Seven Deadly Sins* is usually thought to date from this period because in addition to naming all the major players of the amalgamation with the single exception of Alleyn himself, it included among the lesser parts the name of James's son Richard Burbage. The plot of *The Dead Man's Fortune*, another Dulwich manuscript, also has Burbage's name in it, and probably dates from the same time for the same reason.[16] In May 1591, however, there was a quarrel of some sort between the amalgamated company and old Burbage, over his retention of some of the playhouse receipts. John Alleyn, Edward's brother, subsequently testified in a lawsuit brought by the widow of a

---

5. A detail from the plot for 2 *The Seven Deadly Sins*. A complete facsimile of the plot is reproduced in W. W. Greg, *Dramatic Documents* II, no. 11. The square hole between the two columns of writing marks where the board to which it was fastened hung on a peg in the tiring-house. Presumably it was hung up so that the players could consult it, not the book-keeper. He held a copy of the complete script. Some of the names listed are the parts (Gorboduc, Lidgate, Nicanor) and some of the players (Sincler, Burbage, Cowley). Probably the characters for whom the speeches were written out on the scrolls or 'parts' (see Illustration 17, pages 108–9) have the characters' names, and the bit-part players were given their own names.

The Platt of The Seconde Parte of the Seuen Deadlie Sinns

A tent being plast one the stage for Henry
the Sixt: he in it A sleepe: to him The Lieutenant
A pursevant R Cowly: Io Duke: and i warder
R Pallant: to them Pride Gluttony
wrath and Covetousnes at one Dore: at an other
dore Envie Sloth and Lechery The Three put
back the foure and so Exeunt

Henry Awaking Enter A keeper I sincer to him
a servant T Belt: to him Lidgate and the
keeper Exit then enter againe then Envy
passes over the Stage Lidgate speakes

A Sennit. Dumb show
Enter King Gorboduc wth 2 Counsailers: R Burbadg
mr Brian. Th Goodale. The Queene wth Ferrex and
Porrex and som attendamts follow Saunder wth
Harry A Duke: Kitt: Ro: Pallant: I Holland)
After Gorboduc hath Consulted wth his Lords be
bringes his 2 sonns to to seuerall seates Jhey
envying on on other Ferrex offers to take Porrex his
Crowne. he draws his weapon, The King Queene and
Lord Stay them The Strucke them away
… menacing each other exit … …

Lidgat speakes

Lidgat speakes

Enter Nicanor wth other Captaine: R Nall
A sincer Kitt: A Holland 2 Cowly: to them
Arbactus: mr Pope: to 5 m: will Fowle I Duke
to 5 m: Rodgrerie: Ne: to Ser Sardanapalus
to 5 m: Rodgperie: Ne: to Ser Sardanapalus
Like A woman wth Aspatia Rodope Pompeia
will Fowle to them Arbactus and 3 mr sions
mr Pope A sincer Vincent 2 Cowly to them
Nicanor and other R R Kitt

Exit Sardanapa: wth The Ladies: to Henry A
Messenger Th Goodale to 5 m: will foole
R minge. Alarum

Enter Arbactus pursuing Sardanapalus
and The Ladies fly After Enter Sarda
wth as many Jewels robes and gold as he can
cary.

Alarum

Enter Arbactus Nicanor and The other Captains
in triumphs mr Pope R Pa: Kitt: I Gr: I Sin.

Henry speaks and Lidgate
over the Body

Enter Ferrex Bilencke. …

former gatherer against Burbage for a similar reason that in May 1591, shortly after a fracas with the widow's relatives,

when [Alleyn] . . . came to [Burbage] for certen money which he deteyned from [Alleyn] and his fellowes, of some of the dyvydent money betwene him & them, growinge also by the use of the said Theater, he denyed to pay the same. [Alleyn] told him that belike he ment to deale with them, as he did with the poore wydowe . . . wishing him he wold not do so, for yf he did, they wold compleyne to ther lorde & M^r the lord Admyrall, and then he in a rage, litle reverencing his honour & estate, sayd by a great othe, that he cared not for iii of the best lordes of them all.[17]

The players consequently abandoned the Theatre, moving early in 1592 to a new home, Philip Henslowe's five-year-old Rose playhouse. Henslowe enlarged the Rose at this time, stretching its regular polygon into an irregular egg shape by rebuilding the stage and its gallery scaffolding a few feet further back, increasing the audience capacity by four or five hundred extra customers.[18] Probably this was for the purpose of utilising the evident skills of the new company. They certainly found a welcome with Henslowe. Edward Alleyn's long and profitable association with the Henslowe enterprises was well fixed by this new arrangement, since in October 1592 he married Henslowe's stepdaughter. From this time, as the company's chief player with his personal warrant from the Lord Admiral, he began to take a share in financing and running the company along with Henslowe. Henslowe's records show the Admiral's–Strange's company performing for him regularly from early in 1592 until 1594, except when the plague prohibitions forced the company back to its travels.

Not all the amalgamated company seem to have followed Alleyn to Henslowe. Five of them, Pope, Bryan, Heminges (if he was in the company by 1591), Phillips and Cowley evidently did, since they were travelling with Alleyn as Strange's Men in 1593. But others who appear on the list for the *Seven Deadly Sins* are not mentioned, and their names turn up instead among the debris of the Pembroke's company that is in the records as travelling through Leicester near the end of 1592, at Court that Christmas, and in the country again at York, Rye, Ludlow (their patron's territory), Shrewsbury, Coventry, Bath and Ipswich through the summer of 1593. It seems to have been set up as a travelling company mixing some Strange's Men with some of the 'flag-fallen' Queen's Men.

Even travelling though was difficult at this gloomy time. Henslowe wrote to Alleyn during the Admiral's–Strange's tour in September 1593 that Pembroke's were in difficulties and had been forced to sell their costumes (*Henslowe Papers*, p. 40). A will of one of them, Simon Jewell, tells us that the value to the six sharers of the costumes they sold was

£80.[19] They also evidently sold their playbooks, for Marlowe's *Edward II* was entered on the Stationers' Register in July as a Pembroke's play, and *The Taming of a Shrew* a little later. *Edward I*, published in 1594, was probably another of their texts, and the reported texts of 2 and 3 *Henry VI* were certainly theirs, evidently made up by some of the members of the company once it was broken from their memories of what they had been used to perform. The text of 2 *Henry VI* as printed in the Shakespeare First Folio names John Holland as an actor at IV.ii.1, and John Sincler is named both in 3 *Henry VI* (at III.i.1) and in *The Taming of the Shrew* (Induction I.88). He was later to be named in 2 *Henry IV* as a Chamberlain's man. Both Holland and Sincler appear in the *Seven Deadly Sins* list. There is also a 'Nicke' in that list who may be the same as the 'Nicke' named in the Cade scene in the pirated text of 2 *Henry VI* and in *The Taming of the Shrew* (III.i.82). It would perhaps be stretching coincidence too far to identify these Nickes with Nicholas Tooley, who was to become a sharer in Shakespeare's company and who was once Richard Burbage's boy,[20] but it is at least possible that the Nickes were the same person and that he moved with Sincler and Holland from the amalgamated company in 1590 to Pembroke's in 1592–3, and thence to Shakespeare's company, along with the plays in which all their names appear. The possibility that it was Tooley is strengthened by the probability that his master Burbage did the same. Burbage's break with the amalgamated company must have come when they quarrelled with his father; he is noted in the lawsuit that describes the quarrel as vigorously defending his father's property and profits.[21] He may have formed a new company to play at his father's abandoned Theatre, along with Sincler and Holland, perhaps Tooley, and others from the amalgamation, and taken up with the Earl of Pembroke as a new master. The Earl's son described the player as his 'old acquaintance' in 1619 when Burbage died. Shakespeare may have been another Pembroke's man, if their possession of his plays is any indication of where his early allegiance lay.[22]

Travelling seems to have been the great disintegrator. The size of company that could thrive in London was impossibly cumbersome on the road, and most of the changes in personnel seem to have happened when a company 'broke and went into the country' as Henslowe put it of the Queen's, or when they returned to a foot-hold in London. Pay in the provinces was markedly less than in London – Henslowe paid hired men 5s. weekly when they were travelling as against 10s. in London – and any player who could join a well-placed London company when his own was forced out of town would presumably have done so. The amalgamation of Strange's and the Admiral's seems to have related to these circumstances, as we learn from their plea to the Privy Council of 1591 or 1592,[23] which pointed out that 'oure Companie is greate, and thearbie our chardge intollerable, in travellinge the Countrie, and the Contynuaunce thereof wilbe a meane to bringe us to division and seperacion'. When the amalgamated company went on its travels it does seem sometimes to have divided into its constituent parts – the records show a joint tour in the summer of 1593 and separate tours in 1592 and the spring of 1594.[24]

We can see, then, a shifting population amongst the companies, players moving from group to group as their financial circumstances pushed them. If the *Seven Deadly Sins* dating of 1590 is to be trusted, we can recognise among the Admiral's–Strange's combination at that time the following players: Edward and John Alleyn, George Attewell, James Tunstall, Pope, Bryan, Phillips, Cowley, Burbage, Sincler, Holland, Will Sly, John Duke, the boy Robert Gough, and a 'Harry', 'Nicke', 'Kit' and 'Sander' who may or may not have been Henry Condell, Nicholas Tooley, Christopher Beeston and Alexander Cooke respectively, all of whom turn up later in the Chamberlain's company. Kemp and Heminges had joined by 1593, and were leading members along with Alleyn, Pope, Bryan and Phillips. Cowley and Thomas Downton were also in the amalgamation in 1593, and Attewell and Tunstall, who reappear in the Admiral's in 1595, were probably members throughout the period too. We have no record of John Alleyn playing after 1591, but there is no reason for him to have left his brother's company for any other. Of Burbage, Holland, Sincler, Sly, Duke, Gough, Condell, Tooley and Beeston there is no positive record until they reappear in the Chamberlain's Men after the reshuffle of 1594. They may have gone to Pembroke's when the amalgamated company quarrelled with old Burbage. The 'Bevis' who appears in 2 *Henry VI* with John Holland was certainly a member of the Pembroke's that pirated the play (the reported version has a gratuitous reference to 'Bevys of South-hampton'), and two other players named by Shakespeare, 'Humfrey' (along with Sincler in 3 *Henry VI*, III.i.1) and 'Gabriel' (3 *Henry VI*, I.ii.48, and *Taming of the Shrew* with 'Nicke' at III.i.82), are likely to have been the Humphrey Jeffes and Gabriel Spencer who turn up in the later Pembroke's of 1595–7. The presence of Shakespeare's histories with *The Taming of the Shrew* and others of his plays in the repertory of the Pembroke's players would strongly suggest that either Shakespeare himself or a player such as Burbage, able to afford his playbooks, or both, were in the company in 1593 when they broke.[25] Eventually either or both moved to the Chamberlain's Men, who were the later owners of the plays. Strange's had none of Shakespeare's plays in 1593, so far as we can tell from Henslowe's records of their repertory.[26]

The only Shakespeare play that can be positively identified in Henslowe's lists is *Titus Andronicus*, which is noted as performed by

Sussex's Men for the first time on 23 January 1594. This was after Pembroke's had broken. If the sequence of companies performing the play that is listed on the title-page of the 1594 quarto is correct, then it went from Derby's (i.e. Strange's), to Pembroke's and thence to Sussex's. This may indeed reflect the changing allegiances of either Shakespeare himself, or of Burbage if he bought the play from its author, and probably some others of their fellows, between the play's composition, in about 1590, and 1594, when it was printed. Sussex's were travelling in the summer of 1593 but came to London for the winter, including a six-week season with Henslowe for which they may well have needed reinforcement from the better remnants of the broken Pembroke's.

4. THE STRONG COMPANIES

What may have caused the next reshuffle and the break-up of the amalgamation in the middle of 1594 we cannot tell. The Queen's Men broke in May 1594, and mergers were obviously then desirable, but none of the Queen's Men except the clown John Singer, who joined the new Admiral's, seems to have been involved in this last reshuffle. The membership of the Admiral's and Chamberlain's Men, the two companies that from this date came to bestride the London scene like the monopolistic colossi they were, is known in reasonable detail. They appeared together for Henslowe between 5 and 15 June 1594, probably playing on alternate days, and after that settled in their separate homes for good. Alleyn's new Admiral's stayed on with father-in-law Henslowe at the Rose, and Burbage's new Chamberlain's went to father Burbage at the Theatre.[27] Alleyn, Attewell, Tunstall and Downton of the old Admiral's in the amalgamation were joined by Richard Jones, who had been a fellow of Alleyn and Tunstall in Worcester's in 1583–9, and who had spent 1592–3 travelling on the continent, and Singer from the Queen's, together with Thomas Towne, Martin Slater and Edward Juby, whose names are all recorded in a list in Henslowe's *Diary* amongst memoranda for 1594–6 (pp. 87, 136). Other entries made by Henslowe and additional evidence such as the 1597 plot of *Frederick and Basilea* identify the new names of Edward Dutton, Richard Alleyn, Thomas Hunt, Robert Ledbetter and a number of boys, some of whom ('Sam', 'Pyk' and 'Will') can perhaps be traced back to the earlier Admiral's.

The Chamberlain's Men consisted of Pope, Bryan, Kemp, Phillips, Heminges and Cowley from Strange's, together with Sincler, Holland and 'Nicke' (if it was Tooley) whose names are preserved in Shakespeare's early plays and who probably came through Pembroke's; plus Burbage, Sly, Duke and Gough, who like most of the others had been in the *Seven Deadly Sins* company some years before and after that probably in Pembroke's; and Condell, Cooke and Beeston, who may have been too. Shakespeare, whose name is not in the *Seven Deadly Sins* list, had probably been a fellow of at least some of the new company in Pembroke's.

The years that followed for the reborn companies were exceptionally stable in comparison with the flux caused by the frequent prohibitions of the previous five years. The Admiral's, for instance, according to Henslowe's records, were able to play through six days a week for forty-nine weeks, breaking only for thirty-seven days of Lent, during which the Rose was renovated. A summer tour of eight weeks or so in 1595 was again followed by forty-two weeks of playing broken only by Lent (*Henslowe's Diary*, pp. 21–37). Such an unprecedentedly trouble-free run in London, shared as it was by only the two companies, provided a stability of conditions in which they laid the basis of their mutual prosperity and predominance for the rest of the reign. Their joint predominance, affirmed by a Privy Council decree of 1598, which limited the number of London companies to the two of them, was not challenged for the next twenty-five years.

One challenge that they did face just before their monopoly was sealed with official approval in 1598 is worth noting for the light it throws on the financial organisation and problems, as well as the profitability, of the companies, and also of the government's attitude to playing in London. A new Pembroke's company had appeared in the country in 1595–6, and near the end of February 1597 Francis Langley, owner of the new Swan playhouse, made an agreement with a company calling themselves Pembroke's Servants to play for twelve months at the Swan. They included Gabriel Spencer (probably the 'Gabriel' of *2 Henry VI*), probably Humphrey Jeffes (the 'Humfrey' of *3 Henry VI*), Robert Shaw and William Bird, together with Jones and Downton who up to then had been with the Admiral's. The Rose was left unoccupied by the Admiral's for three weeks from 12 February, an occurrence that may be connected with the departure of Jones and Downton, either as cause or effect. Each of the named Pembroke's Men gave Langley a surety of £100 to guarantee their staying the stipulated length of time. In July, however, the Privy Council produced a drastic and probably unexpected prohibition: it gave orders not only that playing should stop but that all the playhouses should be pulled down. Langley was a special target, perhaps the only real target of the order, most likely as a result of his dubious dealings over a large diamond that the Privy Council had reason to suspect he had illegally in his possession (he claimed to be a goldsmith or financier, and was probably a fence).[28]

Even so Langley might have escaped – the other companies were relicensed in October, and carried on as prosperously as before. But in July Pembroke's Men performed *The Isle of Dogs*, possibly even giving new offence by staging it actually after the prohibition had been announced. It was declared to be 'seditious', and one of its authors, Ben Jonson (who probably also acted in it), was put in prison, along with Spencer and Shaw from the company. Whether the Privy Council was conducting a personal vendetta against Langley or merely trying to restrict the number of London-based companies, either way the result was the destruction of Langley's attempt to set up a third London playhouse. In August Jones fled back to Henslowe, followed by Shaw and Spencer on their release, then Bird, and in October Downton. Humphrey Jeffes and an Anthony Jeffes also turn up in Henslowe's books for the first time after this date. The refugees seem to have taken their playbooks with them to Henslowe, though a renewed or more likely a residual Pembroke's did start touring again at the end of 1597. Langley was subsequently unable to get a licence for playing at the Swan, and so began to sue the departed players for their £100 bonds. Henslowe records loans made to Bird to reach a settlement with Langley (*Diary*, p. 76).

What is illuminating about these varied fortunes is the relationship it reveals between Langley, as theatre impresario, and his tenants. Length of tenure was as important a financial matter to the owner as to the players, and was valued by Langley for insurance purposes at 5 × £100 for a three-year contract. The agreement specifically laid it down that the company was to perform only at the Swan when within five miles of London, except for performances 'in private places'. Langley claimed during the litigation to have spent £300 on apparel for the players and on preparing the playhouse, and in return was to receive half of the gallery takings and to be repaid for his expenditure on apparel out of the players' half. Langley's expenditure was considerable, though of course he expected his returns would be, too. All these arrangements are very like Henslowe's dealings with his companies, and on the evidence of the 1591 lawsuit also like James Burbage's with his (*Henslowe's Diary*, p. xxxii), except that Henslowe seems to have been involved to the extent of owning a number of playbooks himself. Some plays, such as *Friar Bacon* and *The Jew of Malta*, keep on appearing in his lists whatever the company performing on his premises. Henslowe also took out individual bonds with his players to guarantee their continued service. Richard Jones, for instance, was bound on these terms:

Memorandom that the 6 Aguste 1597 I bownd Richard Jones by & a sumsett of ii^d to contenew & playe with the companye of my lord Admeralles players frome Mihelmase next after the daye a bowe written untell the eand & tearme of iii yeares emediatly followinge & to playe in my howsse only known by the name of the Rosse & in no other howse a bowt London publicke & yf restraynte be granted then to go for the tyme into the contrey & after to retorne agayne to London yf he breacke this a sumsett then to forfett unto me for the same a hundreth markes of lafull money of Ingland wittnes to this E. Alleyn & John Midelton.[29]

In return for such bonds Henslowe offered security and such side benefits as his moneylending business – which helped Bird extricate himself from Langley, for instance. There seems to have been a rather blurred line drawn between loans made to the company, for which Henslowe repaid himself out of the players' half of the gallery takings, and loans to individuals. With the personnel of the company likely to fluctuate as it did, this is understandable.

On the company side, the distinction between sharers, those players with a direct financial interest in the company, sharing profits and expenses alike, and hired men, paid on a weekly basis, seems to have been clear-cut. It is usually assumed that a prefatory 'mr' in Henslowe's accounts denotes a sharer as distinct from a hireling.[30] There were probably ten or so sharers in the full-size London companies through the 1590s; those of the Admiral's after 1597, were Jones, Downton, Singer, Juby, Towne, Shaw, Bird, Spencer and the two Jeffes.[31] Alleyn, who retired from acting late in 1597, after the Pembroke refugees had been re-enlisted, lived more or less as Henslowe's partner in his theatrical and bull- and bear-baiting affairs. His taking a share in the financial side probably explains why Henslowe's own records are so much more sparse for this period than they are before 1597 or in 1600–2, when Alleyn briefly returned to the stage.

The sharers of the Chamberlain's Men by 1596 seem to have been eight in number: Burbage, Shakespeare, Kemp, Pope, Bryan, Phillips, Sly and Heminges. Bryan dropped out soon after 1596, and Pope was dying by 1603; they were replaced by Condell and Cowley. Kemp left in 1599 to dance his famous morris to Norwich, and was replaced by Robert Armin from Lord Chandos's Men. In 1603, once they had become the King's Men, the number was increased to twelve with the elevation of Alexander Cooke and Nicholas Tooley, the addition of John Lowin from Worcester's, and Laurence Fletcher, who had been favoured by James when he took a company touring in Scotland, and whose addition to the King's Men in 1603 may have been a further mark of royal favour. His name does not recur in the company's actor-lists, and it is not clear who may have replaced him. The number of sharers remained at twelve for the rest of the company's long life.[32]

The Chamberlain's Men's relationship with the owner of their playhouse was probably at first similar to that of the Admiral's with

Henslowe, and Pembroke's with Langley. The Chamberlain's leading player Richard Burbage was the son of the company financier, as the Admiral's Alleyn was son-in-law to Henslowe. But when he died in February 1597 James Burbage bequeathed his son and the company not a stable home for their playing but a disastrous financial mess. Knowing that the lease of the Theatre was due to expire in April 1597, and that the landlord was noisily hostile to its use for playing, he ventured all his capital to build a new playhouse. The occasional use of City inn-halls for playing had been finally stopped in 1595, and a memory of the first Blackfriars theatre, used by the Children of the Revels for several years up to 1584, may have set his mind on a novel course. He was evidently concerned by the loss of the roofed venues which the inns seem occasionally to have provided up to then. So in 1596 he bought the upper frater in the Blackfriars precinct, and converted it into a hall playhouse. It was inside the City but safe from the Lord Mayor in a 'liberty' where, as in the suburb of Shoreditch, his authority did not run. But unfortunately Burbage had not allowed for the attitude of the wealthy and influential residents in that central west-end enclave. They petitioned the Privy Council to ban the performance of plays at the new playhouse. The Lord Chamberlain, a Privy Councillor and resident in the Blackfriars himself, gave his support, as did the company's new patron, Lord Hunsdon, who also lived there, and who signed the petition to stop the players. Burbage died two months before the Theatre's lease expired, with all his cash tied up in an unusable playhouse.

The company struggled for the next two years, renting other play-houses while the Theatre stood empty and the two Burbage sons tried fruitlessly to negotiate a renewal of the lease. In the end, probably in some sort of despair, they leased a new plot of land near the Rose in Southwark, and hired a builder to secretly dismantle the Theatre and use its frame timbers as the basis for a new amphitheatre, the Globe. The decision to build another amphitheatre instead of a hall, as well as the theft of the old timbers, is a measure of how desperate their situation was.[33] The landlord promptly took them to court over the trespass on his land to steal the timbers, and the case struggled on for years. Another measure of their desperation is the novel decision they took to finance the new construction by bringing in five of the other sharers in the company to help raise the cash for their new home. The two young Burbages put up fifty per cent between them, and five sharers, Heminges, Kemp, Phillips, Pope and Shakespeare, put up ten per cent each. The six company sharers thus became not only 'sharers' in the company's fortunes but 'housekeepers' in their playhouse, entitled to a share in the owner's traditional half of the gallery takings. Shakespeare's housekeeper share, which soon increased when Kemp sold out to the other sharers, was in the long run to prove one of his most profitable investments.

This arrangement, whereby members of the playing company also became the company's landlords, was a unique device forced on them by the desperate financial straits the company went through in the years from November 1596, when the petition of the Blackfriars residents was granted by the Privy Council, until mid-1599 when they began to use the Globe. Viewed in commercial terms, it may have been the company's salvation. It was almost certainly this fortuitous underwriting of their finances that was to make them the most durable playing company that English theatre has ever seen. And yet all the events in the story seem to have happened by chance rather than design. The Burbages made some money from the lost Blackfriars playhouse by leasing it out in 1599, when cash was urgently needed to build the Globe. They gave it to an impresario who started a new boy company in it. These 'little eyases', as Hamlet called them on the Globe stage a year or two later, did not attract the hostility of the local gentry as did the adult players, and they helped the Burbages to recoup some of their father's investment. More to the point, in the long run the boys made the performance of plays in the Blackfriars precinct once again into a routine activity. Consequently by 1608, when the boy company was in deep trouble and their impresario surrendered the lease back to the Burbages, they had cleared the way for the adults to start acting at Blackfriars. At last the adult company, now the King's Men, could perform in the hall playhouse that old Burbage had built for them twelve years before.

The company then sensibly extended the ownership arrangements set up for the Globe, and cut in the leading sharers to become housekeepers of the Blackfriars as well. From then on, the company ran the two playhouses for the one company, alternating between them by using the Globe in the summer and the Blackfriars in the winter. This arrangement was not unlike the early practice, blocked in 1595, of using the amphitheatres most of the time, but turning to the city inns when the weather did not encourage outdoor trudges through the mud to the playhouse for outdoor viewing. Extravagant in

---

6.   A panorama of London engraved by Braun and Hogenberg, and printed as no. 2 in *Civitates Orbis Terrarum* (1572). The approximate location of each playhouse built between 1567 and 1629 has been added. The City walls are clearly marked with a thick black line. Westminster sprawls to the west of the City walls, and the main road north through Middlesex, where the Theatre and Curtain were shortly to be built, can be seen flanked by open fields, as are the baiting-houses on the Bankside in Surrey to the south of the Thames. See Ida Darlington and James Howgego, *Printed Maps of London* (London 1964).

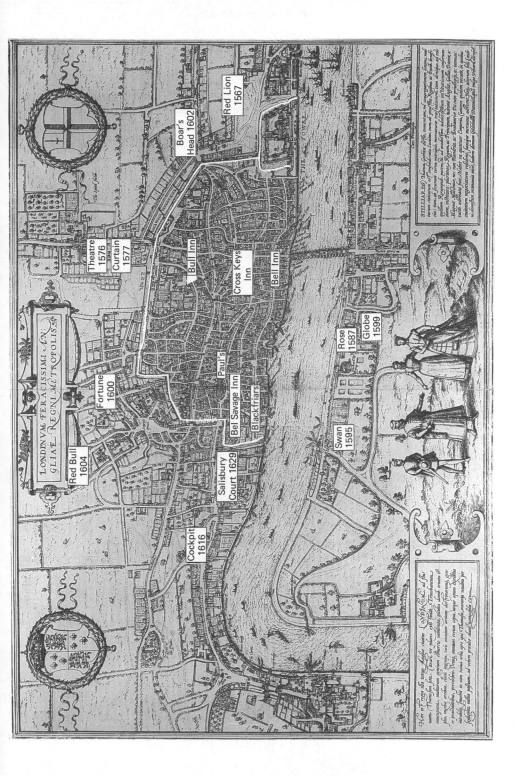

LONDINVM FERACISSIMI AN
GLIÆ REGNI METROPOLIS.

Theatre 1576
Curtain 1577
Boar's Head 1602
Red Lion 1567
Bull Inn
Cross Keys Inn
Bell Inn
Fortune 1600
Red Bull 1604
Paul's
Bel Savage Inn
Blackfriars
Salisbury Court 1629
Cockpit 1616
Swan 1595
Rose 1587
Globe 1599
TO THE TOWER

resources though it was, this new system of alternating between playing in the amphitheatre and the hall evidently suited them, because when they lost one of the playhouses by fire in 1613 they promptly rebuilt it at great expense. They could have played through the year just at the Blackfriars, but by then the Globe was evidently a feature of their activities they could not dispense with. So they dug deep into their pockets and rebuilt it, to continue the alternating pattern of summer and winter seasons.

The year 1599 was important for the Chamberlain's Men, because it secured their new venue, and started their new system of company management and financing. It was also important for their new neighbour Henslowe and his company. Henslowe wasted no time once the Globe became a close competitor. Although the land on which the Rose stood still had six years of its lease to run, he reversed their relative locations by taking his company to the northern suburbs now deserted by the Chamberlain's Men, and built the Fortune a little to the west of the old Theatre site. The year 1600 was particularly important for Henslowe and his company. Not only did their new playhouse, the Fortune, enable them to move from the Bankside to the north-western boundary of the city, but also Alleyn returned to the fellowship, at the wish, so it was claimed, of the Queen herself.[34] The times were still favourable to playing, and there does not seem to have been any more travelling until after the Queen's death in 1603. Henslowe's accounts over these years reveal mainly such minor matters as 10s. paid in May 1601 'to geatte the boye into the ospetalle which was hurt at the fortewne', 24s. in July to buy 8 pounds of copper lace, 6s. 7d. to mend a tawny coat 'which was eatten with the Rattes' in November, and on Christmas Day hose for a boy 'to tumbell in be fore the quen' (*Diary*, pp. 169, 177, 184, 186). The repertory gained thirty-one new plays between 1600 and 1603, a lower number than in the three years up to 1597, partly because of the extremely large number of new plays bought immediately before 1600, and partly (one would assume) because Alleyn, back in the company, was content to revive his old favourites.

Meanwhile another company, Worcester's, came under Henslowe's spreading wing. He built the Fortune in 1600 to rival the new Globe, and so his old playhouse, the Rose, was going vacant. Worcester's Men can be traced around the country throughout the decade or so after 1589 when Alleyn, Tunstall and Jones left them to become Admiral's Men. They appeared at Court in January 1602, and in March were admitted by the Privy Council as a third London company together with Oxford's, 'being joyned by agrement togeather in on companie'.[35] They appear in Henslowe's *Diary* in August, receiving advances for playbooks and apparel. Henslowe, who often did business over food (there are frequent entries in the summer the Fortune was being built for meals with the builder), records that the supper at the famous Mermaid Tavern when he reached his agreement with Worcester's cost him 9s., a sum he characteristically debited to his new company (Diary, p. 214). The Admiral's were now permanently at the Fortune, and Worcester's moved into the Rose.

The Worcester's company may have been new to London, but its membership was not. Players who authorised payments for Henslowe were Kemp, John Duke and Christopher Beeston, all former Chamberlain's Men, Robert Pallant, once of the amalgamated Admiral's–Strange's and probably subsequently of the Admiral's, John Lowin, who was soon to join the Chamberlain's Men, and Thomas Heywood, who was an Admiral's man as player and poet in 1598. Richard Perkins had joined by the time Elizabeth died, and Heywood and Perkins together formed the core of the company, as leading poet and player, from the time they became Queen Anne's Men early in James's reign. They were occupying the new Red Bull playhouse by the middle of the decade. In 1609 their licence to play was drafted, on the familiar Leicester's model with the now standard addition of their customary playing place, as follows:

Knowe yee that wee of our especiall grace certayne knowledge and meere mocion have lycenced and aucthorised and by these presents doe lycence and aucthorize Thomas Greene, Christofer Beeston, Thomas Haywood, Richard Pirkyns, Richard Pallant, Thomas Swinnerton, John Duke, Robert Lee, James Haulte, and Roberte Beeston, Servantes to our moste deerely beloved wiefe Queen Anne, and the reste of theire Associates, to use and exercise the arte and faculty of playinge Comedies, Tragedies, historyes, Enterludes, Moralles, Pastoralles, Stageplayes and suche other like, as they have already studied or hereafter shall use or studye, aswell for the recreacion of our loving Subjectes as for our solace and pleasure when wee shall thinke good to see them, during our pleasure. And the said Comedies, Tragedies, histories, Enterludes, Moralles, Pastoralles, Stageplayes and suche like to shewe and exercise publiquely and openly to theire beste commoditye, aswell within theire nowe usuall houses called the Redd Bull in Clarkenwell and the Curtayne in Hallowell, as alsoe within anye Towne halles, Mouthalles and other convenient places within the libertye and freedome of any other Citty, universitye, Towne or Boroughe whatsoever within our Realmes and Domynions.[36]

5.   THE LATER BOY COMPANIES

The position that the Privy Council had spasmodically struggled to maintain after 1598, of keeping two pre-eminent adult companies, was complicated in the new decade not only by the arrival of the third adult company, and a fourth, the Duke of York's, at the end of the decade, but also by the return of the two boy companies. A new company of

7.   Richard Perkins, from a painting in the Dulwich Collection, artist unknown.

Paul's Boys was back in operation by 1599, and Henry Evans the scrivener once again established a company in Blackfriars in 1600. To some extent the size of the part that the boy companies played in this decade has been exaggerated, at least so far as the history of the companies is concerned. Rosencrantz's claim that the 'little eyases' were carrying it away, even 'Hercules and his load', that is, the Globe's patronage, has helped this. Also relatively more of their repertory is extant than there is of the adults'. As a theatrical fashion, the one company lasted only until 1606, the other until 1608, when James decided, as Elizabeth had before him, that their services could be dispensed with. They really carried it away only in the first of the three phases of their career, up to the death of Elizabeth, at which time Henry Evans was on the point of giving up his venture altogether. By 1608 there was only one company, no longer boys but young adult players, their leaders aged about twenty. Boy companies as such never reappeared. Their chief mark of distinction was that they secured the services of the three most ambitious and opinionated poets of the day – Jonson, Chapman and Marston – and that they were well placed to carry out the tasks these three laid on them. Jonson for one obviously valued the children because he could order them to do what he wanted more easily than his adult employers. Beaumont, Fletcher, Middleton and Dekker also wrote for them.

Paul's were the first to return to the surface, as they had been the last to sink beneath it. Theirs was a smallish enterprise – they seem to have begun by charging only a hesitant 2d., whereas at the close in 1590 they had been charging 4d. or 6d.[37] Their playhouse was a small one and they performed only on Sundays and Mondays. They may have started in a small way over Christmas 1597–8. By 1599, though, Marston had written *Antonio and Mellida* for them, a piece strikingly self-conscious about its venue and its presentation, as if it was their first venture into the openly commercial playing world.[38] Jonson wrote a similarly introductory play, *Cynthia's Revels*, for a second boy company, located at the Burbage venue in Blackfriars and reminding Londoners of old history by calling itself the Chapel Children.

The nature of the enterprise of reviving the boy actors is shown by the membership of the backers of this second company. The manager was Evans, the former associate of Lyly with the old Blackfriars company. He enlisted to help him two men, Nathaniel Giles, who had been appointed Master of the Chapel Children at Windsor three years before, and Edward Kirkham, the Yeoman of the Revels. Giles had the authority necessary for getting the acting personnel, the power to 'take up' children for service in his choir school, and Kirkham, as officer in charge of the Revels wardrobe, had the necessary materials for acting at his disposal. A fourth associate was Evans's son-in-law Alexander Hawkins. Evans clearly believed in the familiar Elizabethan practice of keeping business affairs in family hands, and the subsequent wrangles over the company's finances give point to his faith in family loyalties.

Of the original four associates, Giles seems to have dropped out with some haste. His authority was to take up boys for singing, not acting, and was clearly going to be abused. A complaint brought against him

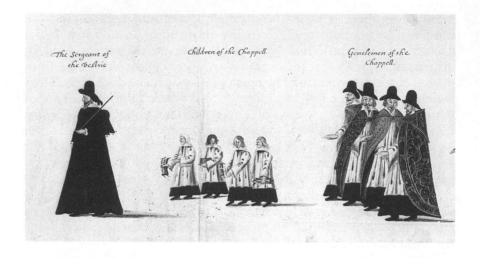

8. A manuscript drawing of the Children of the Chapel Royal in Queen Elizabeth's funeral procession in 1603, British Library MS.35 324 fol. 31v. Chorister garb has been slow to change.

by one Henry Clifton shows that it was. Clifton alleged that his son had been abducted while on his way to school and forced to 'exercyse the base trade of a mercynary enterlude player, to his utter losse of tyme, ruyne and disparagment'. When the case was heard in 1602 Giles was not summoned and may already have made his peace with the authorities. His powers of taking up boys were renewed with all the other renewals of the new reign in 1604, but somebody had evidently remembered the Clifton case by 1606, for in that year he lost the powers for good.[39] He remained as Master of the Chapel Children at Windsor until his death at the rare age of seventy-five in 1634, but seems never again to have meddled with playing.

The brunt of the censure over the Clifton abduction fell on Evans, who temporarily dropped out of the company's management in 1602, after making over his lease of the Blackfriars to his son-in-law. According to a later lawsuit, he subsequently enlisted two more backers, William Rastell and Thomas Kendall, to join Kirkham, who between them apparently paid out £200 for apparel and other playing materials, and £400 on the premises. Evans in return made a verbal promise to transfer half the lease to them, but of course did not do so; it was already in Hawkins's name. The associates drew up articles on 20 April 1602 whereby the three financiers gave Hawkins, as front man for Evans, a bond of £200 to guarantee their payment of half the rent and repairs to the premises, in return for which they would get half the profits of the company. It does seem a little odd that, as Kirkham testified in 1612, the financiers were satisfied with a verbal understanding over the lease when they were drawing up articles for the company's finances, especially since they seem to have been already on difficult terms with Evans. At the same time as they drew up the company articles they agreed to pay Evans 8s. for every week the company performed, apparently to stay out of the way. Perhaps they thought that would be enough to leave them in charge.

Evans did not stay out of the way, for during the prohibition on playing in 1603 he took the pessimistic initiative of discussing with the Burbages, from whom he had a twenty-one-year lease for his playhouse, whether he should give up the lease. In December 1604 he was in the way enough to lock up the 'Chamber called the Schoolhouse' on the premises in order to keep Kirkham and the others out, because they had not paid their share of a £10 repair bill.

The company restarted after the distractions of 1603, and in February 1604 James gave them a new patent as the Children of the Queen's Revels, naming Kirkham, Hawkins and Kendall, with a new man, Robert Payne, in place of Rastell. An additional feature of the patent was to make Samuel Daniel, the poet, their licenser of plays. This was a unique arrangement, which may have had something to do with the boy company insistence that they were a 'private' company, not a 'public' company like the adults. The public companies had to be licensed by the Master of the Revels, and it is possible that the 'private' companies at the 'private' playhouses were left free of this control by the fiction that they were not a commercial operation in the way that the adult companies were. The appointment of Daniel to be master of the revels of this one company may have been a device to accompany the fiction of private performances.

Daniel did not enjoy this distinction for long, because his own play *Philotas*, which the boys performed in 1604, got him into trouble for its resemblance to the Essex rebellion, and cost him the job. Despite this warning the boys seem to have continued to play without licence or control, and the next year another of their plays, *Eastward Ho!*, also unlicensed, got two of its authors into prison. The third, Marston, who had a financial interest in the company, had to flee for safety. In February 1606 John Day's *Isle of Gulls* got them into trouble again, for a more extreme version of the same offence, satire against James and the long tail of Scotsmen who had followed him to the English Court. A contemporary account reported that 'all men's parts were acted of two divers nations'.[40] The company now lost the patronage of Queen Anne, and had to drop her name from their title. Whereas over *Eastward Ho!* it had been the poets whom the government pursued, in this case the leading boys of the company were put in Bridewell prison. The management was reconstructed. Evans still kept himself in the background, and Robert Keysar, another goldsmith, moved in to take control. Under his rule the company became known as the Children of the Blackfriars, and the system of impressment which was originally employed on Giles's authority seems to have been replaced with an indenture system rather more like the system followed by the adult companies with their boys.[41] At about this time the Paul's company found it expedient to retire from playing altogether, and it is possible that the changes in the Blackfriars company system may have been partly designed to allow for the admission of some members from Paul's.

It is not really clear whether, at this late point in the Blackfriars Boys' career, the Master of the Revels had now taken over control of their 'private' activities, and put them under the same constraints as the 'public' players. Possibly he had not, because it was not long before the troubles of 1606 were renewed. In March 1608 the French Ambassador took offence over one or both of Chapman's *Byron* plays. The Ambassador took particular exception to a scene (not in the surviving texts) where the French king's mistress slaps the queen's face. To sharpen his complaint he added that 'a day or two before, they had slandered their king, his mine in Scotland, and all his favourites in a most pointed fashion; for having made him rail against heaven over the flight of a bird and have a gentleman beaten for calling off his dogs, they portrayed him drunk at least once a day'.[42] The result of this was that James 'vowed they should never play more, but should first begg their bread . . .' and gave orders 'to dissolve them, and to punish the maker besides'.[43] Chapman escaped, but Marston, involved over a related offence, and several players in the now almost adult company, were imprisoned. Evans then surrendered the residue of his twenty-one-year lease of the Blackfriars playhouse to the Burbages, apparently without consulting Keysar.

The company was not entirely destroyed. It performed at Court the next Christmas, for the first time in four years, a striking mark of royal forgiveness, or forgetfulness, and soon found a new playhouse just outside the City walls in Whitefriars. In 1610 Keysar allied himself with Phillip Rosseter the lutenist and several adult players, including Richard Jones of the Admiral's, to organise a new company, which he was allowed once again to call the Children of the Queen's Revels. By this time of course some of the 'boys' were not even youths. Nathan Field, who had been the leading actor since 1600, was twenty-two. Two others of the original company, William Ostler and John Underwood, left after 1608 for the King's Men where they had full adult status. In the very earliest days the boys had performed only weekly, as against the daily performances of the adults; after 1610 their practices in this as in all other respects cannot be distinguished from the adults. The King's Men even had the same kind of indoor playhouse, because they moved into the Blackfriars once the children had relinquished it. As a 'Children's' company the Queen's Revels may have had a larger proportion of boys than usual, but there were at least six full adults, some of them with decades of acting behind them.

Apart from the age of the players, and their use of indoor playhouses located inside the City walls, the chief distinctions the boy companies enjoyed came from their repertory. A large proportion of the plays they gave, after a few unsuccessful attempts to revive their pre-1590 repertory, were satirical comedies of a kind likely to give enjoyment to the Court gallants by their mockery not only of citizen values but also of the King and his Scottish followers. Scandal purveyed from the theoretical safety of 'their juniority', as the offended Heywood put it, was the staple diet from early on, when the so-called War of the Theatres was fought out between their poets.[44] The poets had, in all probability, a much larger say in the company's repertory and a freer hand than the poets of the adult companies enjoyed.

6.   THE LATER ADULT COMPANIES

Once the Burbages had reclaimed their Blackfriars playhouse for their own adult company, all the boys turned out to have accomplished was the re-entry of adult players into the city itself, the restoration of the right to play in the City which had been lost when the inns were finally closed to them in 1595. The inhabitants of the Blackfriars precinct stopped the Burbages in 1596 by petitioning the Privy Council, but no protest was raised when they and their adult company took over from the boys twelve years later. In 1608, too, the whole Blackfriars precinct, which had for centuries been exempt from City jurisdiction although inside the City walls, now came into the scope of City government, and yet nothing was done to prevent the adults from playing there.

It was an unparalleled stroke of good fortune for the King's Men. They could revive their old practice of separate winter and summer venues, this time with not an inn for the bad-weather season but an already well-patronised indoor theatre. The King's Men's predominant position was never again to be seriously challenged so long as the theatres lasted, even when the indoor Cockpit and Salisbury Court were used by other adult companies with a similar object. From 1609 the picture becomes a pyramid, with the King's Men (at the Globe for five months of the summer and Blackfriars the rest of the year) at the apex, and the companies of the Fortune and Red Bull maintaining a fairly constant position along the base line. The Cockpit companies rivalled the King's Men in later years, but generally floated somewhere between the apex and the base line occupied by the Red Bull companies.

The story of the London companies for the last thirty years of playing is basically one of consistent tenure and prosperity, though the prosperity came more to the managers than the companies themselves, and with the exception of the King's Men, the only company to last unaltered throughout, there was a fairly regular turnover of companies. Apart from two disastrous fires, at the Globe in 1613, which the King's Men were able to survive, and at the Fortune in 1621, which the Palsgrave's, descendants of the Admiral's, were not,[45] the chief disturbances were in litigation over company finances, and in the relations of companies with their theatre-owners and impresario-backers.

The Queen Anne's company's is a characteristic story of the decade after 1609. The last eleven years of their existence, 1612–23, began with the death of one of the sharers, Thomas Greene, who left his widow his share in the company, valued at £80, and a credit of £37 owed to him by the company. After some argument, the widow and her next husband, James Baskervile, agreed with the company in 1615 to give them an investment of a further £57 10s. in return for a pension of 1s. 8d. every playing day for the couple's lifetime. A year later the company, not having honoured its agreement and still short of ready money, managed to get another £38 from Mrs Baskervile for a further pension of 2s. for her and her son's lifetime. The agreement was revised again a year later for the widow and another of her sons, who was a player with the company and had not been paid his wages. At length, in 1623, Mrs Baskervile took the three players who still survived in the company since the time of the original agreements to Chancery in order to enforce payment of their bonds, and the company had to break.

The Chancery records contain a number of revealing depositions about the company's affairs at the time the bonds were made. In the first place they show that the original £80 that the company admitted they owed the widow of their former fellow was the value of a current share, and their payment to her was to cover the value, not to buy back the share. This automatically remained with the company. The value of a share of course depended entirely on the state of the company's health, and their difficulties grew largely because they were committed to repay a healthy value in time of sickness. As C. J. Sisson has described it,

The accepted and agreed value of a share was a safeguard of the interests of the individual sharer and of his family, being part of a body of assets, including goodwill as well as properties, playbooks and costumes, to which he had contributed either in money or by his skill, or both. But it was also a pawn or hostage by which the whole body of sharers safeguarded the general interests of the company. The actual and real value of a share depended upon the condition of the company and of the trade in which it was engaged. It seems pretty clear that it was not an asset likely to justify itself in a Court of Law. It was very different, of course, with a share by lease in a playhouse building or ground.[46]

The villain of this particular piece, and the only player to come out of it with any profit, was Christopher Beeston, the former Chamberlain's man, who had been a member of the company since its arrival on the London scene and increasingly through the second decade of the century its financier. He rose to power as James Burbage and Alleyn had done before him, by supplying his fellows with money for play-books and properties, and by renting other properties to them. At times, judging by the depositions in the Baskervile case, it looks as if he rented them properties which he had in fact bought with company funds; considering the fluctuating condition of company membership, the verbal nature of many of the agreements and the secretive nature of the accounting, this is not unlikely. One might attribute some of the success of the King's Men to the patent honesty of the man who did their paperwork, John Heminges. It seems to have been Beeston who was instrumental in milking Mrs Baskervile, and his adroitness in departing from the company without himself being bound to answer for repaying her is of a piece with the other indications of his character. The depositions of the players in 1623 actually allege that Beeston, upon whom the players 'at that tyme and long before and since did put the managing of their whole businesses and affaires belonging unto them joyntly as they were players in trust',[47] had been bribed by Mrs Baskervile to commit the company in her favour.

In 1619 Queen Anne died, and the company was divided. Perkins and others remained at the Red Bull and Beeston went to Prince Charles's Men as manager. An otherwise unknown mercer by the name of John Smith promptly took them all to court to get payment for 'tinsell stuffes and other stuffe' delivered on Beeston's instructions to the company between 1612 and 1617. The other players charged Beeston in this lawsuit with consistently looking after himself before he served the company, while he 'much enritched himself', and falsely billed the company for £400. Furthermore he had taken all the company's property with him when he left the Red Bull. He may even have taken a whole playhouse with him, for the recently constructed Cockpit, at which the Red Bull company played for a while in 1617, remained at Beeston's disposal. But of the financing of the Cockpit we know nothing except that the lease taken out in 1616 was in Beeston's name. In this case, as with the 1623 suit, the players were all too anxious to rid themselves of the burden of bills that they felt Beeston had unfairly left them with, and were certainly interested in shifting the onus on to him.

We need not feel that Beeston was the only unscrupulous mismanager of company finances at this time. Philip Henslowe's records of his operations at the Rose and the Fortune mainly concern his financial dealings with his companies, and show little evidence of his feelings for his business. In the 1590s, the period when he maintained the records of his day-to-day dealings in his so-called 'Diary', he evidently worked closely with the players, and had consistently good relations with them. He kept careful records of the material possessions, playbooks, apparel and other properties acquired for the companies. He carefully recorded the income from his gallery rents as well as the outgoings, and the loans he made to the companies while they built up their resources for playing. The pawnbroking and moneylending side of his business made him technically a usurer, since he made loans at more than ten per cent interest, but on occasions he lent money to the players without charging any interest at all. Lending money to get a player out of debtor's prison was good business, of course, since a player could not play his parts while in gaol, but the fact that Henslowe's records are all about his financial transactions does not mean that he took a narrowly commercial view of his activities. There are a few hints that he indulged in this relatively novel sport of sponsoring plays out of a genuine enthusiasm for playgoing.[48]

As time went on, however, and Alleyn took over more and more of the running of the companies, Henslowe became a civic dignitary and more distanced from playing. Under James he became a Court officer as Gentleman Sewer of the Chamber, and in 1607 he was made a vestryman in the Southwark parish of St Saviour. He seems to have become more distanced from his players as well as the business of running the plays and more autocratic in his management.[49] The Dulwich papers left by Alleyn include a pungent document, dating from 1615, drawn up by the Lady Elizabeth's Men as 'Articles of Grievance and Oppression against Philip Henslowe'. Lady Elizabeth's Men had come to London in the Christmas season of 1612–13, when they merged with Phillip Rosseter's Queen's Revels, the former Blackfriars children. Nathan Field was their star player, with other old boys from the Blackfriars company, including Joseph Taylor and William Ecclestone, all later to become King's Men. Field seems to have had generally very good relations with Henslowe. He addressed one letter to him as 'Father Hinchlow', and signed several as his 'loving son'. But he must have shared at least some of the anger voiced in his company's paper in 1615. The articles of complaint read like a catalogue of long accumulated grievances. Overstated though they are, they make a compendium of everything that the players thought could be said against Henslowe as a manager. They are a victim's critique of his increasingly casual and autocratic dealings after twenty-eight years as the first of London's great theatre impresarios (*Henslowe Papers*, pp. 86–90):

Imprimis in March 1612 uppon m^r: Hynchlowes Joyninge Companes with m^r: Rosseter ye Companie borrowed £80 of one m^r: Griffin and the same was put into m^r: Hinchlowes debt; which made itt sixteene score poundes whoe [a]fter the receipt of the same or most parte thereof in March 1613 hee broke the saide Comp[any a]lgaine and Ceazed all the stocke; under Culler to satisfie what remayned due to [him]; yet perswaded M^r: Griffyne afterwardes to arest the Companie for his £80: whoe are still in daunger for the same; Soe nowe there was in equitie due to the Companie £80

Item m^r Hinchlowe having lent one Taylor £30: and £20 to one Baxter fellowes of the Companie Cunninglie put theire said privat debts into the generall accompt by which meanes hee is in Conscience to allowe them £50

Item havinge the stock of Apparell in his handes to secure his debt he sould tenn poundes worth of ould apparrell out of the same with out accomptinge or abatinge for the same; heare growes due to the Companie £10

Also uppon the departure of one Eglestone a ffellowe of the Companie hee recovered of him £14: towardes his debt which is in Conscience likewise to bee allowed to the Companie £14

In March 1613 hee makes upp a Companie and buies apparrell of one Rosseter to the value of £63: and valued the ould stocke that remayned in his handes at £63: likewise they uppon his word acceptinge the same at that rate, which being prized by M^r: Daborne justlie, betweene his partner Meade and him Came but to £40: soe heare growes due to the Companie £23

Item hee agrees with the said Companie that they should enter bond to plaie with him for three yeares att such house and houses as hee shall appointe and to allowe him halfe galleries for the said house and houses; and the other halfe galleries towardes his debt of £126: and other such moneys as hee should laie out for playe apparrell duringe the space of the said 3 yeares, agreeinge with them; in Consideracion theareof to seale each of them a bond of £200: to find them a Convenient house and houses; and to laie out such moneies as fower of the sharers should think fitt for theire use in apparrell which att the 3 yeares, being paid for: to be delivered to the sharers; whoe accordinglie entered the said bondes; but M^r: Henchlowe and M^r: Mead deferred the same; an in Conclusion utterly denied to seale att all.

Item M^r: Hinchlowe havinge promised in Consideracion of the Companies lying still one daie in forteene for his baytinge to give them £50: hee havinge denied to bee bound as aforesaid gave them onlie £40 and for that M^r: ffeild would not consent thereunto hee gave him soe much as his share out of £50: would have Come unto; by which meanes hee is dulie indebted to ye Companie £10

In June followinge the said agreement, hee brought in M^r: Pallant and shortle after M^r: dawes into the said Companie; promisinge one 12^s a weeke out of his part of the galleries; and the other 6 a weeke out of his parte of the galleries; and because M^r: ffeild was thought not to bee drawne thereunto; hee promissed him six shillings weekelie alsoe; which in one moneth after unwilling to beare soe greate a Charge; he Called the Companie together; and told them that this 24ˢ was to bee Charged uppon them; threatninge those which would not Consent thereunto to breake the Companie and make upp a newe with out the[m] Wheareuppon knowinge hee was not bound; the threequarters sharers advauncinge them selves to whole shares Consented thereunto by which meanes they are out of purse £30 and his parte of the galleries bettred twise as much £30

Item haveing 9 gatherers more then his due itt Comes to this yeare from the Companie £10

Item the Companie paid for [Arra]s and other properties £40 which Mr: Henchlow deteyneth £40

In ffebruarie last 1614 perceav[ing]e the Companie drew out of his debt and Called uppon him for his accompts hee brooke the Companie againe; by with drawinge the hired men from them: and selles theire stocke (in his hands) for £400 giveinge under his owne hand that hee had receaved towardes his debt £300: Which with the juste and Conscionable allowances before named made to the Companie which Comes to £267: makes £567

Articles of oppression against Mʳ: Hinchlowe./

Hee Chargeth the stocke with £600 and odd; towardes which hee hath receaved as aforesaid £567 of us; yet selles the stocke to strangers for fower hundred poundes; and makes us no satisfaction./

Hee hath taken all boundes of our hired men in his owne name whose wages though wee have truly paid yet att his pleasure hee hath taken them a waye; and turned them over to others to the breaking of our Companie./

ffor lendinge of £6 to p[ay] them theire wages; hee made us enter bond to give him the profitt of a warraunt of tenn poundes due to us att Court./

Alsoe hee hath taken right gould and silver lace of divers garmentes to his owne use with out accompt to us or abatement./

Uppon everie breach of the Companie hee takes newe bondes for his stocke; and our securitie for playing with him Soe that he hath in his handes, bondes of ours to the value of £5000 and his stocke to; which hee denies to deliver and threatens to oppresse us with.

Alsoe haveing apointed a man to the seeinge of his accomptes in byinge of Clothes (hee beinge to have viˢ. a weeke; hee takes ye meanes away and turnes the man out./

The reason of his often breakinge with us; hee gave in these wordes should these fellowes Come out of my debt, I should have noe rule with them

Alsoe wee have paid him for plaie bookes £200 or thereaboutes and yet hee denies to give us the Coppies of any one of them./

Also with in 3 yeares hee hath broken and dissmembred five Companies./

Henslowe died at the end of the year, probably not of a broken heart, and Alleyn then amalgamated the various companies into one, Prince Charles's Men. Membership was reshuffled considerably. Field left to take Shakespeare's place as a King's sharer, Taylor and Robert Pallant moved to the new company, which took up third place in eminence behind the always predominant King's and the Fortune company. From about this time there were four companies consistently licensed to play in London, and it seems to have been in the brief of the Revels Office to maintain that number. In January 1618 the Revels records carry a note of the payment of 44s. by Heminges 'in the name of the four companys, for toleration in the holdy-days'.[50] Further references to 'the four companys' appear in 1623 and 1636, when the Master of the Revels noted that warrants were sent ordering 'the four companys of players' to stop playing because the plague bill had risen to fifty-four. Other companies (including in 1629 and 1635 a celebrated French troupe) might visit, but no more than four were in residence. The four in 1618 were the King's at the Globe and Blackfriars, Palsgrave's at the Fortune, the Queen's at the Cockpit, and the Prince Charles's, who had probably replaced the Queen's at the Red Bull when they left for the Cockpit, and then succeeded them at the Cockpit when Beeston left the Queen's to join them.[51]

The next important year for change was 1619. For the King's it was a difficult time: Burbage died in March, and the citizens of Blackfriars renewed their protest about the presence of the theatre and the effect of the carriages that thronged the streets around the playhouse and blocked trade:

there is daylie such resort of people, and such multitudes of Coaches (whereof many are Hackney Coaches, bringinge people of all sortes) That sometymes all our streetes cannott containe them, But that they Clogg upp Ludgate alsoe, in such sort, that both they endanger the one the other breake downe stalles, throwe downe mens goodes from their shopps, And the inhabitantes there cannott come to their howses, nor bringe in their necessary provisions of beere, wood, coale or haye, nor the Tradesmen or shopkeep[er]s utter their wares, nor the passenger goe to the comon water staires without danger of ther lives and lymmes, whereby alsoe many times, quarrelles and effusion of blood hath followed; and what further danger may bee occacioned by the broyles plottes or practises of such an unrulie multitude of people yf they should gett head, your wisedomes cann conceave; Theise inconveniences fallinge out almost everie daie in the winter tyme (not forbearinge the tyme of Lent) from one or twoe of the clock till sixe att night, which beinge the tyme alsoe most usuall for Christeninges and buryalls and afternoones service, wee cannot have passage to the Church for performance of those necessary duties, the ordinary passage for a great part of the precinct aforesaid beinge close by the play house dore.[52]

This move was eventually checked by a renewal of the company's patent of 1604, in which the name of the Blackfriars theatre was added to the Globe as the licensed playing place. They sailed on as before.

Burbage's place was filled by the acquisition of Joseph Taylor, once of the Revels children, from Prince Charles's, and this in turn seems to have led the Prince's to welcome Beeston from the flag-fallen Queen

Anne's, who were reorganised when their patron died, also in March 1619. Beeston's transfer in the long run proved to be a major event in company history, for Beeston gave the Prince's Men the Cockpit, the first indoor playhouse to offer a chance of rivalling Blackfriars as the playhouse favoured by the moneyed section of the London audiences.

The change understandably proved more to Beeston's advantage than his company's. As property-owner and theatre manager Beeston's practice seems to have been to run a company for only so long as it remained amenable to his dealings – usually three years – then deliberately break it, as the Lady Elizabeth's Men accused Henslowe of doing, reforming it later with a few survivors from the old company and a large infusion of new blood. One can only speculate darkly on his motives. The Prince's Men lasted until 1622, when they were supplanted by a new group called the Lady Elizabeth's Men, drawing Andrew Cane, destined to be one of the leading Caroline actors, from Palsgrave's, Joseph Moore from the original Lady Elizabeth's, and William Sherlock and Anthony Turner from unknown groups. The year 1625 brought not only the death of James but the worst visitation of plague in London's history, and an eight-month closure period for all theatres. Beeston reopened with a company patronised by the new Queen, Henrietta. It was headed by Richard Perkins, perhaps the most famous actor of his day, formerly of the Red Bull and since then briefly a King's man, and others from the Red Bull company, together with Sherlock and Turner from the old company.

The new Cockpit company rose steadily in prosperity and reputation for the next ten years, the only company to stay at Beeston's playhouse for more than three. The Master of the Revels signalled his judgement of their success in the winter season 1629–30 by giving them ten Court performances compared with twelve for the King's Men, who up to then had given as much of the Court entertainment as all the other companies put together. Shirley was the dramatist for Beeston, and more popular than Davenant or the other young wits currently providing for the Blackfriars. In the 1630–1 season they gave sixteen plays at Court, and were the only company besides the King's to receive the grant of royal liveries.

In 1637 the Lord Chamberlain forbade the printing of any plays without

some Certificate in writeing under the handes of John Lowen & Joseph Taylor for the Kings servantes & of Christopher Bieston for y^e. Kings & Queenes young Company.[53]

This 'young Company' was Beeston's latest. In 1636 during a nine-month-plagued interruption of playing Beeston deliberately broke the

Queen's company and in 1637 reopened with a new group largely made up of young actors. As the Master of the Revels noted:

At the increase of the plague to 4 within the citty and 54 in all – This day the 12 May, 1636, I received a warrant from my Lord Chamberlain for the suppressing of playes and shews, and at the same time delivered my severall warrants to George Wilson for the four companys of players, to be served upon them.

On thursday morning the 23 of February the bill of the plague made the number at forty foure, upon which decrease the king gave the players their liberty, and they began the 24 February 1636 [1637].

The plague encreasinge, the players laye still untill the 2 of October, when they had leave to play.

Mr Beeston was commanded to make a company of boyes, and began to play at the Cockpit with them the same day.

I disposed of Perkins, Sumner, Sherlock and Turner, to Salisbury Court, and joynd them with the best of that company.[54]

The old company was broken, though it later came together again and played at Salisbury Court. As that theatre's manager, Richard Heton, noted,

When her Majesties servants were at the Cockpit, beinge all at liberty, they disperst themselves to severall Companies, soe that had not my lord of Dorsett taken care to make up a new Company for the Queene, she had not had any at all.[55]

Perkins, Sherlock and Turner went to Salisbury Court with the revived company, five others went to the King's Men, and at least six returned to Beeston. The new company was known to the Revels Office as Beeston's Boys, and seems to have consisted of a much larger than usual ratio of boys to adults,[56] rather like the Queen's Revels Children after 1610. There were enough adults for five to be summoned before the Privy Council in 1637 and three to be committed to Marshalsea prison in 1640. They managed their own affairs in a sufficiently adult way for Beeston to bequeath them two of the six company shares, half his own holding, when he died in 1638. In addition to the adults retained from the old Queen Henrietta's Men, two came from the King's Revels, and two had been in Prince Charles's as early as 1631–2. Of the other recruits, two had been boys with the King's.

Beeston's Boys may have been modelled on the company put together by Richard Gunnell when he built the Salisbury Court playhouse in 1629. This was a group of fourteen youngsters, trainee players, who were given bed and board while they were being fattened for the market. The object was, ostensibly,

to train and bring up certain boys in the quality of playing not only with intent to be a supply of able actors to his Majesty's servants of the Black Friars when there should be occasion . . . but the solace of his Royal Majesty when his Majesty should please to see them and also for the recreation of his Majesty's loving subjects.[57]

Apart from the idea of a school to train boys for the King's Company, this sounds very like the formula for the boy companies of the first decade of the century. The training school may have been something of a pretext to gain the company an entrée into London playing. One or two of the boys do seem to have gone on to the King's Company. Stephen Hammerton, who was playing girl's parts for them in 1633[58] and later became the idol of the women in the audiences for his young romantic leads, was bought by Gunnell's partner in 1629 from his apprenticeship to a merchant tailor for the sum of £30.[59] But the primary return from such investments was in playing, and the boys appear to have been supplemented quite soon after they got started with six adult players, who became sharers with Gunnell in the enterprise. Boys were an investment, and were cheaper to maintain than adults. A lawsuit in 1632 claimed that after the long closure through plague the fourteen boys only had seven shirts between them, and that one had died because of their poor diet. Beeston might well have seen the financial advantages of a mixture of boys with adults when he set up Beeston's Boys in 1636–7.

When Beeston died in 1638 his son William took over management of the company's affairs. William was a less adroit diplomat than his father, who is recorded by Herbert, the opinionated and self-satisfied Master of the Revels, as on one occasion giving 'my wife a payre of gloves, that cost him at least twenty shillings'.[60] Beeston no doubt found it money well spent. In the spring of 1640 William fell, like his father before him more than once, into trouble with Herbert for failing to consult him over a play that contained political matters. The play was almost certainly Richard Brome's *The Court Beggar*, which satirised the courtier and wit of the Queen's circle John Suckling, his friend Davenant and several other members of the circle. The times were getting warmer as they moved nearer the explosion, and William was unable to mollify Herbert for his audacity as his father had done. He was visited with a total prohibition:

Wheras William Bieston and the Company of Playerrs of the Cockpitt in Drury Lane have lately Acted a new play without any Licence from the M^r of his Ma^{tes} Revells & beeing commaunded to forbeare playing or Acting of the same play by the sayd M^r of the Revells & commaunded likewise to forbeare all manner of playing have notwithstanding . . . Acted the sayd Play & others . . . Theis are therfore in his Ma^{tes} name, & signification of his royall pleasure to commaund the sayd William Bieston & the rest of that Company of the Cockpitt Players from henceforth & upon sight heerof to forbeare to Act any Playes whatsoever untill they shall bee restored by the sayd M^r of the Revells unto their former

Liberty. Wherof all partyes concernable are to take notice & to conforme accordingly as they and every of them will answere it.[61]

Furthermore William lost his position as 'Governor & Instructer' to the company, and with two of his company was put in the Marshalsea. Ironically, he was replaced by Davenant himself, the putative son of Shakespeare, former King's poet, current Court masque-writer and Poet Laureate, and founder of the most ambitious theatre project to date, one that had been squashed (ironically again with Herbert's connivance) only a year or so before. Davenant had little time to work as manager, for he was soon away at the so-called Bishops' Wars against the Scots, and after the collapse of the second campaign it was obvious that he along with all he stood for were on the losing side in a conflict that was more and more quickly coming into the open. In May 1641 Suckling was summoned before the House of Lords about a band of soldiers he had gathered together in London, supposedly to rescue the King's strong man, Strafford, from the Tower, where Parliament, with mortal intent, had put him. Suckling gained time by declaring with characteristic smoothness that he was raising a force for service in the Portuguese army, and by the time Parliament had obtained a denial from the Portuguese Ambassador Suckling and his fellow-conspirators in what became known as the Army Plot were on their way out of the country. Four of the five named by Parliament escaped; Davenant, with an ostentation as characteristic as Suckling's smoothness, managed to get himself captured in Kent. His famous 'saddleback' nose perhaps made him easily recognisable. He was held until Parliament realised it could not decide what to do with him and allowed him to depart into exile.[62] Beeston meanwhile seems to have slipped back into his managership – his mother still had the lease of the playhouse and a one-third holding in the company – but in any case the end was too near for either profit or delight, and at the beginning of September 1642 Parliament put a stop to both.

The authority the Master of the Revels had over the theatre impresarios is signalled by Herbert's part in the transfer from Beeston to Davenant. His degree of control, and the extent to which the impresarios had taken over a directly managerial role, is shown in a document drawn up in 1639 by Richard Heton for the Salisbury Court company. According to this document, Heton was to have the sole patent for the company, and he stipulated moreover

That such of the company as will not be ordered and governed by me as of their governor, or shall not by the Mr of his Mts Revells and my selfe bee thought fitt Comedians for her Mts service, I may have power to discharge from the Company, and, with the advice of the Mr of the Revells, to putt new ones in their places; and those who shalbe soe descharged not to have the honor to be her Mts servants, but only those who shall continew at the aforesaid playhouse.

Io. Grenhill pinx.   W. Faithorne Sculp.

Sir William D'avenant K.

And the said Company not to play at any tyme in any other place but the forsaid playhouse without my consent under my hand in wryting, (lest his M^{ts} service might be neglected) except by speciall comand from one of the Lo. Chamberlaines, or the M^r of his M^{ts} Revells, &c.[63]

7. COMPANY STRUCTURE

A recognition of the pattern of change in the history of the London companies is necessary before any meaningful generalisation about their organisation and practices sufficient to apply over the whole seventy years can be set up. Subject to the conditions of perpetual change, some picture can be made of the primary features, that is, the management of company finances and the pattern of governmental regulations by which the companies were bound. Between these tangible matters some filling in of the more human company affairs, the customs, corporate tastes and traditions might be attempted.

The chief distinction of London companies from travelling companies was their greater size. This in turn made their financial organisation different from that of the travelling groups, which had no more than six or eight players, few properties other than costumes, and which were led by a player who was at once leading man, manager, financier and warrant-holder. The London companies after about 1580 consisted of a core of between eight and twelve co-owning players, 'sharers', who shared both profits and costs, such as properties and apparel, rent, and the wages of hired men. Most plays required casts of at least twenty, and the companies had in addition in London the extra costs of stage-keepers, tiremen, gatherers, musicians and other assistants. The Admiral's 1 *Tamar Cam* of 1596 ended with a procession of twelve pairs representing a number of different races, made up from the players not already on the stage. The biggest companies in the seventeenth century had a total personnel of forty or more, of whom thirty were hirelings of one kind or another. Sometimes, as in that peak of stage spectacle, Heywood's *Ages*, two companies might join forces for a particular production. Heywood noted in his preface to *The Iron Age* that the *Ages* were 'often . . . Publikely Acted by two Companies, uppon one Stage at once'. The cast-list of *The Silver Age* has forty-one named parts, with additional 'servingmen, swaines, Theban ladies, the seven Planets and the Furies'. But such amalgamations were extremely rare. It was quite costly enough in terms of extras to perform an ordinary play. Even with

9. Sir William Davenant: an engraving in the frontispiece to the Folio edition of his *Works* (1673).

the maximum doubling of parts a 'normal' London company would need to employ, in addition to the eight, ten or twelve sharers, three or four boys for the women's parts, and six or more hired players, plus stage hands and musicians. To be a shareholder in a London company was to be involved in a commercial enterprise with a substantial turnover in expenditure as well as income.

In a normal situation a company sharer would be expected to buy his way into the company, and if the company remained a going concern he could sell his share when he left, providing he left with the agreement of his fellow-sharers.[64] A share in the Admiral's Men, with ten sharers, in 1597 or 1602, was worth £50; in its successor in 1613 with twelve sharers it was worth £70. A Queen Anne's share in 1612 was valued at £80; the former Blackfriars company in 1610 had less than an adult company, six shares, but they were valued at £100 each, a total of £600 against the £840 in 1613 of the Palsgrave's. The income on a King's Company share in 1634 was £180 for the year.[65] If a sharer died, the company reimbursed his widow for the value of her husband's share, and resold the share to a new active member of the company. It was an essential feature of the share system that it should operate not only as an investment for the sharer but as a commitment binding the owner to play for the company and to keep its interests his own. If a sharer left without his fellows' consent he was not reimbursed for his share. A begging letter from Charles Massey to Henslowe in 1613 describes the traditional sharers' agreement (*Henslowe Papers*, p. 64):

I know [you] und[er]stande th[at ther] is [the] composisions betwene oure compenye that if [any] one gi[ve] over with consent of his fellowes, he is to r[ece]ve thr[ee] score and ten poundes (antony Jefes hath had so mu[ch]) if any on dye his wi[dow] or frendes whome he appoyntes it tow reseve fyfte poundes (m^res pavie, and m^res round hath had the lyke) be sides that lytt[ell] moete I have in the play housses, which I would willing[ly] pas over unto you by dede of gifte or any course you [w]ould set doune for your securete, and that you sho[ul]d be sure I dow it not with oute my wiffes consenn[te] she wilbe willinge to set her hand to any thinge that myght secure it to you, Ser fifte poundes would pay my detes, which for on hole twelve month I would take up and pay the intreste, and that I myght the better pay it in at the yeares ende, I would get m^r Jube to reseve my gallery mony, and my qua[r]ter of the house mony for a yeare to pay it in with all, and if in [six] monthes I sawe the gallerye mony would not dow [then in] the other six monthes he should reseve [my whole] share, only reservinge a marke a wekke to furnish my house with all.

In the later years, when verbal agreements were supplemented by written articles, the bonds committed the sharer to stay with the company for a specified number of years, usually three, and gave financial penalties for such unco-operative actions as missing perform-

ances or rehearsals or being drunk. This, at least, is what Henslowe got
Robert Dawes to agree to when he joined the Henslowe enterprises:

the said Robert Dawes shall and will plaie with such company, as the said
Phillipp Henslowe and Jacob Meade shall appoynte, for and during the tyme
and space of three yeares from the date hereof for and at the rate of one whole
share, accordinge to the custome of players; and that he the said Robert Dawes
shall and will at all tymes during the said terme duly attend all suche rehearsall,
which shall the night before the rehearsall be given publickly out; and if that he
the saide Robert Dawes shall at any tyme faile to come at the hower appoynted,
then he shall and will pay to the said Phillipp Henslowe and Jacob Meade, their
executors or assignes, Twelve pence; and if he come not before the saide
rehearsall is ended, then the said Robert Dawes is contented to pay Twoe
shillings; and further that if the said Robert Dawes shall not every daie,
whereon any play is or ought to be played, be ready apparrelled and – to begyn
the play at the hower of three of the clock in the afternoone, unles by sixe of
the same company he shall be lycenced to the contrary, that then he, the saide
Robert Dawes, shall and will pay unto the said Phillipp and Jacob or their
assignes Three [shillings]; and if that he, the saide Robert Dawes, happen to be
overcome with drinck at the tyme when he [ought to] play, by the judgment of
ffower of the said company, he shall and will pay Tenne shillings; and if he,
[the said Robert Dawes], shall [faile to come] during any plaie, having noe
lycence or just excuse of sicknes, he is contented to pay Twenty shillings . . .
And further the said Robert Dawes doth covenant, [promise, and graunt to and
with the said Phillip Henslowe and Jacob Meade, that if he, the said Robert
Dawes], shall at any time after the play is ended depart or goe out of the
[howse] with any [of their] apparell on his body, or if the said Robert Dawes
[shall carry away any propertie] belonging to the said company, or shal be
consentinge [or privy to any other of the said company going out of the howse
with any of their apparell on his or their bodies, he, the said] Robert Dawes,
shall and will forfeit and pay unto the said Phillip and Jacob, or their
administrators or assignes, the some of ffortie pounds of lawfull [money of
England][66]

The sharers had to pay for the rental of their playhouse, the purchase
of costumes and other playing materials, the wages of all their hirelings,
and the various fees exacted by the Revels Office. It was also usual, at
least in the early days, to show good-neighbourliness by making
customary payments to the parish poor. The burlesqued company Sir
Oliver Owlet's Men in *Histriomastix* (c. 1598) is accosted by the local
constable for their 'taxe mony,/To releeve the poore'. The rent for the
playhouse was traditionally half of the gallery takings. If the playhouse-
owner was loaning the company money to buy properties he took his
repayments from the other half of the gallery takings, the gathering of
which was usually his concern rather than the company's. Much of the
function of impresarios like old Burbage, Henslowe, Langley and
Beeston lay in financing the purchase of such properties. It was an

exceptionally stable company that could afford its own; apart from the King's Men not many seem to have done so. They usually began with a loan from the impresario to buy playbooks and apparel, and never got out of his debt. It was in the interests of the Henslowes and Beestons to maintain a turnover of companies since each fresh company needed fresh finance to renew its apparel and repertory.

The system whereby several sharers of a company bypassed the impresario and themselves became playhouse owners or house-keepers began when Shakespeare and some of his fellows were called in by the Burbages, who needed a guarantee of tenure and capital for their new Globe in 1599. It was copied by some companies – the Queen's Men at the Red Bull and the Prince's at the Fortune after 1615 are the chief examples – but it was less common than single managerial ownership, and it frequently led to difficulties. A share in a playhouse was more durable than a share in a company, and could easily pass out of the company's possession. When that happened it almost always led to trouble and ofteñ litigation in order to secure for the householder his proportion of the rent, or for the company or other householders the part of the cost of repairs and maintenance that went with a property share.

It was a litigious age, of course, and the opportunities for human backsliding and inhuman sharp practice were omnipresent. The valuation of a company share was a subjective consideration, depending on the appearance of the company's health and prospects. The proportion of a householder's obligation for payment of a small repair bill was difficult to assess as well as to collect if, as not infrequently happened, a share had been passed on by inheritance and the original holding split into several fractions. The opportunities for a single financier to play on the fallible memories of verbal agreements made by a corporate organisation over several years amongst a changing membership were numerous. Even the gatherers might prove less than reliable, if a reference in 1643 to gatherers who 'seeme to scratch their heads where they itch not, and drop shillings and half croune-pieces in at their collars'[67] is any guide.

The sums of money involved were enormous by the standards of the time in comparison with the social class of those involved. Henslowe is reckoned to have spent £1,317 between 1597 and 1603 directly on the Admiral's Men's properties, of which playbooks took a half.[68] This, on a unit of comparison of a normal working-man's wage as 1s. a day[69] is equivalent to the wages of thirteen or fourteen such men over the whole six years. In 1631 a committee studying the Blackfriars property in an attempt to get the playhouse removed noted that the players had presented an itemised account valuing the property at £21,990. The committee's own valuation, covering loss of rent and interest in the site, was £2,900 13s. 4d.[70] The householders' price was understandably high and the committee's understandably low, but even the low figure is impressive for simply the estimated rental value of a single playhouse for the fourteen years that remained of the lease.

On the day-to-day level we have detailed records of Henslowe's gallery receipts near the turn of the century and more fragmentary records of other enterprises. The Admiral's Men's gallery takings were averaging £20 a week in 1597 (*Diary*, p. xxxv). To build the Fortune, possibly on the framework of an existing building, cost £520; to rebuild the Globe in 1614 about £1,400. Ground-rent was £16 for the Fortune, £14 10s. for the Globe. The licensing fee for playhouses rose from 10s. a week in 1596 to £3 a week in 1600 (for the new Fortune). A King's Company housekeeper in 1615 took £20 for one-fourteenth of the Globe and a similar amount for one-seventh of the Blackfriars, the combined takings from half the galleries of both houses therefore amounting to £420 in the year. By 1635 the Blackfriars was yielding £700–£800 a year and the Globe rather less, though it was still worth twice as much as the Rose in the 1590s.[71] A single performance at Court brought the company £10.

At the lowest level the pay of a player was little different from a journeyman's daily shilling. Henslowe in 1597 contracted to pay William Kendall 10s. weekly for playing in London, and 5s. 'in ye Cuntrie' (*Diary*, p. 269), while *Ratsey's Ghost* (anon., 1606) claimed that 'the very best' of provincial actors 'have sometimes beene content to go home with fifteene pence share apiece' (A4r). A reference in 1620 to 'twelve-penny hirelings' at the Fortune suggests that even Kendall was lucky while playing in London (John Melton, *Astrologaster*, E4r). Richard Jones wrote to Alleyn in 1592 to borrow £3 to get his clothes out of pawn, so that he could join a company about to travel in Germany, complaining that 'some tymes I have a shillinge a day, and some tymes nothing, so that I leve in great poverty' (*Henslowe Papers*, p. 33). Hired men none the less had the promise of shareholding in their future, and were even prepared to furnish bonds of £40 to guarantee their stay with their company (*Henslowe's Diary*, p. 242).

Boys were paid less than hired men. Henslowe charged the company 'a Ratte of iii s A wecke' in 1600 for their use of his boy James Bristow (*Diary*, p. 167). The *Articles of Oppression against Mr Hinchlowe* record 6s. weekly for the man responsible for 'bying of Clothes', which compares with the wages of the hired players. The other hirelings would hardly have been paid more, unless perhaps the 'book-keeper' was felt to be especially responsible. Musicians were more generously rewarded, but in any case often existed in a separate organisation; they had to be licensed separately by the Revels Office. In every case, of course, the wage would have to vary according to the company's takings and general prosperity. Nobody was paid during inhibitions. Roger Clarke joined the Red Bull company for a 6s. wage, as was 'sett downe in their booke', but in the hard times that followed his income went down to a half-crown or 2s. weekly.[72] Even the hired men were sharers in a company's misfortunes.

The Red Bull appears to have found even cheaper labour on occasions. Pepys records how he heard of

Thos. Killigrew's way of getting to see plays when he was a boy. He would go to the Red Bull, and when the man cried to the boys, 'Who will go and be a devil, and he shall see the play for nothing?' then would he go in, and be a devil upon the stage, and so get to see plays.[73]

One other matter of company finances is of interest. Poets were often directly employed by Henslowe, and their products were a regular and major drain on company finances. Thomas Dekker in 1598 had a busy year, during which he shared in the writing of sixteen plays; his total payment from Henslowe was £30, representing a weekly income of a little over 12s. Henslowe at this time was paying about £5 for a play purchased outright. By 1615 his prices had been pushed up to £20. The Court was paying £50 for masques. In later years the Restoration practice of benefit nights seems to have been used in some cases.[74] Companies had a necessary appetite for new plays; the Admiral's absorbed roughly one a fortnight in the years up to 1600; the boys at Blackfriars after their initial period took about four a year. In the last twenty years of playing the incomplete records of the Revels Office suggest a rather lower rate of consumption by each of the four companies.

8.   GOVERNMENT CONTROL

Government regulation of the companies grew up as a natural concomitant of both the government's and the companies' interests. The government gained by its power to limit plays, players and playhouses in what was spoken and by whom, and by the incidental command of the quality of the players who entertained the Court. The players gained above all protection from hostile local authorities. In the later years they profited by the security of the artificially monopolistic situation maintained under the Revels Office, and by such protection as the Master of the Revels could offer in preventing unauthorised performing or printing of the various companies' repertories.

The Crown's interest was exercised through the Privy Council, with the Lord Chamberlain as the Council's officer delegated to watch over plays and playing matters. His executive came to be the Revels Office, originally run intermittently under Henry VIII to organise Court shows, with a Master in the managerial role, one and a half clerks, and a Yeoman, who in the early days was a tailor concerned to maintain the extensive Revels Office wardrobe.[75] Under the Stuarts he seems to have been more of a stage manager. Once the adult theatres were permanently established in London it became expedient to extend the powers of the Office, and in 1581 the Master was granted wide powers, including the censorship of plays. The licensing of plays for performance had been required by proclamations of as early as 1559, when licences were to be issued 'within any Citie or towne corporate, by the Maior or other chiefe officers of the same, and within any shyre, by suche as shalbe Lieuetenauntes for the Quenes Majestie in the same shyre, or by two of the Justices of peax inhabyting within that part of the shire where any shalbe played'.[76] The royal patent to Leicester's Men in 1574, as we have seen, specified that their plays should be 'sene & allowed' only by the Master of the Revels. The 1581 commission to the Master, after specifying his rights to employ 'propertie makers and conninge artificers and laborers' and to buy materials for Court shows, laid it down that he was to take over all licensing authority:

we have and do by these presents authorize and command our said servant, Edmunde Tilney, Master of our said Revels, by himself, or his sufficient deputy or deputies, to warn, command, and appoint in all places within this our realm of England, as well within franchises and liberties as without, all and every player or players, with their playmakers, either belonging to any nobleman, or otherwise, bearing the name or names or using the faculty of playmakers, or players of comedies, tragedies, interludes, or what other showes soever, from time to time, and at all times, to appear before him with all such plays, tragedies, comedies, or shows, as they shall have in readiness, or mean to set forth, and them to present and recite before our said servant, or his sufficient deputy, whom we ordain, appoint, and authorise by these presents, of all such shows, plays, players, and playmakers, together with their playing places, to order and reform, authorise and put down, as shall be thought meet or unmeet unto himself, or his said deputy in that behalf.

And also likewise we have by these presents authorized and commanded the said Edmunde Tilney that in case if any of them, whatsoever they be, will obstinately refuse upon warning unto them given by the said Edmunde, or his sufficient deputy, to accomplish and obey our commandment in this behalf, then it shall be lawful to the said Edmunde, or his sufficient deputy, to attach the party or parties so offending, and him or them to commit to ward, to remain without bail or mainprise until such time as the same Edmunde Tilney, or his sufficient deputy, shall think the time of his or their imprisonment to be punishment sufficient for his or their said offences in that behalf; and that done, to enlarge him or them so being imprisoned at their plain liberty, without any loss, penalty, forfeiture, or other danger in this behalf to be sustained or borne by the said Edmunde Tilney or his deputy, any act, statute, ordinance, or provision heretofore had or made to the contrary hereof in any wise notwithstanding.[77]

This commission formally extended Tilney's powers, from the arrangement of all royal entertainments to the regulation of all the playing companies. It proved an effective form of control. The Privy Council edict of 1598, which limited the London companies to two, strengthened the Master's position. Subsequent commissions, in 1603 and 1622, simply renewed these terms. Later Masters extended their functions, taking on the licensing of plays for printing as well as performance, but that seems to have been more for the additional revenue than better control.

On the whole, the system was beneficial to both controller and controlled. Tilney prospered as Master of the Court entertainments largely because he supported the playing companies. More and more he introduced the players at Court to fill the long Christmas season instead of mounting masques. This was to their mutual advantage, because plays were much cheaper for the Revels Office than masques. The three masques in the 1573–4 season cost £75 each. In 1579–80 Tilney put up nine plays at £25 each.[78] Increasingly too, as the players began to bring their own costumes and properties, plays drew less and less on the coffers of the Revels Office. The chosen players gained a healthy status and Court favour, while the Office improved its financial health. It was a hard but a profitable collaboration. George Buc's bill for four months' work in 1615 specified 'for his owne attendaunce and his fower men viz from and for the laste day of Oct 1615 untill and for the xiiijth of Febr following for Rehearsalles and making choice of playes & Comedies and reforming them by the space of Cvij daies and xix nightes . . .'[79] Choosing, rehearsing and reforming plays kept the Master, his yeoman, his groom and two secretaries well occupied.

Censorship was now centralised, and the censor had close contact with the London companies. Not only did he license all plays but in effect he also licensed the companies. Each royal patent was issued through the Revels Office and specified his control. His exercise of his function is indicated in a warrant of 1616, which was evidently sent round the country and has survived because the local authorities in Norwich copied it into their records:

Whereas Thomas Swynnerton and Martin Slaughter beinge two of the Queens Ma^ts company of Playors havinge sep[ar]ated themselves from their said Company, have each of them taken forth a severall exemplification or duplicate of his ma^ts Letters patente graunted to the whole Company and by vertue thereof they severally in two Companies with vagabonds and such like idle p[er]sons, have and doe use and exercise the quallitie of playinge in div[er]se places of this Realme to the great abuse and wronge of his Ma^ts Sub^ts in generall and contrary to the true intent and meaninge of his Matie to the said Company And whereas William Perrie haveinge likewise gotten a warrant whereby he and a certaine Company of idle p[er]sons with him doe travel and play under the name and title of the Children of his Ma^ts Revels, to the great abuse of his Ma^ts srvice And whereas also Gilberte Reason one of the prince his highnes Playor^s having likewise sep[ar]ated himselfe from his Company hath also taken forth another exemplification or duplicate of the patent granted to that Company and lives in the same kinde & abuse And likewise one Charles Marshall, Homfrey Jeffes and Willm Parr: three of Prince Palatynes Company of Playo^rs haveinge also taken forthe an exemplification or duplicate of the patent graunted to the said Company and by vertue thereof live after the like kinde and abuse Wherefore to the and [sic] such idle p[er]sons may not be suffered to continewe in this course of life These are therefore to pray, and neatheless in his Ma^ts name to will and require you upon notice given of aine of the said p[er]sons by the bearer herof Joseph More whome I have speciallye directed for that purpose that you call the said p[ar]ties offendo^rs before you and thereupon take the said sev[er]all exemplifications or duplicats or other ther warrants by which they use ther saide quallitie from them, And forthwith to send the same to me.[80]

From the 1590s the Master's powers included the licensing of play-houses, and early in James's reign he began to license plays for printing as well as performing. The main point of licensing companies and playhouses seems to have been not so much the control it established as the revenue it gave the Master. Every extra duty brought him extra income. By the time of Henry Herbert, the last and most eager fulfiller of the office, the playhouse fee and the company fee were lumped together in a single annual payment, either from a benefit performance or as a lump sum. The King's Men gave him one day's takings each from the Blackfriars and Globe up to 1633, when they replaced them with a lump sum of £10 every Christmas and Midsummer. Beeston seems to have made a single payment.[81] Herbert's predecessor, Sir George Buc, noted in 1613 a payment of £20 for licensing the new Whitefriars playhouse, but this was a rare windfall, and in contrast we should note at least two occasions when the Master had to prevent a playhouse going up: Buc stopped Rosseter from building in Blackfriars in 1615; Herbert stopped Davenant in 1639.

The licensing of plays was also profitable for the Master, but in this case the ostensible object, censorship, was also a very real one, and the Master's labours were a serious duty taken seriously. The ordinance of 1559 had specified censorship of 'matters of religion or of the gover-naunce of the estate of the common weale'.[82] The hand of the censor can be seen descending on such matters in four extant manuscripts, *Sir Thomas More* (1594?), *The Second Maiden's Tragedy* (1613), *Sir John Van Olden Barnavelt* (1619) and *Believe as you List* (1628), the last of which was prohibited altogether. The deposition scene in Shakespeare's *Richard II* is missing from the early quartos, evidently for censorship reasons, and the texts of *The Isle of Gulls* and Chapman's *Byron* plays are obviously censored.

It is not certain what degree of control the Master of the Revels exercised over the 'private' boy companies in the first years of the seventeenth century. The likelihood that he did not control them as he did the adult companies has already been mentioned. He may have authorised the censorship cuts which show in the printed texts of their plays, but this may have been a retrospective action after spectators at the plays in performance complained of them. The trouble which *Eastward Ho!*, *The Isle of Gulls* and the Byron plays roused may have led the Master to take over responsibility for licensing the plays for printing. Certainly the years from 1605 to 1608 produced enough scandals to warrant an intensified concern for official control of plays, whether it was to restrain the satires about Scottish behaviour at Court or to curb more general offensiveness, either against the state or the church.

In 1606 an Act 'to Restraine Abuses of Players' ordered the censorship of profane oaths:

If . . . any person or persons doe or shall in any Stage play, Interlude, Shewe, Maygame, or Pageant jestingly or prophanely speake or use the holy name of God or of Christ Jesus, or of the Holy Ghoste or of the Trinitie . . . shall forfeite for everie such Offence by him or them committed Tenne pounds.[83]

This is one reason why the pagan gods begin to be called on with more frequency in the drama after this date. Herbert, the censor whose judgements we have most record of, in 1634 clarified the interpretation of the statute of oaths in a tiff with his royal master. As he noted,

This morning, being the 9th of January, 1633 [i.e. 1634], the kinge was pleasd to call mee into his withdrawinge chamber to the windowe, wher he went over all that I had croste in Davenants play-booke, [*The Wits*] and allowing of *faith* and *slight* to bee asseverations only, and no oathes, markt them to stande, and some other few things, but in the greater part allowed of my reformations. This was done upon a complaint of Mr Endymion Porters in December.

The kinge is pleasd to take *faith, death, slight,* for asseverations, and no oaths, to which I doe humbly submit as my masters judgment; but, under favour, conceive them to be oaths, and enter them here, to declare my opinion and submission.[84]

Herbert's basic concerns are revealed in a few of the opinions he recorded, such as these:

1623, August 19. 'For the king's players. An olde playe called *Winter's Tale*, formerly allowed of by Sir George Bucke, and likewyse by mee on Mr. Hemmings his worde that there was nothing profane added or reformed, thogh the allowed booke was missinge, and therefore I returned it without a fee, this 19 of August, 1623.'

1624, January 2. 'For the Palsgrave's Company; *The History of the Dutchess of Suffolk*; which being full of dangerous matter was much reformed by me; I had two pounds for my pains: Written by Mr. Drew.'

1632, November 18. '18 Nov. 1632. In the play of *The Ball*, written by Sherley, and acted by the Queens players, ther were divers personated so naturally, both of lords and others of the court, that I took it ill, and would have forbidden the play, but that Biston promiste many things which I found faulte withall should be left out, and that he would not suffer it to be done by the poett any more, who deserves to be punisht; and the first that offends in this kind, of poets or players, shall be sure of publique punishment.'[85]

His one detailed note on the reforming of matters of governance of the commonwealth again followed his master's voice:

> Monys? Wee'le rayse supplies what ways we please,
> And force you to subscribe to blanks, in which
> We'le mulct you as wee shall thinke fitt. The Ceasars
> In Rome were wise, acknowledginge no lawes
> But what their swords did ratifye, the wives
> And daughters of the senators bowinge to
> Their wills, as deities, &c.

This is a peece taken out of Phillip Messingers play, called *The King and the Subject*, and entered here for ever to bee remembered by my son and those that cast their eyes on it, in honour of Kinge Charles, my master, who readinge over the play at Newmarket, set his marke upon the place with his owne hande, and in thes words:

> This is too insolent, and to bee changed.

Note, that the poett makes it the speech of a king, Don Pedro, king of Spayne, and spoken to his subjects.[86]

Don Pedro was only slightly exaggerating the King's practices over money in the 1630s.

The payment for licensing a play was 7s. under Edmund Tilney, the first regular Master of the Revels. His successor, George Buc, started licensing plays for printing in 1606, and added that duty to his licences for performing when he took over the Mastership at Tilney's death in 1610. He charged £1 for both a licence to perform and a licence to print. Henry Herbert, who bought the reversion of the office in 1622, charged the same, doubling it for plays needing a lot of correction, and charging £2 regularly after 1632. Herbert paid £150 a year for the privilege of fulfilling the Master's duties, so his total income must have amounted altogether to substantially more than that.

The companies were not obliged to the Revels Office only for the licences which regulated and protected them. The Master also safe-guarded public health by enforcing the plague regulations, and safe-

guarded religion by enforcing the prohibitions on playing through Lent,
though in the later years Mammon was worshipped as well, in the form
of profitable Lenten dispensations to play issued by Herbert.

Plague regulations so far as the theatres were concerned followed
simply from the general requirement that places of public assembly
should be closed in time of infection. The City made the point as early
as 1569:

Forasmuch as thoroughe the greate resort, accesse and assembles of great
multitudes of people unto diverse and severall Innes and other places of this
Citie, and the liberties & suburbes of the same, to thentent to here and see
certayne stage playes, enterludes, and other disguisinges, on the Saboth dayes
and other solempne feastes commaunded by the church to be kept holy, and
there being close pestered together in small romes, specially in this tyme of
sommer, all not being and voyd of infeccions and diseases, whereby great
infeccion with the plague, or some other infeccious diseases, may rise and
growe, to the great hynderaunce of the comon wealth of this citty, and perill
and daunger of the quenes majesties people, the inhabitantes thereof, and all
others repayrying thether, about there necessary affares.[87]

The battles between City and Court in the 1570s and 1580s inevitably
included the plague question. The Leicester's patent of 1574 forbade
playing 'in the tyme of common prayer, or in the tyme of great and
common plague'. The clashes ten years later that produced the Queen's
Men and the City's 'Remedyes' over playing concluded that playhouses
should not open until the weekly bill of plague victims had been less
than fifty for three weeks. In 1604 the Privy Council brought this down
to thirty a week. The King's Men's patents of 1619 and 1625 specify
forty. The limits were not always very exactly enforced, but the
visitations of plague none the less were by far the most severely limiting
phenomenon the players encountered. The prolonged closures of the
really bad years, 1581–2, 1592–3, 1603–4, 1608–9, 1609–10, 1625, 1630,
1636–7, 1640 and 1641 never failed to endanger the companies and
usually caused major reshuffles of membership.

The worship of God was less disruptive than the visitations of plague.
The Privy Council ordered the closing of theatres through Lent in 1579,
and Henslowe's records show an obedient closure in 1595 and 1596. In
1597 however the Admiral's Men played through twelve days of Lent
and observed the closure for less than the whole period again in the
following year. In 1600, 1601 and 1604 the Privy Council renewed its
orders about Lenten playing, yet in 1605, though Lent began on 13
February, the Prince's Men played before royalty at Whitehall on the
19th. In 1607 the King's Men similarly played before James nine days
after Lent had begun. In 1615 there were substantial violations of the
closure order, and there is little evidence in later Revels Office records
of any very strict enforcement. There is actually some evidence to

suggest that the Master of the Revels took a fee for a 'Lenten dispensation', allowing playing throughout Lent excepting only 'sermon days', that is, Wednesdays and Fridays, and Holy Week. The performances are often noted as being displays of fencing or acrobatics rather than the more directly provocative stage-plays.[88] Dispensations of this kind make it readily understandable that in 1642 the whole business of playing should be taken out of the Privy Council's and its deputy's hands by Parliament's firm pronouncement that

Whereas the distressed Estate of Ireland, steeped in her own Blood, and the distracted Estate of England, threatned with a Cloud of Blood, by a Civill Warre, call for all possible meanes to appease and avert the Wrath of God appearing in these Judgements; amongst which, Fasting and Prayer having bin often tryed to be very effectuall, have bin lately, and are still enjoyned; and whereas publike Sports doe not well agree with publike Calamities, nor publike Stage-playes with the Seasons of Humiliation, this being an Exercise of sad and pious solemnity, and the other being Spectacles of pleasure, too commonly expressing lacivious Mirth and Levitie: It is therefore thought fit, and Ordeined by the Lords and Commons in this Parliament Assembled, that while these sad Causes and set times of Humiliation doe continue, publike Stage-Playes shall cease, and bee forborne.[89]

3.   The Players

1.   THE SOCIAL STATUS OF PLAYERS

IN AN EPIGRAM to Robert Armin, a King's player, John Davies of
Hereford wrote:

> Wee all (that's Kings and all) but Players are
> Upon this earthly Stage.
>> (*The Scourge of Folly* (1610), Q2v.)

Kings might well be compared to players. Comparing players to kings,
however, was a very different matter. The standard attitude to players
was that put by an anonymous author in the mouth of the highwayman
Gamaliel Ratsey, whose execution in 1605 was the occasion for the
publication of several pamphlets about his life and opinions. One
anecdote involved his exploitation of a troupe of travelling players
(*Ratsey's Ghost* A3v-B1v). Ratsey, according to the pamphleteer, came to
an inn where

that night there harbored a company of Players: and Ratsey framing himselfe to
an humor of merriment, caused one or two of the chiefest of them to be sent for
up into his chamber, where hee demanded whose men they were, and they
answered they served such an honorable Personage. I pray you (quoth Ratsey)
let me heare your musicke, for I have often gone to plaies more for musicke
sake, then for action. For some of you not content to do well, but striving to
over-doe and go beyond your selves, oftentimes (by S. George) mar all; yet
your Poets take great paines to make your parts fit for your mouthes, though
you gape never so wide. Othersome I must needs confesse, are very wel
deserving both for true action and faire deliverie of speech, and yet I warrant
you the very best have sometimes beene content to goe home at night with
fifteene pence share apiece.

    Others there are whom Fortune hath so wel favored, that what by penny-
sparing and long practise of playing, are growne so wealthy, that they have
expected to be knighted, or at least to be conjunct in authority, and to sit with
men of great worship, on the Bench of Justice.

Evidently for this playgoing highwayman the idea of a player becoming
a knight or a magistrate was deplorable (Ratsey himself was the son of
a wealthy Lincolnshire gentleman). This last jibe seems to be a direct

allusion to Edward Alleyn, since the reference to 'Others . . . whom Fortune hath so wel favoured' would fit his brief return to the stage of the new Fortune playhouse in 1600, and the social ambitions that began to appear after his subsequent retirement.

Having patronised his guests, Hamlet-fashion, and sympathised with their hard lot, Ratsey rewards them for listening to him and goes his way. A week later, still in his humour of merriment, he meets them again in a different disguise, like the players themselves, who were now masquerading under another name:

lying as they did before in one Inne together, hee was desirous they should play a private play before him, which they did not in the name of the former Noblemans servants. For like Camelions they had changed that colour; but in the name of another, (whose indeede they were) although afterwardes when he heard of their abuse, hee discharged them, and tooke away his warrant. For being far off, (for their more countenance) they would pretend to be protected by such an honourable man, denying their Lord and Master; and comming within ten or twenty miles of him againe, they would shrowd themselves under their owne Lords favour.

Ratsey heard their Play, and seemed to like that, though he disliked the rest, and verie liberally out with his purse, and gave them fortie shillings, with which they held themselves very richly satisfied, for they scarce had twentie shillings audience at any time for a Play in the Countrey.

Ratsey has other ideas of what they deserved, of course, and they become targets for his Robin Hood-like rough justice. The next day he overtakes them on the road and retrieves his bounty, taking the opportunity to reprove them for their 'idle profession'. The leader he singles out for gratuitous good counsel:

And for you (sirra saies hee to the chiefest of them) thou hast a good presence upon a stage, me thinks thou darkenst they merite by playing in the country: Get thee to London, for if one man were dead, they will have much neede of such a one as thou art. There would be none in my opinion, fitter then thy selfe to play his parts: my conceipt is such of thee, that I durst venture all the mony in my purse on thy head, to play Hamlet with him for a wager. There thou shalt learne to be frugall (for Players were never so thriftie as they are now about London) & to feed upon all men, to let none feede upon thee; to make thy hand a stranger to thy pocket, thy hart slow to performe thy tongues promise: and when thou feelest thy purse well lined, buy thee some place or Lordship in the Country, that growing weary of playing, thy mony may there bring thee to dignitie and reputation: then thou needest care for no man, nor not for them that before made thee prowd, with speaking their words upon the Stage. Sir, I thanke you (quoth the Player) for this good counsell, I promise you I will make use of it; for I have heard indeede, of some that have gone to London very meanly, and have come in time to be exceeding wealthy. And in this presage and propheticall humor of mine, (says Ratsey) kneele downe, Rise up Sir Simon two shares and a halfe: Thou art now of my Knights, and the first Knight that ever was Player in England. The next time I meete thee, I must share with thee againe for playing under my warrant, and so for this time adiew.

How ill hee brooked this new knighthood, which hee durst not but accept of, or liked his late counsell, which he lost his coine for, is easie to be imagined. But whether he met with them againe after the senights space, that he charged them to play in his name, I have not heard it reported.

The Ratsey anecdote provides a common view of the common player in his own times, though the pamphleteer evidently had a special anti-pathy to players, which might be explained by his fellow-feeling with 'them that before made thee prowd, with speaking their words upon the Stage'. The poets knew how generously the players treated them; Heywood's company paid out more for the heroine's dress in *A Woman Killed with Kindness* than for the play itself.[1]

The social standing of players, or rather the range of social attitudes to them, can be seen in a comparison of the Theophrastan characterisa-tion 'A Common Player' of 1615 with its counter 'An Excellent Actor'. The first was written by a law student called John Cocke from Lincoln's Inn. It claimed that

The Statute hath done wisely to acknowledg him a Rogue, for his chiefe essence is, *A daily Counterfeit*: He hath beene familiar so long with out-sides, that he professes himselfe, (being unknowne) to be an apparent Gentleman. But his thinne Felt, and his silke Stockings, or his foule Linnen, and faire Doublet, doe (in him) bodily reveale the Broker: So beeing not sutable, hee proves a *Motley*.[2]

The Player Cocke characterised was not necessarily so common either; he might be a King's Man. But he would be, none the less, a rogue:

howsoever hee pretends to have a royall Master or Mistresse, his wages and dependance prove him to be the servant of the people. The cautions of his judging humor (if hee dares undertake it) be a certaine number of sawcie rude jests against the common lawyer; hansome conceits against the fine Courtiers; delicate quirkes against the rich Cuckold a Cittizen; shadowed glaunces for good innocent Ladies and Gentlewomen; with a nipping scoffe for some honest Justice, who hath imprisoned him: or some thriftie Tradesman, who hath allowed him no credit.

Such an imputation was too much for one company with a royal master, and a reply soon appeared in print, probably written by Webster, whose *Duchess of Malfi* had recently been performed by the King's Men. It describes in conventional terms the qualities of a good actor as Heywood had set them down in his *Apology for Actors*, stressing their educational value:

By his action he fortifies morall precepts with example; for what we see him personate, we thinke truely done before us: a man of a deepe thought might apprehend, the Ghosts of our Ancient *Heroes* walk't againe, and take him (at severall times) for many of them. Hee is much affected to painting, and tis a question whether that make him an excellent Plaier, or his playing an exquisite painter.[3]

The last reference is meant to remind us of Richard Burbage, still the leading King's player, who was well enough known as a painter to have been commissioned in 1613 and 1616 to paint escutcheons for the Earl of Rutland.[4] Cocke was being unwarrantably snobbish.

The imitating Characterist was extreame idle in calling them Rogues. His Muse it seemes, with all his loud invocation, could not be wak't to light him a snuffe to read the Statute: for I would let his malicious ignorance understand, that Rogues are not to be imploide as maine ornaments to his Majesties Revels.

Cocke subsequently backpedalled, overlooking his explicit reference to the King's and Queen's companies, and protested that he meant only common players. He was let off a good deal more lightly than a later opponent of the theatre, William Prynne, whose *Histrio-mastix* of 1633 was one of the more trenchant Puritan blasts against plays and players. It attacked such decadences as women appearing in Court presentations. Henrietta Maria herself had recently graced a masque with her participation, so Prynne was taken up by the Star Chamber, who stripped him of his academic degrees, fined him, pilloried him, cropped his ears and sentenced him to the Tower for life.

The descriptions of Cocke and Ratsey were probably not entirely inaccurate with regard to the great majority of professional players who travelled for their living and whose 15*d*. or 2*s*. were rarely as ready to hand as the craftsman's shilling. It was an exceptional player who could profess himself to be even an apparent gentleman and conceal his dyer's hand in a courtier's glove. Shakespeare purchased a coat of arms for his father, but he earned a dig from Jonson in the process. In *Every Man Out of his Humour* Jonson parodied the Shakespeare motto, 'Non Sans Droict', as '*Not without mustard*'. A more intimate sign of status, or rather of the player's consciousness of where his way of life put him, is in Shakespeare's Sonnet 29. One of a group written to his aristocratic patron and friend and expressing his awareness of the distance between a playhouse and a great house (27 and 28 were written while he was travelling) it describes how he can move from misery to joy simply by shifting his thoughts from his own 'state' to his friend. It ends

> For thy sweet love remember'd such wealth brings
> That then I scorn to change my state with kings.

This final couplet is not so simple an assertion as it looks. The poet's 'state', he says at the beginning of the poem, is 'outcast'. A 'state' of course was not only a condition of mind but also a throne, a 'chair of state'. As a player-king Shakespeare's state was 'outcast' in the sense that like all players he was kept away by a socially unbridgeable gulf from the 'lord of my love' (Sonnet 26). He could accept the fact that his 'state' was so low as that of a player-king only by the assurance of his lord's love. Love alone can span the gulf between the player-king's and a real king's 'state'. Every sonnet written to the young aristocrat shows Shakespeare's awareness of how wide that gulf truly was.

Ratsey's gibe at the aspiration of prosperous players to knighthoods or at least to the 'Bench of Justice' would probably have been taken as an allusion to Alleyn, Burbage's peer, and the wealthiest of the famous London players at the turn of the century. The Ratsey reference to Hamlet must apply to Burbage, so it is not unlikely that the player favoured by 'Fortune' should be Alleyn. In 1605 he was Master of the Royal Game (or Bear-warden), a post that Henslowe's father had held before him, and he was already laying plans for the foundation of his great benefaction, Dulwich College. Alleyn failed in his ambition for a knighthood,[5] though in 1610 he did become a Churchwarden, a position carrying with it some judicial functions. His past as a player did not prevent him making his second marriage in 1623 to a daughter of the Dean of St Paul's. The fifty-two-year-old Dean, who in his days as Jack Donne had seen *Tamburlaine* and therefore presumably Alleyn on the London stage (in *The Calme*, line 33, he speaks of seeing Bajazeth in his cage), was less than amiable to his sixty-year-old son-in-law, but the quarrels were built on financial grounds rather than social.

James's fund-raising with such devices as his notorious £30 knighthoods at the beginning of his reign had confirmed the extent to which money was a major determinant of status. In 1630 Charles found a new source of income by fining those subjects with annual incomes of £40 a year who had not taken up knighthoods at the time of the coronation in 1625. One subject reluctant to have honour thrust upon him in such a fashion was a Cuthbert Burbage, almost certainly Richard's brother and still a proprietor of the Blackfriars and Globe.[6] If your source of income was from plays it was no barrier to the purchase of gentility.

2. FAMOUS CLOWNS

To locate players fairly precisely in the strata of Elizabethan and Jacobean society we should look first at the relationships of the great players to the great nobles. Phillip Sidney was not ashamed to be godfather to the son of Richard Tarlton the clown, and when Burbage

---

10. The full-length portrait of Edward Alleyn, founder of Dulwich College, in the Dulwich College Collection, artist unknown.

died in 1619 the Earl of Pembroke wrote to the Earl of Carlisle that he had stayed away from a play at Court 'which I being tender-harted could not endure to see so soone after the loss of my old acquaintance Burbadg'.[7] On the other hand one of the signatories to the petition of residents that prevented the Burbages and their company from moving into the Blackfriars playhouse in 1596 was their own patron, Lord Hunsdon, shortly to become the Lord Chamberlain himself.[8] Some at least of the lords of society were not prepared to tolerate the antics and dispositions of the public players except at a distance from home, and there is no evidence that many common players rose beyond their immediate circumstances in the tiring-houses and taverns of London and the provinces. It is probably not an over-statement to say that to the aristocracy they were at best befriended parasites.

Something of the history of acting as well as actors can be found in the careers of the famous players. The first great names of the 1580s were the clowns of extempore, Tarlton and Robert Wilson, whose fame far exceeded that of their contemporary straight actors in the Queen's Men, Bentley and Knell. By 1600 the position was reversed, and the reputations as tragedians of Alleyn and Burbage dominated the theatre world; in 1599 Kemp jigged his way out of the 'world',[9] and his successor Armin was as renowned for being a playwright as for being a clown. Subsequently fame fell not so much on the tragedians who inherited Alleyn's and Burbage's famous roles, Perkins or Taylor, as on the actor-managers like Beeston or actor-playwrights like Nathan Field. First the witty entertainers, next the great tragedians, lastly the impresarios. Like gentility, fame proved increasingly a commercial consideration.

Tarlton was not only a stage clown but a man of many parts, a maker of plays and ballads, a drummer, tumbler and qualified Master of Fencing.[10] He became famous in the 1570s, a byword in the 1580s, and a popular legend for a century after his death for his extemporised jests. Howes's additions to Stowe's *Annales* in 1615 characterise his facility as 'a wondrous plentifull pleasant extemporall wit', as distinct from that of his fellow-member of the Queen's and fellow-playwright Robert Wilson, whose wit was 'quicke delicate refined extemporall' (p. 697). His 1585 play, *The Seven Deadly Sins*, enormously popular though it was, has not survived in print (we have only the 'plot' of the second part), and the bulk of the evidence for his facility appears in the numerous jestbooks published after his death and purporting to record the witticisms of his life. Jestbooks were extremely popular reading fare in the sixteenth century, and since the usual practice of fathering common tales on semi-legendary wits like Skelton was also applied to Tarlton few of the anecdotes can be relied on. Fortunately some of his jokes were distinctive enough to be repeated by more reputable authorities than the

11. Richard Tarlton in clown's rustic apparel, with pipe and tabor. From a sepia wash drawing in the Pepysian Library, Cambridge.

jestbook writers. John Manningham noted one he heard, in his *Diary*, (1602):

Tarlton called Burley House gate in the Strand towardes the Savoy, the Lord Treasurers Almes gate, because it was seldom or never opened.[11]

This was very likely heard at second or third hand, if not at a further remove, since it was noted down fourteen years after Tarlton's death. Henry Peacham (*Truth of our Times* (1638)) told one at first hand:

I remember when I was a schoolboy in *London, Tarlton* acted a third son's part . . . His father being a very rich man, and lying upon his death-bed, called his three sonnes about him . . . To the third, which was *Tarlton* (who came like a rogue in a foule shirt without a band, and in a blew coat with one sleeve, his stockings out at the heeles, and his head full of straw and feathers), as for you, Sirrah, quoth he, you know how often I have fetched you out of *Moorgate* and

Bridwell, you have beene an ungracious villaine. I have nothing to bequeath to you but the gallowes and a rope. *Tarlton* weeping, and sobbing upon his knees (as his brothers) said, O Father, I doe not desire it, I trust in God you shall live to enjoy it your selfe.[12]

The reply may or may not have been extempore; certainly Tarlton's reputation did not entirely rest on his ability to extemporise. He is described as having a squint eye and a flat nose, and his very appearance, as Peacham also noted, was often funny enough:

> Tarlton when his head was onely seene,
> The Tire-house dore and Tapistrie betweene,
> Set all the multitude in such a laughter,
> They could not hold for scarse an houre after.[13]

As early as 1592 Nashe in *Pierce Penilesse* had described a similar reaction and its consequences when the Queen's company was travelling in the country;

A tale of a wise Justice. Amongst other cholericke wise Justices, he was one, that having a play presented before him and his Towneship by *Tarlton* and the rest of his fellowes, her Majesties servants, and they were now entring into their first merriment (as they call it), the people began exceedingly to laugh, when *Tarlton* first peept out his head. Whereat the Justice, not a little moved, and seeing with his beckes and nods hee could not make them cease, he went with his staffe, and beat them round about unmercifully on the bare pates, in that they, being but Farmers & poore countrey Hyndes, would presume to laugh at the Queenes men, and make no more account of her cloath in his presence.[14]

Tarlton's compeer, Wilson, a more scholarly wit, played in the same company with him.[15] Evidently the value of having extemporising wits and versifiers in the group was sufficient to justify two such performers sharing the same performance. Wilson also spent some time with Leicester's Men, touring the Netherlands with them in 1585–6, when he shared his work with 'my lord of Lesters jesting plaier' as Sidney described him, Will Kemp, the clown who later became the resident extemporising comedian in Shakespeare's company and probably the first actor of Falstaff.[16]

Kemp was the last of the famous Elizabethan clowns. He was better known for harlequinade and jigs than wit, and probably served his turn mainly for the dances and jigging sketches that normally accompanied performances on the public stages. He is rightly or wrongly thought to have been the culprit charged by Hamlet with speaking more than was set down for him, and it has even been suggested that his departure from the Chamberlain's Men in 1599 was because he had a hand in the piracy of the last Falstaff play, *The Merry Wives of Windsor*.[17] What is clear is that the role of the clown in adult company plays had diminished

12.   Will Kemp dancing a jig, from the title-page of *Kempes Nine Daies Wonder* (1600). The accompanist has the same gear (pipe and drum) as Tarlton.

markedly in value as plays began to offer more scope for the tragic actors. Hamlet's reprimand simply reflects an aristocratic impatience with knockabout and extempore. Kemp's duties as a clown with a role in almost every play of his company's repertory probably did not decline, but his occupancy of the stage during the performance proper was probably less. The parts we know he played include Peter in *Romeo and Juliet* and Dogberry in *Much Ado*, where he was given no more than a couple of scenes in which to indulge himself.

His successor had significantly different talents. Robert Armin was a playwright as Tarlton and Wilson had been, but much less an extemporiser. He was known for his singing rather than his wit. Where Shakespeare had written Falstaff and Dogberry with Kemp in mind, for Armin he produced Feste and Lear's Fool.[18] Both Kemp and Armin claimed descent from Tarlton, but between 1580 and 1600 the inheritance had dropped sharply in value. Alleyn's Tamburlaine now bestrode the stage.

13.   Robert Armin in the long coat of a 'natural' fool, from the title-page of his
History of the Two Maids of More-clacke (1609).

3.   FAMOUS TRAGEDIANS

Alleyn was born in 1566, the son of a London 'innholder'. Possibly his
father's occupation brought him into early contact with the players, for
he was already with a leading company, Worcester's, by the time he
was sixteen. By 1592 he was the outstanding player of his day. As
Henslowe's son-in-law and business partner, both in the theatrical
affairs and in the bull- and bear-baiting business, he rose to an
unparalleled prosperity, not only for himself but for the reputation of
the stage as a whole. He became famous as Tamburlaine, Faustus and
Barabbas in Marlowe's plays, as Orlando in *Orlando Furioso*, Muly
Mahomet in *The Battle of Alcazar* and Tamar Cam in the play of that
name.[19] His 'stalking Tamburlaine' drew similes from several pamphlet-
eers at the end of the century. His own self-mocking name for himself
in a family letter was 'the fustian king'.[20] Fuller remembered him as 'the
Roscius of our age, so acting to the life, that he made any part (especially
a majestick one) to become him' (*Worthies* (1662), Fff2v). He took the
part of Genius in King James's triumphal pageant through London in
1604; Dekker records that 'his gratulatory speech was delivered with
excellent Action, and a well tun'de, audible voyce' (*The Magnificent
Entertainment* (1604), C1r). Early in the new century he gave himself up

wholly to his business interests, retaining his shares in the Admiral's Men as manager rather than as player. He began negotiations to purchase the manor of Dulwich in about 1605, when he was thirty-nine, the year of Ratsey's anecdote, and began the school and hospital which have since become Dulwich College as a work of piety in 1613. The property cost £10,000 initially, and subsequent expenditure was about £1,700 a year, all of which derived in the first instance from Alleyn's theatrical interests.[21] He and his College were the age's highwater mark for the commercial and pietistic respectability of his first profession.

The name linked with Alleyn's by the early historians of the Elizabethan stage as the greatest of its players was of course Burbage. Baker's *Chronicle* (1674) celebrates *'Richard Bourbidge* and *Edward Allen*, two such Actors as no age must ever look to see the like'.[22] Two years younger than Alleyn, Burbage was a younger son of the carpenter turned impresario who built the Theatre in 1576, and first appears at the age of twenty-three, named in a lawsuit as defending his father's takings. He protected them with 'a broom staff' when the deponents came to collect their share in accordance with a Chancery Court order, and

scornfully and disdainfully playing with this deponent's nose, said that if he dealt in the matter, he would beat him also, and did challenge the field of him at that time.[23]

He was then in Alleyn's company with the Strange's–Admiral's amalgamation of 1590. He probably left them for Pembroke's after this, as we have seen, and reappeared with the new Chamberlain's Men in 1594, as their leading actor and a major shareholder.[24] His father left the Theatre and his Blackfriars property to Richard and his elder brother Cuthbert when he died in 1597.

Burbage seems to have been far less commercially minded than Alleyn. He avoided the temptations of managership and remained in acting until his death in 1619, when he left his wife according to contemporary rumour 'better than £300 land',[25] which though considerable for his day hardly compares with Alleyn's holdings or even with those of his fellow-player Shakespeare in Stratford. He was fifty when he died, by which time he had made famous such roles as Richard III, Jeronimo, Hamlet, Lear, Othello, and Ferdinand in Webster's *Duchess of Malfi*; his name appears in all the King's Men's plays for which lists of players survive between 1599 and 1618. He was Ratsey's Hamlet as Alleyn was the one hoping to be knighted.

In the second decade of the seventeenth century Nathan Field came to rival Burbage in fame. Jonson linked the two names in *Bartholomew Fair* in 1613, and Richard Flecknoe in a retrospective comment in 1664 spoke of them as the leading players at the time when Jonson, Shakespeare and Beaumont and Fletcher were the leading playwrights.

14.   Richard Burbage, from the painting in the Dulwich Collection, thought to be a
self-portrait.

'It was the happiness of the Actors of those Times to have such Poets as
these to instruct them and write for them; and no less of those Poets, to
have such docile and excellent Actors to Act their Playes, as a *Field* and
Burbidge.'[26] Field was a contemporary of Burbage in the King's Men for
the last four years of his life, and died only a few months after him. His
fame was not entirely for playing. He died a bachelor with a considerable reputation, of the kind not uncommon among players, for success

15.   Nathan Field, from the painting in the Dulwich Collection, artist unknown.

with women. A story circulating in 1619 reckoned that the Earl of Argyll had paid 'for the nourseing of a childe which the worlde says is a daughter to my lady and N. Feild the Player'.[27]

After Burbage and Field the names most prominent in theatre affairs were those of such men as Beeston and Richard Gunnell, who was a leading player with Palsgrave's in 1622 – Alleyn leased the rebuilt Fortune to the company with Gunnell and Charles Massey as the chief sharers – and who built the Salisbury Court playhouse in 1629. Gunnell and Beeston were not directly involved in playing, so far as we know, in their years as impresarios. The chief fame of the last years was mainly reserved first of all for the King's Men's trio of Taylor, Lowin and Swanston, and then for the clowns of the leading companies – Shank at the Blackfriars, Timothy Reade at Salisbury Court and Andrew Cane at the Fortune. In a number of ways the notes we have on them curiously echo the praise given to the clowns of the 1580s. Shank's fame was for his knockabout and dancing, as was Cane's. The latter was remembered as late as 1673, when Henry Chapman excused the presence of an appendix in his pamphlet by saying it was the fashion, 'Without which a Pamphlet now a dayes, finds as small acceptance as a Comedy did formerly, at the *Fortune* Play-house, without a Jig of *Andrew Kein's* into the bargain'.[28] Reade is linked with Cane in a pamphlet of 1641, '*The Stage-Players Complaint*, in a Pleasant Dialogue between Cane of the *Fortune* and Reed of the *Friers* [i.e. Whitefriars, or Salisbury Court]'. In the pamphlet Cane is called '*Quick*' and described as able to 'outstrip facetious Mercury in your tongue', while Reade is '*Light*', and described as nimble-footed, with heels 'as light as a *Finches* Feather'. Reade seems to have used the same trick of poking his head through the curtain as Tarlton in Nashe's anecdote. In Goffe's *The Careless Shepherdess* (1656) a character reminisces

> I never saw *Rheade* peeping through the Curtain,
> But ravishing joy enter'd into my heart

and claims to have preferred Reade's 'Craps and Quibbles' to 'the gravest speech in all the *Play*'.[29]

In noting the memories of the last decade of the Shakespearean tradition of acting, it is also worth remembering the French actors whom Beeston entertained in 1629 and 1635. Their fashion struck their contemporaries as somewhat exaggerated. In Glapthorne's *The Lady's Privilege* (1640), a character describes them as inclined to affectation:

> Very ayry people, who participate
> More fire than earth; yet generally good,
> And nobly disposition'd, something inclining
> To overweening fancy.

The same character then demonstrates their playing by mimicking a 'Comick scene', in which he '*Acts furiously*' (II.i).

4. STYLES OF ACTING

The question of degrees of affectation or exaggeration in acting raises the next matter in the consideration of players and playing: the question of the boy players and the difference between their playing and that of the adults. To begin with we must distinguish between the boys of the boy companies and the boy trainees in the adult companies. The backgrounds of the two kinds of boy player were originally quite different. The boys apprenticed to the adults were bound for a period of several years' training in their profession before graduating to be hired men and eventually perhaps sharers in their company. They entered their bonds between the ages of ten and thirteen, usually playing the women's parts which their small stature and unbroken voices equipped them for. The most positive instances we have show that one boy carried on playing women's parts until he was at least twenty-one, while another had changed to men's parts by nineteen. There was no set pattern, and nothing like the seven-year apprenticeships that boys in the guilds went through before rising to the status of journeyman.[30] Burbage according to his brother's account must have been acting by the time he was seventeen,[31] and Alleyn was already outstanding by sixteen.

The boys of the children's companies on the other hand acted only with their own age group and were trained and directed not by their fellow-actors but by the managers for whose profit they worked. In 1599 and 1600 they came into existence as a venture backed by a tradition of boy playing in the choir-school companies older and far more respectable than that which the professional adult tumblers-turned-players had behind them. In actual fact by 1576 when Farrant started the Chapel Children at the first Blackfriars their contribution to the Court Revels had already diminished and the once predominant chorister function had been separated off altogether from the playing. They were already frankly commercial, though the bland pretence to be rehearsing for her majesty's pleasure was retained as an obvious bulwark against the hostile local authorities.

Between the boy company actors and the boy players in the adult companies there was no difference of interest, though there was some difference of organisation, since instead of being bound to individual sharers as in the adult companies the boy players were all bound to their manager.[32] The major difference lay in their educational backgrounds. The descendants of the chorister groups played normally only two or three times a week, and some at least of the remaining time not given to rehearsing was given over to formal education. When Paul's discreetly closed down in 1606 the boys who did not join the other company returned to their nominal occupations without great difficulty.

The production of plays by boy actors had always been a schoolmaster's art, and the pupils of the best schoolmasters were anxiously sought after by the managers; in some cases too anxiously, as we know from the case of the kidnapped Thomas Clifton, who was a pupil at Christ Church school. Most of Evans's boys probably came from St Paul's Grammar School, where Nathan Field was certainly a pupil. He was then thirteen, and evidently already an expertly trained player. The Master of St Paul's School was Richard Mulcaster, celebrated for several decades for the shows his boys produced at Court and elsewhere. The Citizen's Wife in *The Knight of the Burning Pestle* asks one of the boy players (of the Blackfriars company) if he is not one of 'Maister *Monkesters* scholars' evidently a matter for some pride. Richard Brinsley, another schoolmaster, wrote a book in 1612 called *Ludus Literarius*, praising the value of playing in the education of schoolchildren.

The background of even the post-1599 boy companies was therefore more academic than that of the professional adult players, and their training accordingly was probably not so much in pure acting practice as in the declamatory arts of rhetoric, specifically pronunciation and gesture. Acting in plays was customary in many schools in the sixteenth century as a tail on the necessary dog of oratory. The growth of commercial interests made the acting tail wag the educational dog, but the link between the two was not entirely severed in the process.[33] Heywood in his *Apology for Actors* (1612) cited his own experience at Cambridge as a major part of his justification of his profession.

In the time of my residence in *Cambridge*, I have seen Tragedyes, Comedyes, Historyes, Pastorals and Shewes, publicly acted, in which Graduates of good place and reputation, have bene specially parted: this is held necessary for the emboldening of their Junior schollers, to arme them with audacity, against they come to bee imployed in any publicke exercise, as in the reading of Dialectike, Rhetoricke, Ethicke, Mathematicke, the Physicke, or Metaphysicke Lectures. It teacheth audacity to the bashfull Grammarian, beeing newly admitted into the private Colledge, and after matriculated and entred as a member of the University, and makes him a bold Sophister, to argue *pro et contra*, to compose his Sillogismes, Cathegoricke, or Hypotheticke (simple or compound) to reason and frame a sufficient argument to prove his questions, or to defend any *axioma*, to distinguish of any Dilemma & be able to moderate in any Argumentation whatsoever.

(C3v)

Readers of the *Parnassus* plays put on by Cambridge students at the turn of the century might feel Heywood's argument to be improbably pious; but the background of formal education in the decorums of speech and its attendant gestures must have had its effect on the theatrical foreground.[34]

We do not know how rare was the transition that brought Nathan Field, Underwood and Ostler into the leading adult companies, but

Field at least was outstanding among his adult brethren for his learning. During his four years with the King's Men they put him to good use not only as an actor but as a playwright. His educational background was far different from that of such unsuccessful players as turned to copying out playbooks in the hard times of the 1590s.[35] The classical learning even of actors competent enough at writing to make up a remembered text was so deficient that they cannot be assumed to have had much schooling of any kind, let alone training in rhetoric, which usually started fairly well on in the Elizabethan school curriculum. One of Alleyn's wryer protests to his father-in-law Dr Donne claimed that his education had not been in sophistry:

Before this violence brake forth you called me a plain man. I desire always to be so for I thank God I could never disguise in my life and I am too old now to learn rhetoric of the curiousest school in Christendom.[36]

Some distinction must have existed between the unschooled professionals on the one hand, descendants of the poor players who toured and tumbled for a living only slightly better than vagabondage, and the academically tutored schoolchildren on the other, practised as they were in the long tradition of Quintilian's rhetoric with its emphasis on careful speech and studied gesture. The social and educational difference provides one reason why the playwrights who produced material for the boy companies in the years after 1600, particularly Marston and Chapman, regularly gave their little eyasses lines to belabour the common players with. Marston gave Paul's Boys in 1600 a chance to demand in *Antonio's Revenge*, I.v:

> would'st have me turn rank mad,
> Or wring my face with mimick action;
> Stampe, curse, weepe, rage, & then my bosome strike?
> Away tis apish action, player-like.

and again in 1605, in *Sophonisba*, IV.i (acted by the Blackfriars Children):

> I should now curse the Gods
> Call on the furies: stampe the patient earth
> cleave my streachd cheeks with sound speake from all sense
> But *loud and full* of players eloquence
> No, no, What shall we eate.

Chapman similarly gave the boys an attack on exaggerated acting in his comedy *The Widow's Tears* in about 1605 (acted by the Blackfriars Children):

This straine of mourning with Sepulcher, like an over-doing Actor, affects grosly, and is indeede so farr forct from the life, that it bewraies it selfe to be altogether artificiall. (IV.i.)

Acting 'to the life' was of course intrinsically a more 'artificiall' business for boys acting men's parts than for the men themselves, and it would be understandable if they bolstered their own performances by using the academically approved conceptions of what was natural, and criticised by that yardstick the acting of the adults that exceeded their capacities. Equally, of course, there may be the taste of sour grapes in their distaste for the adult fustian kings and for the excesses of the 'stalking-stamping Player, that will raise a tempest with his toung, and thunder with his heeles' (*The Puritan* (1607), III.iv, acted by Paul's). They seem to have given a very emphatic preference themselves to satirical prose comedy over the fustian plays with which they tried in the early days to match the adults.

Cynthia's Revels, the first play the Blackfriars Children commissioned from Jonson in 1600, contains a large number of instructions to the boys how they should act, and offers as good a guide as any to what a judicious bystander felt they could do. They are advised to 'studie to be like cracks [i.e. crackropes, boy players]; practise . . . language, and behaviours, and not with a dead imitation: act freely, carelessly, and capriciously, as if our veines ranne with quick-silver.' Amorphus, who was probably played by Field, at one point (II.iii) demonstrates to his fellows 'the particular, and distinct face of every your most noted *species* of persons, as your marchant, your scholer, your souldier, your lawyer, courtier, &c. and each of these so truly, as you would sweare, but that your eye shal see the variation of the lineament, it were my most proper, and genuine aspect'. In the same play, III.v is a full-scale rehearsal scene, a coaching session in acting run by Amorphus. Jonson's opinion of the capacities of the player of Amorphus was evidently high, and of a kind to suggest that the boy company strictures on 'player' acting as 'stalking-stamping' were simply justifiable condemnations of exaggeration.

The condemnations of exaggerated acting were not confined to the boys of 1600–8, however. Shakespeare gave Burbage as Hamlet the most famous condemnation of all in 1601 when the eyasses were carrying it away. He followed it up with Ulysses' speech in *Troilus and Cressida* about the 'strutting player whose conceit / Lies in his hamstring, and doth think it rich / To hear the wooden dialogue and sound, / 'Twixt his stretched footing and the scaffoldage' (I.iii.153–6), which might be construed as stalking-stamping. Shakespeare had produced a detailed account of over-acting much earlier than this in *Richard III*, where Buckingham says contemptuously (III.v.5–11):

> Tut, I can counterfeit the deep tragedian,
> Speak and look back, and pry on every side,
> Tremble and start at wagging of a straw:

> Intending deep suspicion, ghastly looks
> Are at my service, like enforcèd smiles;
> And both are ready in their offices,
> At any time, to grace my strategems.

We might well suspect that academic teaching of pronunciation and gesture was less useful to either the boys or the adults than a direct eye on nature.[37] If anything, the orators learned these aspects of their occupation from the players rather than the reverse. The relationship was certainly described on that assumption by an anonymous writer in 1616 (T. G., *The Rich Cabinet*), who claimed that

as an Orator was most forcible in his ellocution; so was an actor in his gesture and personated action.   (Q4r)

The really important thing for us in the relationship between oratory and acting is its effect on the terminology used to describe acting, and the implications of the changes in terminology.

In the sixteenth century the term 'acting' was originally used to describe the 'action' of the orator, his art of gesture. What the common stages offered was 'playing'.[38] From this distinction came Jonson's bitter jibe when he inscribed the title-page of *The New Inn* as having been 'never acted, but most negligently play'd, by some, the Kings Servants'. That the academic term 'acting' should become so completely the prerogative of the common players as it did early in the seventeenth century is the most striking testimony possible to their predominance over the orators. More significantly perhaps, what the players were presenting on stage by the beginning of the century was distinctive enough to require a whole new term to describe it. This term, the noun 'personation', suggests that a relatively new art of individual character-isation had developed, an art distinct from the orator's display of passions or the academic actor's portrayal of the character-types described by Jonson in *Cynthia's Revels* and by earlier academic play-wrights such as Richard Edwardes, in the prologue to his *Damon and Pithias* (1565). The author of the comparison between oratory and acting quoted above spoke of the player's 'personated action'; Heywood's *Apology for Actors* specified that the good actor should 'qualifie every-thing according to the nature of the person personated' (C4r); even the author of a puritanical reply to Heywood (I. G., *A Refutation of the Apology for Actors* (1615)) told a story in which a 'jesting-Plaier . . . so truely counterfeited every thing, that it seemed to bee the very persons whom he acted' (E3v). The essential virtue of the character of 'An Excellent Actor' was held to be that 'what we see him personate, we thinke truely done before us'. The first use of the term 'personation' is recorded in the Induction to Marston's *Antonio and Mellida*, a play crammed with neologisms, written probably in 1599–1600, at the end of the great decade in which Alleyn and Burbage made their reputations.[39] It is not stretching plausibility too far to suggest that the term was called into being by the same developments – in the kinds of part given the actors to play and their own skill in their parts – that made two great tragedians succeed the extemporising clowns on the pinnacle of theatrical fame. By 1600 characterisation was the chief requisite of the successful player.

To know that natural acting, 'counterfeiting' nature and playing a part 'to the life' or with 'lively action' was the Elizabethan norm[40] is not necessarily to know how an Elizabethan player would have performed his part on stage, of course. Such descriptions as we have of Elizabethan displays of feeling do not entirely correspond with the postures evoked by the same feelings today. The language of gesture is more or less conventional, and therefore as liable to change as any other language. In Field's *Amends for Ladies* (1616), I.i, a gentleman complains that his mistress does not take his love seriously because he uses the wrong actions:

> 'cause I doe not weepe,
> Lay mine arms ore my heart, and weare no garters,
> Walke with mine eyes in my hat, sigh, and make faces.

Field himself is shown with his hand on his heart in his portrait, perhaps acknowledging his success as a lover in life. Like the other gestures, to a modern eye it looks strident. So too are the poses described by the 'country man' who composed *The Cyprian Conqueror* in about 1633, and wrote a preface instructing the potential actors of his play how to perform:

The other parts of action, is in ye gesture, wch must be various, as required; as in a sorrowfull parte, ye head must hang downe; in a proud, ye head must bee lofty; in an amorous, closed eies, hanging downe lookes, & crossed armes, in a hastie, fuming, & scratching ye head &c . . .[41]

Still, the difference between then and now was probably on the whole not too great. In 1644 a teacher of the deaf, John Bulwer, produced a manual of what he called with unconscious irony the 'Natural language of the hand', describing the gesture appropriate to each emotion (*Chirologia* and *Chironomia*, 1644).[42] The thoughtful man is shown scratching his head, threats are made with a shaking of the clenched fist, a finger on the lips asks for silence, and oaths are sworn with raised palm, much as one might expect today if one were to seek out gestures with which to mime such processes. Of Bulwer's illustrations, 120 in all, perhaps 20 would not still be readily recognisable to a modern audience.

Such gestures would also be recognised today of course as more

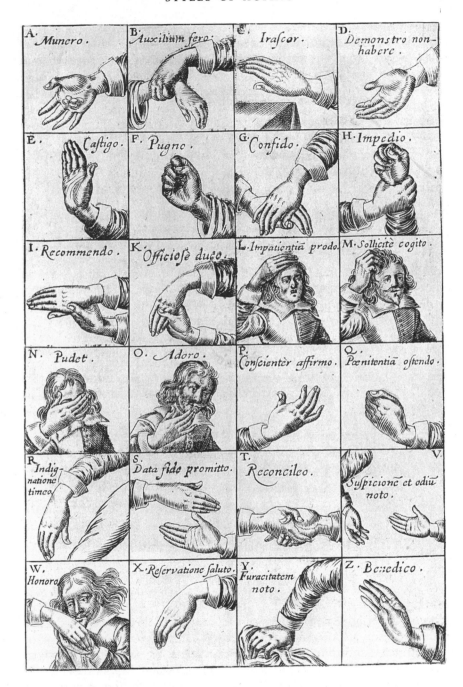

16.   Gestures for miming in John Bulwer, *Chirologia, or the Naturall Language of the Hand* (1644), p. 155.

appropriate to mime than to acting. Bulwer was not writing for the stage, but for the orator, from the standpoint of the inventor of a sign-language for the deaf, and his illustrations belong more properly with dumb-show than acting with words. When the Player Queen in *Hamlet* 'makes passionate Action' of grief during the dumb-show (III.ii.134) she in all probability raised her joined hands to heaven just in the way Bulwer's sorrowful orator does. That Queen Gertrude in the play proper was expected to do the same is unlikely.

By the time *Hamlet* was written, in fact, 'Pantomimick action' was openly condemned as old-fashioned. Thomas Campion in his *Book of Airs* (1601) spoke contemptuously of the old academic acting, the

old exploided action in Comedies, when if they did pronounce *Memeni*, they would point to the hinder parts of their heads, if *Video*, put their finger in their eye. But such childish observing of words is altogether ridiculous.   (B2v)

And in 1602 Thomas Tomkis showed that it looked dated even in Cambridge, where plays in Latin were still performed, when in his student play *Lingua* he produced an affected young man called Phantastes, showing his peers how to 'pronounce':

PHA[NTASTES]. Pish, pish this is a speech with no action, lets here Terence:
    quid igitur faciam, &c
COM[EDUS]. *Quid igitur faciam? non eam ne nunc quidam cum accusor ultro?*
PHA. Phy, phy, phy, no more action, lend me your baies, doe it thus. *Quid igitur, &c.*
    He acts it after the old kinde of Pantomimick action
COM[MUNIS]SEN[SUS]. I shold judge this action *Phantastes* most absurd: unles we should come to a Commedy, as gentlewomen to the commencement, only to see men speake.

                                                                    (IV.ii)

Tomkis at least, one presumes, would have listened to his Shakespeare as well as watching him. Bulwer's concern was primarily with the academic schooling of orators and teachers of the deaf so that their audiences could, literally, 'see men speake'.

Certain conventions of gesture on the Elizabethan stage did clearly differ from what would be familiar today. The conventions were the shorthand of stage presentation, and in a packed repertory, with plays performed at high speed, there can have been little chance for deeply studied portrayals of emotions at work. There were many ways of utilising this shorthand.[43] Such conventions as love at first sight required an established way to convey them on stage. Marston evidently knew of one, since in *The Insatiate Countess* (1611) we find at one point the bald stage direction '*Isabella fals in love*.' Some method of presentation involving mimed gestures was necessary in such cases, especially with love at first sight, since it usually struck the lover dumb.[44] Another convention that seems less than natural today is the tradition of direct address to the audience. Falstaff's catechism on honour is a relic of the clown's role of 'interloquutions with the Audients'.[45] Like explanatory prologues, the explanatory soliloquy or aside to the audience was a relic of the less sophisticated days that developed into a useful and more naturalistic convention of thinking aloud, but never entirely ceased to be a convention.[46]

Theatrical shorthand in the conventions of action that mimed the internal passion must have been essential to the Elizabethan actor. The repertory was hardly ever the same two days running, and the opportunities for rehearsal can have been few in comparison with modern standards. With a part in every play, the leading players can have had little time for doing more while studying their parts than the essential learning of the lines. As Bernard Beckerman puts it of the Globe actor:

There was no opportunity for him to fix a role in his memory by repetition. Rarely would he play the same role two days in succession. Even in the most popular role he would not appear more than twice in one week, and then only in the first month or two of the play's stage life. The consequences of such a strenuous repertory were twofold. First, the actor had to cultivate a fabulous memory and devote much of his time to memorization; various plays testify to the scorn of the playwright for the actor who is out of his part. Secondly, the actor had to systematize his methods of portrayal and of working with his colleagues.[47]

The Chamberlain's Men had barely more than a day to revive the defunct *Richard II* for performance when the Essex conspirators paid them to do so in 1601. The temptation in such circumstances to introduce stock poses must have been strong, and would have been reinforced by the practice of allocating parts according to acting types. Such a procedure would have reduced the strain on the actor's ability to 'personate' and left him to concentrate properly on his memory.

5. THE REPERTORY SYSTEM

The single most characteristic feature of all the companies throughout the period was their repertory system. Nothing can have shaped the nature of playing so much as having to perform a different play every day, and to produce new plays at frequent intervals. The Admiral's in their 1594–5 season, performing six days a week, offered their audiences a total of thirty-eight plays, of which twenty-one were new to the repertory, added at more or less fortnightly intervals. Two of the new plays were performed only once, and only eight survived through to the following season. Even the most popular plays the Admiral's performed, those of Marlowe, would be put on stage not more often than once every month or so. The first part of *Tamburlaine* appears in Henslowe's records for this season fourteen times, its second part six, *Faustus* twelve, *The Massacre at Paris* ten and *The Jew of Malta* nine. The repertory in the next season, 1595–6, was again large – thirty-seven plays, of which nineteen were new – and in 1596–7 thirty-four plays were performed of which fourteen were new. The most popular play over the whole three seasons, *The Wise Men of Westchester*, was performed altogether in the three years thirty-two times, or less than once a month even allowing for Lent.

The Admiral's Men's appetite for new plays was at its height at this time, of course, with security, a quasi-monopoly of London playing, and Marlowe's plays as the most famous of the day performed by the leading player of the day, Alleyn, to draw the crowds to them. Their appetite slackened off markedly later on. None the less, the stringent organisation and the feats of memory required from the company would have involved a number of consistent and traditional practices that must have persisted through the whole period and that we can recognise as characteristic. The most important of these would have been the custom of type-casting parts. It is a ready presumption that each player was allocated the part in each new play that most closely suited his talents. No player would wish to change his part in a play once he had learned it – there were enough new parts in new plays without that – so if one player left the company, his successor would have to take over all his abandoned parts, and would therefore be admitted to the company on the understanding that his type matched that of the departed player. Such a system probably explains the insistence of the company agreements on a player being reimbursed for his share in the company only if he left with his fellows' consent. Sharers had duties too specific to allow easy coming and going.

The most tangible testimony for such a custom is to be found in the plays written by a company's resident poet, most notably in the sequence of plays written first by Shakespeare, and later by the authors of the Beaumont and Fletcher canon, for the King's Men. Such plays might reasonably be presumed to have been tailored to the company's personnel and particular talents at the time of writing. A number of cast-lists that survive from the later years of the company (1623–32) confirm that presumption for at least those years. From these lists it appears that all members of the company were employed in every play; that there were consistently seven or eight major roles, two or three of them for women, who were played by the indentured boys; and that hired men did not take major parts.

The question of type-casting the players' roles in specific acting 'lines' has been much debated since it was first proposed and set out by T. W.

Baldwin in 1927.[48] Baldwin characterised what he saw as the major kinds of role, and fitted the later King's players to them. Heroes would be played by Burbage and later Joseph Taylor, the blunt foil for the hero, tyrants or soldiers by John Lowin, smooth villains by Eyllaerdt Swanston, dignitaries or aged kings by Robert Benfield, young lovers by Richard Sharpe and comic figures by Thomas Pollard. John Shank, the chief clown, did not figure prominently in the cast-lists, and may have been left to his own devices.[49] This interpretation of the repertory system and consistent type-casting of parts has been strongly challenged, on the ground that Baldwin's evidence is used too sloppily, and that he tries to read a nineteenth-century repertory practice into seventeenth-century conditions.[50] It is certainly true that Baldwin's ascription of 'lines' to particular players is grossly overconfident and inaccurate. In the few cases where the parts that players played are known precisely, there is not the consistency of type-casting that he tried to make the evidence show.

None the less, the repertory system was intense, especially in the early years, when each day needed a different play, and some systematisation would have been unavoidable. The same players played in a different play each afternoon. The same players had to fit all the different parts in the different plays, and the most regular way of allocating the parts would have been by type-casting. Hamlet's account of the players who come to Elsinore anticipates some such distribution of typical roles:

He that plays the king shall be welcome; his majesty shall have tribute of me; the adventurous knight shall use his foil and target, the lover shall not sigh gratis, the humorous man shall end his part in peace, the clown shall make those laugh whose lungs are tickle o'th' sere, and the lady shall say her mind freely – or the blank verse shall halt for't. (II.ii.298–302).

On the other hand, we might note Webster's praise of 'an excellent actor' for his versatility. 'All men have been of his occupation,' says Webster, 'and indeed, what hee doth fainedly that doe others essentially: this day one plaies a Monarch, the next a private person. Heere one Acts a Tyrant, on the morrow an Exile.'[51] But Webster is playing games with the world as a stage here, and his comment is concentrated more on the changes of life than of the stage. It is more to the point to consider the likely effects of doubling, and the limits that such a practice would necessarily impose on type-casting. John Sincler played five parts in the Strange's Men's 2 *The Seven Deadly Sins*, and Richard Cowley, later to play Verges in *Much Ado*, took seven. Players taking so many parts could not readily be type-cast. Consistent type-casting of the major roles is the easiest way to cope with the demands of any repertory system, but it could not have been an invariable practice. The illness or

absence from the company of a single player, or someone's fit of pique
in rehearsal might easily cause a square player to be cast in a round
part.

All that can be said positively about the likelihood of type-casting is
that one of the values of the sharer system was to provide insurance
against the casual absence of any of the leading players from the
company and consequent shifts in casting. Henslowe no doubt had that
sort of motive as well as some milk of human kindness when he
advanced William Bird's wife £3 to get her husband out of prison,
where he had been put 'for hurting of a felowe which brought his wiffe
a leatter' (Diary, p. 83). Marital concord and availability for playing set
roles went together.

What we know of the sharer system and the careers of individual
sharers does seem to indicate that fairly distinct playing types were
recognised. The clowns were always a distinct entity. New sharers took
on the parts of the players they replaced. Joseph Taylor joined the
King's Men shortly before May 1619, to replace Richard Burbage, who
died in March of that year, and certainly took over several of Burbage's
parts.[52] Benfield joined the company in 1615 most likely to replace
William Ostler, who died at the end of the previous year, and took over
his part as Antonio in The Duchess of Malfi. There was some consistency
in casting, and consequently in the tying of particular parts to particular
players. On the other hand early in the seventeenth century the
company was enlarged from eight sharers to ten and then to twelve,
and with the larger numbers to draw on the allocation of roles would
have become easier. Some sharers seem never to have taken major
parts. Shakespeare was never noted for his playing apart from a joke by
Davies of Hereford in The Scourge of Folly (1610) about his kingly roles.
It is also true that the many non-resident poets who did not know the
company well or who did not know in advance which company would
buy their work could not have written parts with specific players in
mind. Some plays, possibly Shakespeare's, possibly Jonson's for the
Blackfriars boys, and possibly the later Fletcher and Massinger's for the
King's Men, might have been written in the expectation that certain
players would take certain parts. But casting was never in the hands of
the poets, and especially in the early years the repertory system must
have made it rather more a matter of administrative convenience than
aesthetic choice.

There is a certain amount of evidence that shows how well the
companies worked in this repertory system. This is to be found in the
few cases where a play-text has survived in two versions, one the
author's or the company's original text and the other a version based
on a text copied down from a player's memory. The variant texts of
Faustus and the 'bad' quartos of several of Shakespeare's plays seem to

have been created to some extent from memory. One such revealing text is the 1594 quarto of Greene's *Orlando Furioso*. W. W. Greg, in his edition,[53] maintains that the play was written after August 1591 and played possibly at Christmas 1591 and certainly in February 1592 by Alleyn and Strange's Men for Henslowe. The Christmas performance may have been by the Queen's Men, who would have relinquished the play to Alleyn when they left for the provinces at the beginning of 1592 – unless, as the *Defence of Conny-Catching* maintained, Greene resold the play after the owners had gone. Alleyn took the play as his personal property, since it stayed with him in the Admiral's Company repertoire when he and Strange's Men parted company.

The authoritative piece of text is the 'Part' of Orlando, a fragment comprising two-thirds of a scribal transcript of the leading part. It has corrections made in Alleyn's hand, so was presumably made at the beginning of 1592, since it is unlikely that Alleyn would ever have wanted the part copied for him a second time. The only text of the full play is the quarto printed in 1594. Greg writes:

The text of *Orlando* printed in 1594 proves on examination to be a version severely abridged by the excision of scenes, speeches, and passages of dialogue, as well as by compression and the omission of characters, for performance by a reduced cast in a strictly limited time. Further than this the version has been adapted, by the insertion of episodes of rough clownage and horseplay, to the tastes of a lower class of audience . . . Thus the quarto contains what would appear to be essentially a stage version: the text is dependent on, not antecedent to, actual performance . . . based almost throughout on reconstruction from memory, while there seems likewise to be an oral link in the transmission. Modifying this, however, to some extent is the fact that a couple of short passages appear to reproduce written copies that happened to be preserved in the stock of the company, while a few incidental points reveal a knowledge of the original version, though this knowledge was clearly not obtained directly from any written source. Certain features, lastly, prove that the copy used for the printed quarto was in the first instance prepared for playhouse use.[54]

Greg suggests that the cause of this compilation was the reduced circumstances of the Queen's Men, who made it while on tour, possessing the original properties (for instance the roundelay scrolls that Orlando reads from; these were certainly written out to be read on stage, since Alleyn's Part does not transcribe them), and with a company reduced to seven men and two boys. They lacked the prompt-book, since this had been sold to Alleyn before they left London. Their

---

17.   A detail from the manuscript of Alleyn's part of Orlando in *Orlando Furioso*. In the line below the marginal addition a different hand from the scribe's has written 'scurvy poetry a litell to long'. A complete facsimile is in Greg, *Dramatic Documents*, II, no. C (strip 9).

limited resources made them cut progressively more and more, for fewer players, made them build up the action sequences in place of words, and elaborate the comic scenes. The verse, where it was preserved, was kept with remarkable accuracy, at least in its metre.

The Q text as a whole stands firmly on the 'drumming decasillabon', with a few alexandrines or half-lines to interrupt the flow. Altogether it is not greatly different from Greene's original, though less adroit. It is, however, revealing to see the way Q irons over the patches it puts on badly mangled verses to make them as smooth as their neighbours. It even makes up rhymes. One such case is Q1019–20: ·

> Part 171–2:
> and yet forsooth Medor durst enterprise
> to reave Orlando of Angelica

> Q1019–20:
> And yet forsooth, Medor, base Medor durst
> Attempt to reve Orlando of his love.

Greg conjectures that this corruption started with the change of verb, necessitating the repetition in the first line and the shortening of the second. But the repetition is a characteristic acting exclamation, and the alteration of the second line creates a rhyme with the one following, line 1021, which is identical in both texts. Greg may be right, but the creation of a new rhyme suggests something more positive operating than simply improvising to cover lost metre. It implies a strong concept of the need for high poetry. The result in Q is metrically no less correct than Greene's original as given in the transcript of the Part.

A second instance of patching is equally positive. In Q604 the actor substituted for Greene's abstruse 'Clora' the more familiar 'Flora' from two lines earlier, then added a phrase to make the reference seem more apt, and still kept his metre:

> P10–11:
> kinde Clora make her couch, fair cristall springes
> washe you her Roses, yf she long to drinck

> Q604–6:
> Fair Flora make her couch amidst thy flowres,
> Sweet Christall springs, wash ye with roses,
> When she longs to drinke.

The addition leaves Q with a three-foot line at 606, the first half of a rhymed couplet, but the extra phrase itself is fitted into the metrical pattern and leaves it little more nonsensical than the original.

The provincial players consistently cut long-drawn similes and passages of classical name-dropping such as P410–13:

> Extinguish proud tesyphone those brandes
> fetch dark Alecto, from black phlegeton
> or Lethe waters, to appease those flames
> that wrathfull Nemesis hath sett on fire.

And another seven lines, equally crowded, are cut after Q1550. It is possible of course that the provincial players simply felt they could not match Alleyn's delivery of such lines.

The exclamations that occur regularly in the quarto as player's additions are sometimes absorbed into their line, sometimes not.

> P18: venus hath graven hir triumphes here beside
> Q614: What? Venus writes her triumphs here beside
>
> P22: this gordyon knott together counites
> Q620: But soft this Gordion knot together co-unites

This last exclamation does not fit its context as aptly as it should, because there is no reason for the speaker to be surprised over who is co-united by the Gordian knot. A still more inapt exclamation is one that Q adds to line 1385 – Orlando's 'Sacrepant', a surprised recognition of the villain of the piece, when Orlando already knows perfectly well who it is. Greg calls this 'just the sort of touch that a blustering actor would introduce'. By this criterion there was a good deal of bluster in the performances that helped to make the Q text.

Harold Jenkins has noted a similar tendency of the actors to inflate their lines in the Folio version of *Hamlet*, the classic instance being Hamlet's 'O vengeance!' in his second soliloquy, a cry that appears in the Folio text, based on a playhouse manuscript, but not in the Second Quarto, the text untouched by player's hand.[55]

The memorial quarto of Shakespeare's *Henry V* when compared with the accepted text, the Folio, shows that it was compiled by minor players who probably had the parts of Exeter and Gower in the early performances.[56] On the whole they got their own speeches right, but they had hopeless memories for numbers and for proper names, and sometimes failed to grasp the meaning of what they had been given to speak. Their version as a whole suggests that the play was performed with an urgency that prevented any dalliance. The slow awakening of King Henry from the depths of prayer when summoned by Gloucester, for instance, which is delicately presented in the Folio version, was made through the pirates' memories into a vigorous leap straight back into the action:

> Folio IV.i.323–6:
> GLOUC. My Liege.
> KING. My Brother *Gloucesters* voyce? I:

I know thy errand, I will goe with thee:
The day, my friend, and all things stay for me.

Quarto:
GLOST. My Lord.
KING. My brother *Glosters* voyce
GLOST. My Lord, The Army stayes upon your presence.
KING. Stay *Gloster* stay, and I will goe with thee,
The day my friends, and all things stayes for me.

According to the players' memories, the clowns too would seem to have altered what was set down for them, particularly their comic catch-phrases. Nym's 'and theres the humor of it' turns up on three extra occasions in Q, and Fluellen's catchphrases got even harder wearing: his favourite oath, 'Godes plud', crops up three extra times, and once Q elaborates it to 'Gode plut, and his', when he has just been struck a blow that he has every intention of repaying. 'Looke you' is sprinkled at random throughout all his speeches, and four times he incongruously uses a phrase not found anywhere in F – 'and it shall please your Majesty'. One late entry in the game appears twice in Q to once in F – 'in the worell', an oddity of pronunciation that crops up again in *The Merry Wives of Windsor*. And there is also the peculiar frequency with which Ancient Pistol is faced with his own name in the quarto, perhaps because it was pronounced 'Pizzle'.

When one attempts finally to draw up a composite picture of the characteristics of the Shakespearean actor and the main features of his trade, one is confronted with an impressionist landscape flecked with many colours, the outlines of which are nowhere distinct. The broad lines would suggest that from the 1570s onwards acting was always a trade, one less than wholly respectable but one in which success and money could buy a good name nearly as readily as in other trades. It was more hazardous than the guild occupations but it could also be more profitable. The trade itself always held to a standard of life-like presentation as its artistic aim.

What remains is to attempt an assessment of the quality of the acting in so far as it can be differentiated at separate points in time and among the various companies or individuals. We have already seen the evidence which suggests that discerning critics by about 1600 had rejected the scholastic 'Pantomimick action', recognised a concept of 'personation' and begun to deplore exaggerated or affected acting. After 1600 there appears to have been little substantial change. Richard Brome in 1638 looked right back to the 'dayes of *Tarlton* and *Kempe*' to find the 'barbarisme' that had been successfully purged from his own stage (*The Antipodes*, II.ii.). Through the seventeenth century exaggeration was the only charge commonly flung at the players.

The players of the northern playhouses, the Fortune and the Red Bull, were targets for attacks on 'over-doing' more commonly than any others. Tomkis jibed at them in *Albumazar* (1615), Wither in *Abuses Stript and Whipt* in the same year, and Thomas Carew in verses prefixed to Davenant's *The Just Italian* in 1630.[57] Edmund Gayton ironically claimed in 1654 to have heard that 'the Poets of the Fortune and red Bull, had alwayes a mouth-measure for their Actors (who were terrible teare-throats) and made their lines proportionable to their compasse, which were *sesquipedales*, a foot and a halfe' (*Pleasant Notes upon Don Quixot*, p. 24). Soon after Gayton, Richard Flecknoe showed what a standard comparison for affectation Red Bull acting used to be, writing (in his 'Character' *Of a Proud [Wo]man*) 'She looks high and speaks in a majestique Tone, like one playing the *Queens* part at the *Bull*' (*Aenigmaticall Characters*, B1v).

Breadth of gesture seems to have matched the *sesquipedales*, to judge by such incidents as one in 1622 when Richard Baxter while acting on the Red Bull stage accidentally wounded a feltmaker's apprentice, who was sitting on the stage to watch the play.[58] We might trace the acting tradition to which Baxter's swashbuckling belonged back as far as Alleyn himself. Alleyn after all was owner of the Fortune and creator of the 'majestick' roles that the Red Bull and Fortune players inherited from him (most of his repertoire, including *Tamburlaine* and *Faustus*, went to his Fortune company, but some plays, including *The Jew of Malta*, went to the Red Bull, where they remained in the repertoire till 1642). Alleyn was most remarked on for his characteristic 'stalking and roaring' in his roles as Tamburlaine and Orlando.[59] His peer, Burbage, on the other hand, who spoke Hamlet's words to the Players about unnatural actors strutting and bellowing, was himself never spoken of except as a master of 'lively' or life-like acting. His elegist wrote of his most famous 'personation',

> oft have I seene him, leap into the Grave
> suiting the person, w[ch] he seem'd to have
> of A sadd Lover, with soe true an Eye
> that theer I would have sworne, he meant to dye,
> oft have I seene him, play this part in jeast,
> soe livly, that Spectators, and the rest
> of his sad Crew, whilst he but seem'd to bleed,
> amazed, thought even then hee dyed in deed.[60]

And Thomas May in *The Heir* (1620), also written shortly after Burbage's real death, speaks of him 'painting' another famous role:

ROSCIO . . . has not your Lordship seene
    A Player personate *Hieronimo*?
POL[YMETES]. By th'masse tis true, I have seen the knave paint grief

> In such a lively colour, that for false
> And acted passion he has drawne true teares
> From the spectators. Ladies in the boxes
> Kept time with sighs, and teares to his sad accents
> As had he truely been the man he seem'd.   (I.i)

His technique of personation is suggested by such things as his elaboration in *Hamlet* of the hero's habit of repeating words, as a trait peculiar to a very singular character.[61] and by references like Samuel Rowland's to gentlemen copying his appearance as Richard III (*The Letting of Humours Blood in the Head-Vaine* (1600), A2r):

> *Gallants*, like *Richard* the usurper, swagger,
> That had his hand continuall on his dagger.

In playing as in so many other ways, Shakespeare's company, more restrained than their fellows on the public stages, and more life-size, as well as more life-like, than the boy companies, appear to have been the outstanding company of the age in their naturalism.

4.   The Playhouses

1.   MOBILE PLAYERS

THE MOST well-trodden subject of all the background aspects of the drama is the structure of the playhouses. Playhouse design, being more tangible than other matters, has also attracted the most controversy. It is easier to dispute fixities like the shape of a stage than such intangible matters as an Elizabethan audience's awareness of itself as a visible presence during a performance in daylight. The recent discovery of some real playhouse remains has added greatly to the tangibility of what is known, and further burrowing in the warren of legal papers has yielded up still more evidence. But the weight of the many footprints planted in this part of the terrain has not altered the muddy nature of most of the evidence.

This evidence about the playhouse structures, muddy as it is, needs to be kept in proportion. The playhouses ought to be studied as no more than convenient accessories to the business of playing. Both plays and players operated in London long before there were any permanent structures built for the performance of plays. Throughout the Shakespearean era companies retained the capacity at the end of an afternoon's playing to take their plays off to a nobleman's house or to Court and play again there with no more aids to performance than the arena itself and what they could carry to it. The Revels Office did supply costumes and constructions for performances at Court, but even there most of the work went into erecting stages and seating in halls that were normally used for other purposes.

The adaptability of the early players in their use of playing arenas is part of the whole story of the innovation of commercial playing in London, and its gradual climb up the ladder of social respectability.[1] There were radical differences in the design of the playhouses. The first amphitheatres, built in 1567 and 1576, were simpler structures than the later amphitheatres in the shapes of both stage and auditorium. Each amphitheatre seems to have been quite distinct from the others, whether in size, in the provision of stage features such as trapdoors or 'heavens', or in the kinds of access provided for the audience. The Swan was very different from its near neighbour the Rose, built eight years earlier. Their neighbour the Globe, built four years later, was different from either of them. Hall theatres, the first of which started up along with the first open-air stages, were different again.

The earliest amphitheatres, like the Red Lion in Stepney, built by John Brayne probably for his brother-in-law James Burbage and his company in 1567,[2] were conceived in terms which reveal the traditional practices they catered for. They had a stage like the platforms erected in market-places for travelling players, backed by a curtained booth which concealed the players. The auditorium was a scaffolding of galleries like those provided for the bear-baiting arenas and innyards. This scaffolding served the double function of increasing the quantity of spectators by banking them upwards, and of keeping out anyone who could not pay for admission. Burbage was likely to have been motivated to build his scaffolds chiefly by the control they gave him over his audience's purses. He could now collect money at the door instead of going through the crowd with a hat as the travelling players had to do. This was no more than an adjustment of the practices long familiar to travelling players. The cheapest patrons stood in the yard just as they stood around the stage in market-places, while the wealthier sat more removed, in the galleries which now surrounded the stage and the standing patrons. The highest in social status sat in a special section of the galleries closest to the stage called 'lords' rooms'.

This disposition of the amphitheatre audiences, set by the early traditions of the travelling players, was in total contrast with the hall playhouses. There the audience who paid least sat at the furthest remove from the stage, as they do in modern theatres. The more you could pay the nearer you could be to the action. The halls were also located much nearer the haunts of the wealthy playgoers than the surburban amphitheatres. Paul's playhouse, which started business in 1575, nestled under the walls of the cathedral itself. The first Blackfriars playhouse, which started up within a year of Paul's, was not far away, down Ludgate Hill towards the Inns of Court and the residences of the rich who lived in the Blackfriars precinct and along the Strand. Throughout the period, for reasons that probably started as social snobbery, the halls were called 'private' playhouses, to distinguish them from the licensed 'public' amphitheatres. At the turn of the century their 'private' identity may have become for a time an excuse to keep them free from the supervisory functions of the Master of the Revels. In later years their 'private' label merely renewed the feeling of social difference between the clientele of the expensive and 'private' halls and those who attended the much cheaper 'public' amphitheatres.

The two kinds of playhouse differed radically in the numbers they could hold, too. Johannes de Witt estimated in 1596 that the Swan could hold three thousand people, and the Spanish ambassador gave the same figure as the minimum capacity at the Globe in 1624.[3] The Rose and its successor the Fortune had a smaller capacity, but all the amphitheatres could take in far more customers than the halls could. Paul's playhouse may not have seated more than a couple of hundred, and the first and second Blackfriars playhouses can hardly have seated many more than six hundred. These smaller capacities, however, were more than compensated for by the higher prices which the halls charged. When Shakespeare's company started to run a playhouse of each sort, as they did after 1608, they seem to have made distinctly more money from their hall playhouse than from the Globe.

Hall playhouses were designed for the wealthy both in their auditorium layout and their locations. By contrast the amphitheatres were built closer to the working-citizen parts of the City. The first amphitheatres were built in fields alongside the poorest residential areas, the suburbs of the east and the north. This was probably not so much because of any particular allegiance to the poor, but rather because the suburban location put them under the more lenient care of the justices of Middlesex and Surrey, free from the hostility of the City's magistrates. The first Middlesex amphitheatre, the Red Lion, built before the players had any government protection and probably as temporary in its playing life as in its design, was set up to the east, in Stepney. The first durable building, the Theatre, was built on land leased for twenty-one years in Shoreditch, near Finsbury Fields, nearly a mile north of the City's eastern end. By then, in 1576, its builder, James Burbage, had a patent for Leicester's Company which for the first time secured their status. The Theatre went up when the first halls were opening in the City. Its neighbour the Curtain appeared a year later, a few hundred yards nearer the City. Ten years later, in 1587, Henslowe opened the Rose south of the river in Southwark, near the baiting-houses and under the magistrates of Surrey.

Access across the river for the poor was by London Bridge, and for the wealthier by ferry. All the Southwark playhouses were conveniently accessible by ferry, since the busiest City wharves were directly opposite, below St Paul's. The Swan became the Rose's first playhouse neighbour in 1595. When Shakespeare's company crossed the river and opened nearby at the Globe, a little closer to London Bridge, in 1599, Henslowe promptly moved to the space they had vacated, building the Fortune in Middlesex, still close to the City but some way to the west of where the Theatre had been. The Red Bull opened soon after, still more to the west and a little further north, in Clerkenwell. Meanwhile the Boar's Head had been converted in 1599 from an innyard on the eastern edge of the City, in Whitechapel. Henslowe and Alleyn built the last of the traditional amphitheatres, the Hope, on the site of the old Beargarden in Southwark in 1614, planning to use it as a dual-function playhouse and baiting house. In the event, the players soon gave it up to the bears.

The subsequent playhouses built before the closure in 1642 were all halls. Once Shakespeare's company took over the Blackfriars hall in 1608, others soon set out to imitate them. The Whitefriars was south of Fleet Street, close to the Inns of Court, a little west of Blackfriars. The abortive Porter's Hall was to have been built between Paul's and Blackfriars. The Cockpit was built in 1616 to the north-west of it, in Drury Lane, and the last hall playhouse, Salisbury Court, built in 1629, was again positioned in Whitefriars. The hall playhouses stretched in a line from St Paul's westwards, with the amphitheatres to the north and south, and rather more to the east. All of them were positioned outside the jurisdiction of the city fathers, except for Paul's and the Blackfriars. The Blackfriars precinct was officially made part of the City of London in 1608, when James had to gratify the City because he needed its wealth, but by then the playhouse, originally built in what had been a 'liberty' free from City control, was secure from Guildhall's interference, and its new occupants were under royal patronage.

2.   THE HISTORY OF PLAYHOUSE-BUILDING

The story of where and when the players accommodated themselves in London would make a short history of their lives up to 1642. In the early years, while they struggled to gain a secure footing, they used such scaffolds as they could find or construct, whether custom-built like the Red Lion, the Theatre and the Rose, or buildings converted for playing, like the Bel Savage or the Boar's Head, which used innyards. As often as they could in winter they used City inns like the Bell and the Cross Keys in Gracechurch Street, where they may have had an indoor space to perform in. They kept this up despite Guildhall's opposition until in 1595 all the City's inns were finally barred to them.[4] In the meantime Richard Farrant had rented a hall in Blackfriars, and another chorister company had opened in the City at Paul's by 1576. They ran first as two companies and then as a merged group until the Marprelate troubles closed them down in 1590. In the next decade only the adult companies performed, and only amphitheatres were available for playing. In 1596, probably because access to the City inns had now been lost and certainly because his lease of the land on which he had built the Theatre was due to expire, James Burbage thought that he could combine the adult company practice of occasionally using rooms at inns in winter with the boy company practice of performing in halls. So he built the second Blackfriars as his replacement for the Theatre in 1596. After this scheme failed the two boy companies reopened at Paul's and at Burbage's new Blackfriars while the adult companies reshuffled themselves between the northern and southern suburbs, building a new generation of amphi-theatres there for the purpose. Not until the boy companies had finally faded from the scene in 1609 did the adults gain belated access to a hall playhouse. From then on development almost all went into the building of hall playhouses for adult companies.

This brief history needs amplifying, not only with some detail about the structure of the various playhouses, but with an account of the constraints on building. In order to control the number of playhouses, the Privy Council insisted that each one be licensed. It was the Privy Council's attempts to restrict the number of playing companies and available playhouses in the 1590s that led to the restraint on inns being used for playing, and the consequent formal conversion of the Boar's Head and the Red Bull from inns into playhouses. The Bel Savage had been used for plays, prize-fights and other sorts of show since the 1570s. It had three ranges of galleries like Burbage's Theatre, and a similar system of admission and pricing. All the playhouses had arrangements for selling ale on their sites, so that whether they counted as taverns or playhouses was a matter of name rather than function. The Boar's Head kept not only its taproom but also four parlours and eleven bedrooms when it was formally made into a playhouse. The Globe and the Fortune both had taprooms. Converting the Boar's Head and the Red Bull was in part a matter of altering Elizabethan nomen-clature to suit Jacobean regulations.

The licensing of playhouses around the turn of the century is in some degree a mark of the rise in the status of playing. By 1599 playing had outgrown its early association with inns. The use by Shakespeare's company of the Cross Keys in Gracechurch Street briefly in 1594, a use which required special dispensation, is in fact the last time on record that City inns were used for playing. And yet the policy that the leading company evolved for themselves once they were secure under James was in some ways a throwback to earlier practices. In 1583 the Queen's Men had been assigned to use the Bell in Gracious (Gracechurch) Street near Bishopsgate in the City, and the Bel Savage on Ludgate Hill. The Bel Savage was an open amphitheatre like the Theatre and the Curtain, but it is possible that the Bell and Cross Keys offered roofed venues.[5] Conceivably the Queen's Men were allocated the two inns because one could accommodate large numbers and the other was useful in bad weather. If so, James Burbage's construction of the Blackfriars in 1596 was no more than a premature attempt to reproduce the playing conditions of that greatly favoured first royal company. It makes the King's Men's eventual choice of policy when they had two playhouses for their use less of a novelty than it has been thought to be. To alternate in summer and winter between the Globe and Blackfriars would have merely renewed the privileged routine that Elizabeth allowed her royal players in 1583.

The conversion of the Boar's Head and the Red Bull into playhouses is evidence of the higher status that playing had acquired by the turn of the century. Robert Browne, who leased and converted the Boar's Head, was the leader of a company of players trying to establish themselves as the third of the adult companies normally resident in London. He evidently made a good job of his conversion.[6] When James authorised three adult companies in 1604 Queen Anne's Men chose to use the Boar's Head as their base even though the Curtain, Swan and Rose were available to them. They soon left it for the new Red Bull, however, and that playhouse remained their regular home for the next twelve years, until 1616, when their manager, Christopher Beeston, used his and probably their profits to build himself a hall playhouse, the Cockpit.

The years from 1595 to 1604 were notable for an oversupply of amphitheatres, possibly as a result of the ban on the use of City inns. Burbage had refurbished his Theatre and Henslowe enlarged his Rose early in 1592, but in 1595 a new generation of playhouses began to rise. Langley built the Swan near the Rose in that year.[7] The Theatre was pulled down and rebuilt 'in another forme' on Bankside as the Globe, early in 1599.[8] Henslowe then moved north to build the Fortune in 1600. Meanwhile Browne was developing the Boar's Head at the City boundary in Whitechapel, and the Privy Council stopped another conversion in East Smithfield in 1600.[9] After a year or two when it was closed in favour of the Fortune, the Rose reopened in 1602. The Red Bull was in use by 1604, and the old Curtain, owned by a consortium of players, was also still available. Each of these new constructions competed with the others to be the homes of the two or three companies that Privy Council regulations permitted to exist.

The playhouses that won were the Globe, Fortune and Red Bull. The Curtain and Swan were opened occasionally for prizefights or other types of spectacle, and sometimes plays, but were rarely occupied by resident companies. The Boar's Head got itself entangled in litigation (Langley had a thick finger in that pie too). The Rose was demolished in 1606, though in a sense it grew up again in 1614, when Henslowe and Alleyn decided to replace their other main business venue, its neighbour the Beargarden, with a new multipurpose playhouse-and-gamehouse, the Hope.

The Hope was something less than the last of its kind, for it was designed from the start as a dual-purpose playhouse and bull- and bear-baiting house with a removable stage. Playing was more frequent there at first than baiting, three afternoons out of four, so far as we can tell. The two forms of entertainment did not work well in partnership, however, and there were quarrels over priority, which led to the players more or less giving it up altogether by about 1620.

Three other playhouses were opened along with the second generation of amphitheatres, and another three up to 1629. These were all halls. Paul's started up in the playing business again in about 1599, in a location adjoining the Cathedral, and the Chapel Children in 1600, at the second Blackfriars theatre. In 1608 a private playhouse opened in the Whitefriars; in 1615 another (Porter's Hall) was opened in the Blackfriars precinct, but immediately stopped from being used as a playhouse. In 1616 the Cockpit or Phoenix was opened in Drury Lane near the Inns of Court, based like the amphitheatres on a gaming-house, though this time on the much smaller, roofed hall used for displays of cockfighting. The royal Cockpit in Whitehall – probably a larger building than the commercial ones – had occasionally been used as a venue for plays since Henry VIII first built it. Lastly, in 1629, when the royal Cockpit was being rebuilt by Inigo Jones as a regular playhouse, another commercial venue, Salisbury Court, was opened near to the old Whitefriars. The Whitefriars had closed after only a few years, when its lease fell in, and its impresario then foundered on the abortive Porter's Hall project. The life of the three hall playhouses that existed in 1629 was every bit as healthy as the three public playhouses then still flourishing. It is probably an accurate sign of the times that after 1609, the first year an adult company was able to get possession of an indoor playhouse, the only new ones built or projected were halls.

The whole history of playhouse-building can be summarised in the words of the reviser of Stow's *Annales*:

In the yeere one thousand six hundred twenty nine, there was builded a new faire Play-house, neere the white Fryers. And this is the seauenteenth Stage, or common Play-house, which hath beene new made within the space of three-score yeeres within London and the Suburbs, viz.

Five Innes, or common Osteryes turned to Play-houses, one *Cockpit, S. Paules* singing Schoole, one in the *Black-fryers*, and one in the *White-fryers*, which was built last of all, in the yeare one thousand six hundred twenty nine, all the rest not named, were erected only for common Playhouses, besides the new built Beare garden, which was built as well for playes, and Fencers prizes, as Bull Bayting; besides, one in former time at *Newington* Buts; Before the space of threescore yeares above-sayd, I neither knew, heard, nor read, of any such Theaters, set Stages, or Play-houses, as have beene purposely built within mans memory.[10]

3. EARLY AMPHITHEATRE DESIGN

For the first generation of playhouses, based on baiting-houses, the information is sparse, and not entirely consistent. Samuel Kiechel, a

German merchant visiting London in 1584, noted of its entertainments that

there are some peculiar houses, which are so made as to have about three galleries over one another, inasmuch as a great number of people always enters to see such an entertainment. It may well be that they take as much as from 50 to 60 dollars [£10 to £12] at once, especially when they act anything new, which has not been given before, and double prices are charged. This goes on nearly every day in the week; even though performances are forbidden on Friday and Saturday, it is not observed.[11]

Another traveller, William Lambarde, within a decade or so of Kiechel recorded that

such as goe to Parisgardein, the Bell Savage, or Theatre, to beholde Beare baiting, Enterludes, or Fence play, can account of any pleasant spectacle, [if] they first pay one pennie at the gate, another at the entrie of the Scaffolde, and the thirde for a quiet standing.[12]

The amphitheatres were usually round or polygonal buildings,[13] built on a timber frame with plaster infilling, on brick and pile foundations, with thatch or tile roofing for the galleries. The yard and three ranges of galleries were reached, to judge by Lambarde's account, by one or more gates into the yard, and by stairs into the galleries. To enter the yard cost a penny, to enter the galleries cost another, and to sit in comfort in the higher galleries cost another ('to get a standing' meant to find a viewing-place, whether standing or sitting). There were also lords' rooms costing 6d., partitioned off from the galleries closest to the stage, at the Theatre, Rose and Globe, and presumably at the others too. The stage was a platform measuring as much as 40 feet across and extending out from one side to the middle of the yard. At the rear of the stage was a 'tiring-house' or players' changing-room, the front face of which had two or more openings on to the stage. At the first gallery level in the tiring-house façade was a balcony or gallery (sometimes called the 'tarras' in the seventeenth century), which was occasionally used as a supplementary playing area in conjunction with the stage itself. Near the front of the stage in some playhouses was a large trap-door. Over the stage, extending out from the tiring-house above the balcony or tarras was a cover or 'heavens' supported by two pillars rising from the stage. This was to shelter the stage from the weather and to provide a place from which things could be let down on to the stage. The Hope's stage was built in 1614 with a 'heavens' but no pillars, so that the stage could be removed for the baiting. Set on top of the heavens or cover was a 'hut' or huts, within which stage hands operated the machinery for 'flights' or descents on to the stage, and where they produced thunder and lightning effects. Alongside the hut was a small platform, level with the gallery roof, from which a trumpeter announced the beginning of a performance. A flagstaff beside the platform or on the hut flew a flag during the performance. These last details appear to be true of the Swan, and were probably not dissimilar in the other playhouses.

The decor of these playhouses was 'sumptuous' and 'gorgeous' according to the Puritan preachers of the 1570s and 1580s, though unless they put themselves at risk by visiting plays we must assume their testimony to have been second-hand. We do know, from contemporary documents such as the building contract for the Fortune, that the woodwork of the interior was painted, in at least one case in order to imitate the appearance of marble, like the Italian theatres.[14] Some of the woodwork was carved. The underside of the 'heavens' was painted with sun, moon and stars, and probably the signs of the zodiac. Curtains or 'hangings' covered part of the tiring-house façade, and green rushes were strewn on the stage itself.[15]

These generalisations probably do not apply to all the early amphitheatres. There is some precise and tangible evidence about three of them: the foundations of the Rose and part of the Globe, and a Dutch tourist's sketch of the interior of the Swan. The two different types of evidence tell different stories, and seem to indicate that the three Southwark playhouses differed from each other in numerous ways. Balancing the different stories and assessing the value of each kind of evidence is a difficult exercise made more difficult by the uniqueness of each kind of evidence and probably of each playhouse. Even the amount of corroborative evidence about the playhouses is widely different. The Rose was the venue where more than thirty extant plays of the 1590s were staged, and the papers concerned with the running of the playhouse have survived too. No more than one play definitely staged at the Swan has survived, and little else about its operations besides a flysheet for an event which turned out to be a con trick. Weighing the evidence about these two playhouses, and using it to find something about the history of playhouse design, is a delicate and unrewarding labour.

Much of the groundplan of the Rose was identified early in 1989, when a team of archaeologists, given access to about 60% of the ground area, found the foundation walls and the yard surface. An office had been built on the site in 1957, and its piles had penetrated some sections of the site. The eastern flank was not then available for digging, but enough of the rest was exposed to make the basic shape and structure of the design clear. It was a thatched polygon, originally built with about fourteen sides, roughly seventy-two feet in outside diameter, with a yard slightly under fifty feet across. The yard was covered in mortar, and seems to have been raked down towards the stage. The stage was markedly smaller than the measurements given for other amphitheatres, and its sides were tapered. The tiring-house wall was probably angled to match the inner walls of the surrounding galleries. The foundations also give evidence of a major reconstruction at some time in its life which turned the originally symmetrical polygon into a bulging tulip-shape.[16]

Henslowe's *Diary* preserves a mass of information about the operations of the Rose. It lists his takings from the galleries; it names many of the plays performed there; it details the loans he made to the players and includes inventories of their properties. It includes Henslowe's copy of the agreement with John Cholmley, his fellow-financier, to build the Rose in 1587, and detailed accounts of the moneys paid and the items paid for when the Rose was altered in 1592. These records help to make sense of the groundplan of chalk and rubble on the site.

Henslowe's *Diary* starts with the arrival of Strange's Men to join Alleyn at the Rose in February 1592. It was shortly before this event, and evidently because of it, that Henslowe undertook the major alterations which became evident during the final days of the Rose excavation in May 1989. This reconstruction entailed levelling the original gallery walls and stage foundations on the northern side down to the pile caps, and rebuilding them in a bulge some way further out. The symmetrical polygon thus became a misshapen ovoid, elongated so as to extend the yard and the side galleries, and pushing the stage area back so that the new stage and tiring-house frame covered the pile caps of the original foundations and repositioned themselves six feet six inches further north.

This peculiar extension was made at what was probably the most crucial time in the history of the evolution of Shakespearean playhouse design. Burbage refurbished the Theatre at the same time. Besides *Tamburlaine*, *The Spanish Tragedy* and *Dr Faustus*, the two theatres had the heroic Talbots in Shakespeare's first *Henry VI* play, and *Titus Andronicus* (the latter two probably staged at the Rose) all first appearing in those years, and setting a fashion that was still able to draw London playgoers to similar amphitheatres for the same plays fifty years later. We do not know what use was made of the Rose from 1587 to 1592, when it was altered. But five years can hardly have been long enough to wear it out and justify such expensive refurbishing. Presumably the original design, only the fourth amphitheatre playhouse ever built in London, was found unsatisfactory in some way. Why else should Henslowe lay out so much money after only five years?

Henslowe's *Diary* includes an itemised list of the costs of the 1592 alterations, headed

A note of suche carges as I have layd owt a bowte my playe howsse in the yeare of o^r lord 1592 as ffoloweth[17]

18. The foundations of the Rose as excavated in 1989, seen from above. The photograph was taken by Andrew Fulgoni from the top of the ten-storey office on the south side of Park Street, facing north.

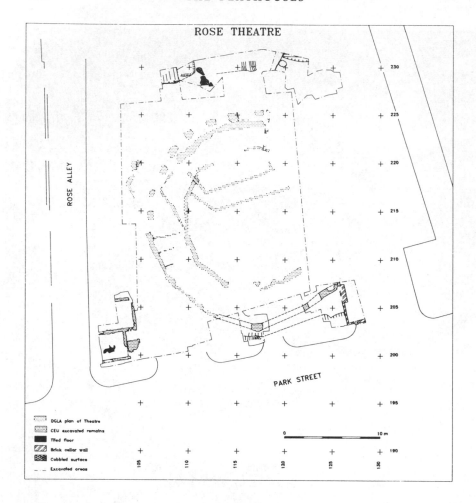

19. A plan by English Heritage of the groundwork on the Rose site, as uncovered by September 1989. The building in the bottom left-hand (south-west) corner is John Cholmley's tenement. On its surviving floor tiles was run the grocery business which led him to partner Henslowe in putting up the cost of building the Rose, in return for which he had the exclusive right to sell food and drink in the playhouse. All the remains from the 1587–92 period are shown stippled. The section of the playhouse to the right (east) still awaits excavation.

The list contains a number of items confirming many of the details about the design of the remade playhouse. Lime and sand was used along with loads of chalk and brick to cement in the new foundation walls and probably some of the brick partition walls too. Deal boards and laths supplied the materials for the walls and floors. The walls, if not the ceilings, were made of timber frames infilled with lath and plaster. Some ceilings were plastered too – the 'Rome over the tyer-howsse' and 'my lords Rome' are specified. A series of payments to a thatcher confirm the type of roofing used for the galleries, and probably the stage roofing too (there are no payments for a tiler, and no remains of any tiles were found on this site). A note about buying dozens of turned balusters tell us what the gallery fronts facing the yard were fenced with. The stage was painted, though we are not told in what colours.

The list also shows what care Henslowe took in supervising the work. John Grigg, the builder, who was on good terms with the Henslowes as we know from family letters which have survived, supplied some of the building materials himself, but most of them were bought by Henslowe directly from his regular suppliers, whether it was nails from the ironmonger at the sign of the Frying Pan, or from 'braders', or loads of timber brought in by boat. He paid the workmen, including the bricklayer, the thatcher and the plasterer, himself. Evidently by this time his original partner Cholmley had retired, or had been bought out, since Henslowe bore all the costs from his own purse. The whole job, ending with payments to the plasterers and the painter, took about two months to complete.

This evidence confirms the large scale of the 1592 extensions, but it does nothing to explain why the enlargement was done. From the position of the foundations it seems that the galleries were stretched by six or seven feet on either side of the stage, increasing the likely space there for audience by two hundred or more sitters. If we ignore the possibility that the wooden stage platform was made so that it jutted out into the yard well forward of its chalk foundations, the enlargement also increased the yard space for the audience from roughly 1,400 square feet to nearly 1,800 square feet. This would have admitted rather less than another two hundred understanders. Calculations based on the groundplan as now exposed, and assuming the existence of three levels of galleries, give an audience capacity of about two thousand originally, and about two thousand four hundred at the enlarged Rose. A rough estimate of the audience at a very popular play in the enlarged Rose (the lost play *Hercules*, on 6 January 1596), gives a figure of about two thousand two hundred fee-payers. A more usual attendance figure seems to have been about six hundred,[18] so calculations of the total capacity may not be greatly significant. On the other hand, a normally low attendance only makes the increase in maximum capacity more puzzling.

None the less, increasing the audience capacity is quite a plausible explanation of the changes. In its original capacity the Rose was markedly smaller than the other playhouses. It was only two-thirds the

Rose Phase 1

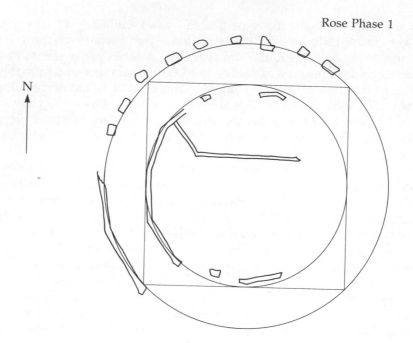

N

20. A simplified diagram, made by John Orrell, of the groundwork of the Rose as originally built in 1587.

size of its 1576 predecessor the Theatre, for instance, which must have had an outside diameter of about one hundred feet if we accept the known Globe measurements as corresponding to the Theatre's framework. The Globe, like its neighbour the Swan, had a capacity of over three thousand spectators according to contemporary estimates, so the Theatre, like the Globe and the Swan, would have made an obvious contrast in size with Henslowe's playhouse. No new playhouses were built between the Rose's first erection in 1587 and its reconstruction five years later, so Henslowe was not forced into a change of mind about the size of his auditorium by any fresh competition on the London scene. The desire to increase his auditorium capacity to something closer to that of the Shoreditch playhouses must have been one consideration behind his financial outlay in 1592. But it is unlikely to have been the sole reason.

The Rose's enlargement presents many puzzles, the greatest of which relates to the stage area. Evidently the enlargement was required to include some redesign of the stage itself, since otherwise it would have been simpler and cheaper merely to extend the galleries at the auditorium end towards Maiden Lane. The Rose's original stage was small,

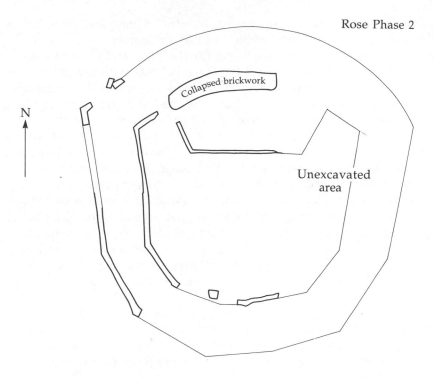

Rose Phase 2

N

Collapsed brickwork

Unexcavated area

21. A simplified diagram, made by John Orrell, of the groundwork of the Rose as it was enlarged in 1592. The gallery walls including the stage and backstage on the northern side were dismantled and re-erected several feet further back, and the side galleries stretched to cover the gap.

noticeably smaller than the stages of the rival playhouses. As early as 1567 the Red Lion's stage had been set out at thirty feet deep and forty feet across. Henslowe's replacement for the Rose, the Fortune play-house, had a stage twenty-seven and a half feet deep and forty-three feet across. But the original stage of the Rose seems to have been thirty-seven and a half feet across at the rear, tapering to only twenty-seven and a half feet at the front, and as little as fifteen and a half feet deep. The replacement in 1592 seems to have been about seventeen feet deep, with the same width as its predecessor, if the angled rear wall was retained. If it was fronted with a flat-planed *frons scenae*, of the sort shown at the Swan in Johannes de Witt's sketch of it in 1596, then the depth of the Rose's stage either in 1587 or 1592 would have been reduced to about twelve feet at most. A *frons scenae* of this kind, built in timber with no foundations (and therefore with no remains surviving on the site, since all the original timbers have gone), is of course possible. But it seems unlikely, because it would have reduced the area of the stage to far less than the five hundred square feet provided by the stage with angled rear walls. Even that compares poorly with the nearly twelve hundred square feet at the Red Lion and the Fortune.

The question of the depth of the stage belongs with the question of the stage pillars. A column base was found just inside the foundation wall of the later stage front, built after the wall itself and abutting closely to it. If the clunch (chalk aggregate) footings of the stage front mark its exact limit then the pillar supported by this column base would have risen from the very edge of the stage. There is no sign of any pillar base having been supplied for the first stage. This may mean that the reconstruction in 1592 was partly done to add supports for the stage heavens, though that would be a large deduction from the inadequate evidence so far available, and two plays performed at the Rose before 1592 seem to require stage posts. The question of the heavens and a stage roof is in any case complicated by the large drain which was found to run from the tiring-house northwards to a large ditch crossing the site. This square wooden drain was positioned too high in the ground to drain the yard, and most likely functioned as a drain for the run-off of water from the stage roof. However, thatch cannot be provided with guttering, and there is no mention of lead for gutters in Henslowe's records of the 1592 alterations. The roofing of the reconstruction, and many questions about the shape of its redesign above ground level, are still a mystery.

The erosion trenches found in the mortar which surfaced the yard, and the evidence they supply about driplines from the eaves of the thatched gallery and stage roofs, are also enigmatic. A circular erosion trench, about eighteen inches in from the inner gallery walls, is easily explained as the dripline from the gallery thatch. A straight erosion trench across the front of the stage is more puzzling, because its depth, which is comparable to that around the galleries, suggests that the water that made it also dropped from a high roofline. Water dripping off the wooden surface of the stage platform itself if it projected forward of the stage foundation could not have made such a deep trench, because the platform would have been only five feet or so above the yard surface, compared with the thirty or so feet of the gallery roof thatch. The trench's position, a foot in front of the stage foundation wall, suggests that it was the wall that marked the forward limit of the stage platform, and that well above it at about the level of the gallery roof there was a hipped stage roof positioned to drip water onto the members of the audience pressing closest to the platform.

The evidence about the auditorium is also incomplete. The galleries were constructed in segments, with partition walls at each angle. There may have been an entrance to the yard opposite the stage on the south side, by Maiden Lane. No signs of stair turrets were found, and it therefore seems most likely that access to the galleries was by steps up from the yard, as Lambarde and other tourists described them. This may or may not mean that the stairs to the upper levels would have been constructed inside the galleries themselves, as seems to have been the case at the Swan. If they were they would have reduced the audience capacity of the galleries still further. The mortar-surfaced yard, with its irregular but quite steep rake, supplied an obvious means of coping with the rainwater funnelled in from the surrounding gallery eaves. It would also have helped the viewlines for the standing spectators. The mortar surface itself was covered with a deep deposit of ash and clinker, mixed with hazel-nut shells. This deposit, eighteen inches (40cm) thick, had an equal mix of ash and hazel-nut shells throughout, which probably indicates that the ash was laid at intervals to provide a secure footing on the mud which would have been trampled in daily onto the mortar surface. The audience then scattered its debris into the ash underfoot, stirring it in as they shifted their feet through the performance. The whole deposit built up through the fifteen years (1587–1600 and 1602–3) that the playhouse was in regular use.

One clear deduction can be made about the Rose: its design was in most respects distinctly different from that of its neighbour the Swan and its later neighbour the Globe, as well as its successor the Fortune on the northern side of the city, for which there is a builder's contract, and also from the Boar's Head to the east, about which there is some evidence from legal documents. The Rose therefore has limited value when we try to deduce the features of other playhouses from it. But as an early playhouse, rebuilt at a crucial time in theatre development, with a unique record of its use for performances, its details form a striking testimony to the diversity of Elizabethan thinking about play-house design. Its remains make it look more like a piece of carpentry than careful architecture. It was a patched-up, jerry-built contrivance. The work of the Roman Vitruvius and his resurrection in the sixteenth century by Serlio as a handbook for architects has been inevitably elevated into a model for Elizabethan design. If the Rose was built like its neighbours, we must be cautious about using Vitruvius or Serlio as any sort of serious precedent for the design of these thoroughly home-made constructions.

The second major piece of evidence about early playhouse design needs to be approached with a rather different kind of caution. The Dutch scholar Arend van Buchell made a copy of a sketch sent to him by his friend Johannes de Witt, showing the interior of the Swan. This sketch was made in 1596 shortly after the playhouse was built, and discovered in Amsterdam only in 1880.[19] De Witt was visiting London, and like most foreign tourists took particular note of the playhouses then in use, the Theatre, Curtain, Rose and Swan. As he noted in his diary,

There are four amphitheatres in London of notable beauty, which from their diverse signs bear diverse names. In each of them a different play is daily exhibited to the populace. The two more magnificent of these are situated to the southward beyond the Thames, and from the signs suspended before them are called the Rose and the Swan . . . Of all the theatres, however, the largest and the most magnificent is that one of which the sign is a swan, called in the vernacular the 'Swan Theatre'; for it accommodates in its seats three thousand persons, and is built of a mass of flint stones (of which there is a prodigious supply in Britain), and supported by wooden columns painted in such excellent imitation of marble that it is able to deceive even the most cunning. Since its form resembles that of a Roman work, I have made a sketch of it.

The sketch shows the three galleries noted by other tourists, with two entries to the galleries from the yard. There is a stage, with three players performing on it. The tiring-house façade has two pairs of closed doors, and a partitioned gallery or tarras containing several spectators (or players or musicians). There are two carved stage-posts supporting the cover or heavens. which is tiled.[20] The hut, trumpeter and flag appear above the cover. The various sections are labelled by de Witt with the equivalent names from the Roman theatre, which the Swan reminded him of.

To say that a number of the features illustrated by de Witt are debatable is to put it mildly. Many other items of evidence about the public playhouses seem to conflict with what is shown in the sketch, and have accordingly created doubts about de Witt's accuracy, or that of van Buchell as copyist, or both. For one thing, what is supposed to be happening in the picture is not clear – the trumpeter would seem to be announcing the commencement of the performance, but the players are in full swing. The audience is there (if it is audience) in the tiring-house gallery, but nobody is portrayed in the circular galleries or the yard (it has even been conjectured that de Witt is bearing witness to a rehearsal). If the gallery figures are audience, where is the playing area above the stage? The two double doors are at odds with evidence that there were three or more stage entrances in many Elizabethan and Jacobean plays. There is certainly no 'inner stage' or 'discovery-space', as many plays require, and no hangings. There are curious 'bulks' or 'trestles', as they have been called, underneath the stage, which seem to be upholding it in a very awkward position. And there is the question of the stairs that appear to allow entry to the galleries. Their positioning accords with the contemporary statements that the audience first entered the playhouse, presumably the yard, before going up into the galleries, but they are at odds with the two external staircases which are noted at the Swan in the contract for the Hope. Where would external

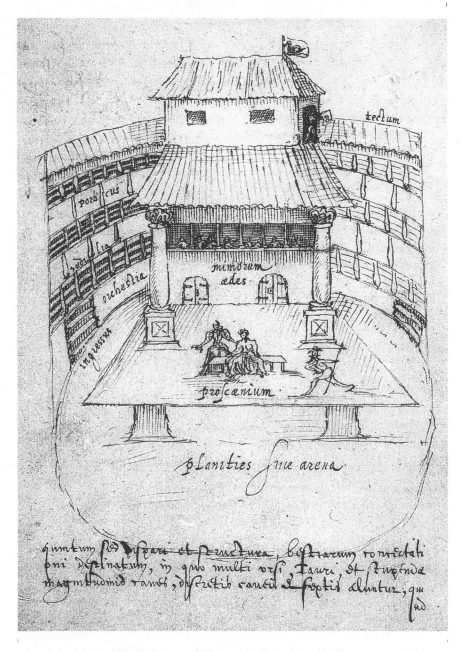

tectum

porticus

sedilia

orchestra

ingressus

mimorum aedes

proscænium

planities siue arena

22. Arend van Buchell's copy of Johannes de Witt's sketch of the Swan. From the original in the Bibliotheek der Rijksuniversiteit, Utrecht.

staircases be going to if not into the galleries? The internal stairs which de Witt illustrated would hardly have been used as exits only. The 'ingressus' label that de Witt gave them might mean either that they were entries to the galleries from the yard, or to the yard, presumably from outside the playhouse. They do look most like stairs up into the galleries from the yard. Some resolution of these questions is necessary before we can accept either that de Witt's sketch is an accurate depiction of the Swan or that it is inaccurate and the evidence that seems to contradict it preferable.

The accuracy of de Witt's sketch, or van Buchell's copy, has been greatly disputed, and with good reason. The perspective varies, so that the viewer seems to be positioned simultaneously above the roof level and at a middle gallery level. The stage roof and trumpeter show an abortive effort to give a view from off-centre. There are six partitions in the stage gallery when there should be five. These indications of a less than exact method of recording by the observer, together with the fact that the surviving drawing is a copy, besides such enigmas as the hatched markings under the stage and the inconsistency of several features with other evidence, have led some commentators to dismiss what the drawing seems to offer altogether. There are too many peculiarities in the drawing for comfort. One anomaly in particular has been strengthened by the archaeological work done on the Rose and the Globe.

De Witt's drawing of the Swan's galleries shows an 'ingressus' or stairway from the yard up into the lowest gallery. This conforms with the evidence for the admission system described by other visitors to London at the time, where spectators first paid one penny for admission to the yard, then a second for admission to the galleries. De Witt shows the access way into the galleries that this early system indicates was necessary. It was a much clumsier and less economical system than the one developed later. At the Rose, and apparently at the Swan, late-comers paid a first gatherer to enter at the back of the yard, but to get into the galleries they had to press through the yard's crowd and then, after paying a second gatherer, force their way up the 'ingressus' through the spectators sitting at the front of the gallery degrees to find a seat at the back. By contrast, at the Globe, as the recent archaeological work has shown, the entrants to the yard and the galleries divided themselves off in the outer lobby. The standers came into the yard at the back, as at the Rose, but unlike the Rose the seekers after seats in the galleries did so too. The gallery patrons paid only once, in the entrance lobby, and then climbed up through a stair turret going directly up from the lobby to enter at the back of the galleries. The firstcomers got the best seats without the fear that they had at the Rose of subsequently being elbowed by latecomers who had to push their way through them to the back. The puzzle about de Witt's drawing is that another piece of evidence about the Swan indicates that it had stair turrets like the Globe's, which would have made the 'ingressus' from the yard unnecessary. The Hope contract (see page 153) orders that its stair turrets be built like those at the neighbouring Swan. It is most unlikely that the Swan ever had such a major overhaul between de Witt's visit and the Hope contract of 1614 as the construction of stair turrets would have entailed, so it must have had them when de Witt gave it an 'ingressus'.

De Witt's drawing may well show features from more than the one playhouse. The square stage and planar *frons scenae* with its two stage doors may have belonged to the Swan, but the 'ingressus' seems to have come from the Rose. Certainly de Witt was not thinking of the Rose's tapered stage when he made his drawing, but he may have conflated his memory for other features. The drawing may be accurate in some respects for the Swan itself, but it would be unwise to use it for general observations about playhouse details. Van Buchell's copy of whatever de Witt drew for him shows the Swan to be as different from the Rose as it was from the Globe and the Fortune. Even the Rose's rake in its yard does not seem to have been copied at the Swan, since the word 'planities' which van Buchell applied to the Swan's yard indicates that it was flat. The inconsistency between features in the Swan drawing and evidence about other playhouses does not mean that the Swan's evidence can be wholly discounted. But it can only be used hesitantly for the Swan itself.

Apart from the doubt over the 'ingressus' and stair turrets, what little other evidence there is about the Swan does not contradict de Witt. The two stage doors are quite sufficient for the staging of the only play we know to have been performed at the Swan. A *Chaste Maid in Cheapside* actually specifies in a stage direction entries '*at one Dore . . . At the other Doore*'. It has been pointed out that one pair of double doors opened out would have been sufficient for any normal 'discovery' or display scene, or for the pushing out of a bed onto the stage, or the carrying out of large properties. The hangings might either have been omitted by de Witt because they would have obscured the location of the stage doors, or possibly they could have hung in the doorways behind the doors, so that when the doors were open the hangings would be visible to conceal a 'discovery', and when they were closed the hangings would be hidden and so would not impede the normal use of the doors.

The figures watching the players from above the stage have caused as much controversy as the non-existent discovery-space. About one-sixth (45 out of 276)[21] of the extant plays written in the period when the Swan was in use require a playing space 'above' or 'aloft', but there is little space apparent in de Witt's sketch. The partitions of the gallery suggest that they are the Swan's equivalent to the 'gentlemen's roomes' of the Fortune contract, or the 'lords roome' that Jonson describes as 'over the stage' at the Globe in *Every Man Out of his Humour*. It has been suggested that the players simply moved into one of the gentlemen's rooms when they required an area aloft, and shared it temporarily with the gentlemen.[22] There would then be no loss of revenue from the rooms, and perhaps a gratifying proximity to the action for the gentlemen. Or one of the rooms might be the musicians' room, in which case there would be no problem in asking them to move over.

The 'bulks' or 'trestles' underneath the stage are curious chiefly because they seem to be drawn so crudely and so out of proportion in comparison with the rest of the sketch. I have a suspicion that they are in fact quite accurately if incompletely drawn, and that they represent not under-stage supports but gaps in the hangings that were draped round the stage to conceal the under-stage area. Some form of concealment there must have been – at the Fortune it was wooden palings – or the operation of the stage trap could hardly be secret. There must have been apertures, because it was from under the stage that devils were expected to run amongst the audience in *England's Joy*, a non-existent play for which an ingenious trickster attracted large crowds to the Swan in 1602.[23] The crowd, when it realised it had been caught by fraud, are said to have revenged themselves upon the playhouse, including the 'hangings', of which the most accessible would have been those surrounding the stage. Such a theory would explain the curiously soft outlines of the shapes and the splay of their feet, as being a depiction of soft material hanging to the ground, in contrast with the sharp outlines of the wooden features in the sketch. All that is missing are the vertical lines at the outer edges of the stage marking the corners of the hangings. De Witt would have sketched the apertures to show where the devils emerged from.

4.   LATER AMPHITHEATRE DESIGN

Besides the Globe evidence, the best information we have of the second generation of public playhouses is the builder's contract for the Fortune. The Fortune was built in about six months, from 17 January 1600, in competition with the Globe. The builder, Peter Streete, was the man who had supervised the demolition of the old Theatre and its reconstruction on the Bankside. Unfortunately much of his contract simply instructs him to copy what he had done in the previous year with the Globe, or to follow a plan that has not survived. It is none the less worth quoting in detail:

Phillipp Henslowe & Edward Allen, the daie of the date hereof, have bargayned, compounded & agreed with the saide Peter Streete ffor the erectinge, buildinge & settinge upp of a new howse and Stadge for a Plaiehouse in and uppon a certeine plott or parcell of grounde appoynted oute for that purpose, scytuate and beinge nere Goldinge lane in the parishe of Ste Giles withoute Cripplegate of London, to be by him the saide Peeter Streete or somme other sufficyent woorkmen of his provideinge and appoyntemente and att his propper costes & chardges, for the consideracion hereafter in theis presentes expressed, made, erected, builded and sett upp in manner & forme followinge (that is to saie); The frame of the saide howse to be sett square and to conteine ffowerscore foote of lawfull assize everye waie square withoutt and fiftie five foote of like assize square everye waie within, with a good suer and stronge foundacion of pyles, brick, lyme and sand bothe without & within, to be wroughte one foote of assize att the leiste above the grounde; And the saide fframe to conteine three Stories in heighth, the first or lower Storie to conteine Twelve foote of lawfull assize in heighth, the second Storie Eleaven foote of lawfull assize in heigth, and the third or upper Storie to conteine Nyne foote of lawfull assize in height; All which Stories shall conteine Twelve foote and a halfe of lawfull assize in breadth througheoute, besides a juttey forwardes in either of the saide twoe upper Stories of Tenne ynches of lawfull assize, with ffower convenient divisions for gentlemens roomes, and other sufficient and convenient divisions for Twoe pennie roomes, with necessarie seates to be placed and sett, aswell in those roomes as througheoute all the rest of the galleries of the saide howse, and with suchelike steares, conveyances & divisions withoute & within, as are made & contryved in and to the late erected Plaiehowse on the Banck in the saide parishe of Ste Saviours called the Globe; With a Stadge and Tyreinge howse to be made, erected & settupp within the saide fframe, with a shadowe or cover over the saide Stadge, which Stadge shalbe placed & sett, as alsoe the stearecases of the saide fframe, in suche sorte as is prefigured in a plott thereof drawen, and which Stadge shall conteine in length Fortie and Three foote of lawfull assize and in breadth to extende to the middle of the yarde of the saide howse; The same Stadge to be paled in belowe with good, strong and sufficyent newe oken bourdes, and likewise the lower Storie of the saide fframe within-side, and the same lower storie to be alsoe laide over and fenced with stronge yron pykes; And the saide Stadge to be in all other proporcions contryved and fashioned like unto the Stadge of the saide Plaie howse called the Globe; With convenient windowes and lightes glazed to the saide Tyreinge howse; And the saide fframe, Stadge and Stearecases to be covered with Tyle, and to have a sufficient gutter of lead to carrie & convey the water frome the coveringe of the saide Stadge to fall backwardes; And also all the saide fframe and the Stairecases thereof to be sufficyently enclosed withoute with lathe, lyme & haire, and the gentlemens roomes and Twoe pennie roomes to be seeled with lathe, lyme & haire, and all the fflowers of the saide Galleries, Stories and Stadge to be bourded with good & sufficyent newe deale bourdes of the whole thicknes, wheare need shalbe; And the saide howse and other thinges beforemencioned to be made & doen to be in all other contrivitions, conveyances, fashions, thinge and thinges affected, finished and doen accordinge to the manner and fashion of the saide howse called the Globe, saveinge only that all the princypall and maine postes of the saide fframe and Stadge forwarde shalbe square and wroughte palasterwise, with carved proporcions called Satiers to be placed & sett on the topp of every of the same postes, and saveinge also that the said Peeter Streete shall not be chardged with anie manner of Pay[ntin]ge in or aboute the saide fframe howse or Stadge or anie parte thereof, nor rendringe the walls within, nor seeling anie more or other roomes then the gentlemens roomes, Twoe pennie roomes and Stadge before remembred. Nowe theiruppon the saide Peeter Streete dothe covenant, promise and graunte ffor himself, his executours and administratours, to and with the saide Phillipp Henslowe and Edward Allen and either of them, and thexecutours and administratours of them and either of them, by theis presentes in manner & forme followeinge (that is to saie); That he the saide Peeter Streete, his executours or assignes, shall & will att his or their owne propper costes & chardges well, woorkmanlike & substancyallie make, erect, sett upp and fully finishe in and by all thinges, accordinge to the true meaninge of theis presentes, with good, stronge and substancyall newe tymber and other necessarie stuff, all the saide fframe and other woorkes whatsoever in and uppon the saide plott or parcell of grounde (beinge not by anie aucthoretie restrayned, and havinge ingres, egres & regres to doe the same) before the ffyve & twentith daie of Julie next commeinge after the date hereof; And shall alsoe at his or theire like costes and chardges provide and finde all manner of woorkmen, tymber, joystes, rafters, boordes, dores, boltes, hinges, brick, tyle, lathe, lyme, haire, sande, nailes, lade, iron, glasse, woorkmanshipp and other thinges whatsoever, which shalbe needefull, convenyent & necessarie for the saide fframe & woorkes & everie parte thereof; And shall alsoe make all the saide fframe in every poynte for Scantlinges lardger and bigger in assize then the Scantlinges of the timber of the saide newe erected howse called the Globe; And alsoe that he the saide Peeter Streete shall furthwith, aswell by himself as by suche other and soemanie woorkmen as shalbe convenient & necessarie, enter into and uppon the saide buildings and woorkes, and shall in reasonable manner proceede therein withoute anie wilfull detraccion untill the same shalbe fully effected and finished.[24]

In summary, the significant points are that the shape was to be square inside and out, unlike the 'round' Globe, probably imitating the inn-yards instead of the baiting-houses, or else making use of an existing framework (it was very cheap in comparison with the second Globe, which had to be rebuilt from foundation level after the fire of 1613). The square measured 80 feet (24 metres) on the outside and 55 feet (16.8 metres) inside. It was built in timber clad with plaster ('lathe lyme & haire') on a brick and pile foundation, and roofed with tiles over the 'fframe, Stadge and Stearecases'. The first gallery was to be 12 feet (3.7 metres) high, the second 11 feet (3.3 metres) and the third.9 feet (2.7 metres), a total height of 32 feet (9.7 metres), each of the upper galleries having a 10 inch (25 cm) overhang into the yard. The stage, tiring-house and cover were set up inside the main framework, the stage measuring 43 feet (13 metres) across and extending half-way, i.e. 27 feet 6 inches (8.4 metres), into the yard. The stage and lowest gallery were 'paled in' with oak boards, and the gallery paling was reinforced with iron 'pykes'. The tiring-house was to have glass windows, presumably at the rear, on the outer face of the framework. Richard Hosley's analysis of the Fortune[25] adds the likelihood that two entrances from the street were on the south flank, probably as part of the staircases that led up into the galleries. The stage would most likely have been on the northern side of the yard, where it would have most light.

The cost of building the playhouse was £520, the total cost to Henslowe and Alleyn £1,320.[26] It cost £120 a year in upkeep between 1602 and 1608. Its sign was a picture of Dame Fortune, who smiled on the building until 9 December 1621, when it was burned to the ground. Alleyn promptly rebuilt it in brick at the cost of £1,000, possibly this time with a circular design. James Wright described it as 'a large, round Brick building'.[27] It was finally dismantled in 1649.

Some information about the Boar's Head is available from legal documents. The wrangles which brought it to the notice of the courts started in 1599, soon after Francis Langley took a share in its finances. Since they concerned the various outlays of cash, and what the cash was spent on, some fairly detailed descriptions of the building works are given in the legal records that survive.[28] The first conversion from an innyard to a playhouse was done in 1598. The Privy Council order to pull the amphitheatres down had wafted away, so with the Theatre standing unused in 'vast silence, and dark solitude'[29] and Langley in trouble at the Swan, only the Rose and the Curtain were then available as regular venues for playing. The locality and perhaps the inn itself were not unused to plays. The Privy Council had intervened many years before, in September 1557, to stop the performance of *A Sackful of News* at 'the Bores hed without Aldgate'.[30] Its position at the eastern gateway to the City made it an obvious candidate. Oliver Woodliffe, owner of the site in 1598, and a yeoman called Richard Samwell joined finances to put up a stage and convert the surrounding structures into galleries and a tiring-house. Woodliffe provided the tiring-house and the gallery over the stage, Samwell two levels of galleries facing the stage and a single gallery down each side of the rectanglar enclosure. Samwell was to be the manager, handling the running costs, the players and the takings, Woodliffe the sleeping partner.

The playhouse they constructed was not large, and seems to have had a stage standing free of the tiring-house, truly a 'theatre in the round', except that it was square. It evidently did not prove adequate, because in 1599 they launched a major improvement, setting the stage six feet back to butt against the tiring-house, putting a roof over it, and increasing the galleries' seating capacity till the theatre could accommodate about one thousand spectators. The total cost was near £500. By this time Samwell had Robert Browne and Derby's Men as clients, and

Browne had come in as a part-financier. In August 1599 Browne bought Samwell out. Trouble started soon after, because Langley had bought Woodliffe out in November of the previous year.

Langley's lawsuits were mostly against Samwell, and ran until 1601. They might have been one cause for Browne and his company to move away. In late 1601 Worcester's Men took a three-month tenure of the playhouse, and on 31 March 1602 the Privy Council allocated Worcester's the Boar's Head when it confirmed them as the third London company. But that arrangement did not last long. By 17 August Worcester's were at the old Rose, and Browne and Derby's Men had returned to their former lodging. Whether because of its small capacity or for other reasons, they did not stay there for many months, since by 1604 they were settled at the Red Bull. After that the Boar's Head died as a playhouse.

The stage at the Boar's Head was rectangular, almost 40 feet across at the front and about 25 feet deep, with two rooms about 12 feet 6 inches deep behind the stage for the tiring-house.[31] Plays written for the Boar's Head stage needed two entry doors, and make no demand for any machinery in the heavens. Only one play needed a trap, and one an 'above'. The yard was similar in size to the Fortune's, measuring 54 feet 6 inches by 55 feet 7 inches. The galleries were originally only three feet deep, making a shallow seating and passageway space that was broadened in 1599 to about six feet. It was the limited gallery space – only one or two levels instead of the three at the Swan and the Fortune – which made it so much smaller in audience capacity than the others. At Samwell's end of the building there was a privy, the only interior privy on record at any of the playhouses. Apart from that feature, it seems to have been not unlike a square version of the Swan as de Witt shows it, with a rectangular stage, two stage doors, and a gallery for audience above the stage.

Our knowledge of the other Elizabethan and Jacobean public playhouses is more fragmentary, deriving mainly from casual mentions in contemporary writing, including the inevitable lawsuits, and from the analysis of stage directions in the plays, filled in with deductions based on the Swan sketch and Fortune contract. Of the original Theatre in Shoreditch we know from lawsuits that it was built in timber with some ironwork, and had a tiring-house and galleries, one of which had rooms for gentlemen to sit in.[32] The leading companies used it regularly in the 1580s, but by 1597 it was empty because of trouble with the lease of the land on which it stood. After Christmas 1598 the players employed twelve workmen under the supervision of Peter Streete to pull it down, and on 20 January 1599 they transported its timbers across the river to a new site near the Rose and Swan. Exit Theatre.

The techniques of building in timber were on the decline in Tudor

23.   Wenceslas Hollar's 'Long View' of the Bankside, engraved in his *Long View of London* (1644). The captions on the Globe and the Hope, or bear-baiting house, were accidentally reversed.

times, partly under the influence of Renaissance brick and plaster construction, partly because timber became more costly as the oak forests were cut back. In Jacobean times new fire regulations added their pressure towards building in brick and tile instead of timber and thatch. We can see the changes at work in theatre-building, in the Swan's marbling, and in the switch from timber framing to brick at the second Fortune and the later private playhouses. Early playhouses like the Theatre, however, belong in the old tradition, understandably enough since James Burbage was by training a carpenter. Building in timber involved highly standardised construction techniques, and a very precise module or dimensional code for interlocking beams. The beams were morticed and tenoned, and held at the joints only by dowel pegs (iron nails were expensive). The component timbers were prefabricated, since construction by means of interlocking pieces required a whole section or bay of a framework to be fitted together before they could stand in their places – the beams could not easily be interlocked once they were in place. The main component beams were numbered if they were prefabricated in large numbers or if they were to be transported from one site to another. This what Streete would have done in dismantling the Theatre's framework.[33]

The playhouse built out of the timbers transported across the Thames early in 1599 is the most misinterpreted piece of hardware the Elizabethan players had. Constructed on a second-hand frame as a second-best option by the company which had hoped to use the Blackfriars hall instead, built for it three years before, the Globe's beginning was unpromising. The fact that subsequently most of Shakespeare's greatest plays were written for it has obscured these origins and has fertilised elaborate fantasies about its design for hundreds of years. This account will try to lop the more extravagant fantasies about the Globe's original shape by examining the only two substantial and reliable pieces of evidence we have.[34]

The story of the company's loss of the Theatre, its abortive replacement with the Blackfriars and the dubiously legal acquisition of the Theatre's frame timbers to build the Globe has been told above (pages 45–8). One feature of that story is the cut-price circumstances in which the first Globe was built, and the contrasting opulence of the rebuilding. That creates difficulties for the evidence about the original Globe, because the two best pieces of evidence both relate principally to the reconstructed playhouse of 1614. To identify the original Globe we have to weigh the likelihood of improvements to the design that were made in the rebuilding against the probability that the nostalgia which persuaded them to rebuild it would have required any changes to be minimal. Testimony in a lawsuit of the 1630s claimed that the new Globe was built on the foundations of the old. This suggests that the groundplan would have been the same. What changes may have been introduced above the foundations is a matter for conjecture.

Only two kinds of good evidence about the Globe survive. One kind is archaeological, like the Rose dig, the other a contemporary's graphic picture, like de Witt's Swan drawing. Both are of the second Globe. The archaeological evidence has uncovered a section of the gallery walls with a stair turret lobby attached to the outer wall. Wenceslas Hollar's drawing for his famous 'Long View' of London from the south shows what he could see of the second Globe in the 1630s from the tower of the church that is now Southwark Cathedral. The archaeological evidence provides information chiefly about the foundations, and Hollar's view shows only the exterior shape of the lavishly built replacement for the original Globe. Such imperfect evidence has to be eked out with thoughts from the plays written for the first Globe, if any secure indications of Shakespeare's workplace are to be found.

The archaeological evidence comes from only a small section of the total foundations, which lie under other buildings.[35] It shows a broad foundation of 'clunch', or chalk stones in an aggregate, which evidently formed the outer gallery wall foundation. Two walls of a polygon have been uncovered, angled at about 158° or 160°. This angle indicates that

24. Hollar's drawing of the second Globe for the 'Long View'.

there might have been twenty sides to the polygon in all. Another angle has been discovered in the inner gallery wall in brick and mortar. It measures the same as the outer wall. Since it is one side round from the outer gallery angle, the likely radius of the outer walls can be measured by bisecting the two angles, subtending a line through them and noting where they intersect. They cross at about fifty feet from the outer gallery wall. It thus appears that the Globe was roughly one hundred feet in its outside diameter, markedly larger than the approximately seventy-two feet of the Rose. The Globe's gallery walls enclose a space a little over ten feet deep, barely larger than the Rose's. Its yard must therefore have been about eighty feet in diameter. The Rose's yard measures three rods, or forty-nine feet six inches. A five-rod diameter at the Globe would make it eighty-two feet six inches.

The Globe remains have other foundations attached to the gallery walls, which appear to form the base of one of the two entrance ways to the playhouse. Part of two crosswalls stretch between the gallery foundations, to the right (looking from the yard) of the outer wall angle. Hazel-nut shell debris was found at the yard end between the two crosswalls, indicating that they formed a passageway into and from the

25. The Globe's foundations from above, a photograph taken by the Museum of London when they were first uncovered, in October 1989.

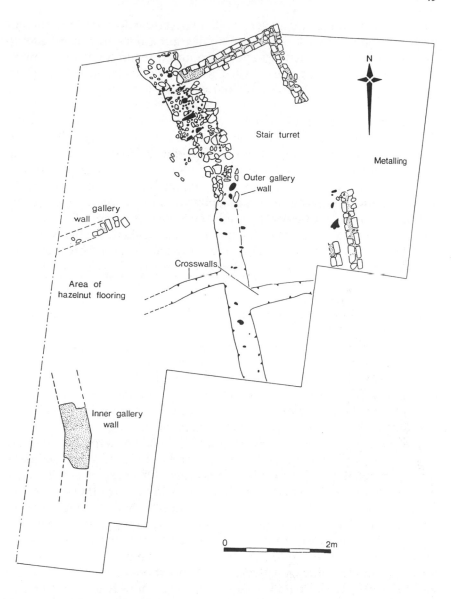

26. A plan of the Globe foundations, based on the area covered in the photograph on p. 144. It is still only a conjectural interpretation of the remains. They show an outer wall of chalk and flint with some timbers embedded, and one angle of the inner wall, made of brick. Outside the outer wall other brick foundations seem to show the entrance lobby. Between the outer and inner gallery walls runs the base of a pair of corridor walls from the lobby to the yard.

yard. Outside the outer gallery wall two sets of foundations jut out from the centre of each side, turning at right angles to run parallel to the faces of the outer gallery and make an enclosure or lobby framing the angle of the outer gallery wall. These parallel lobby walls stop short of the angle, to make an open doorway into the lobby. Outside this doorway a deposit of gravel was found, evidently laid in order to provide a footing for pedestrians arriving from Maiden Lane to the north. The positioning of the lobby walls around the angle of the outer gallery wall suggests that the timber upright in the angle, part of the main structural frame for the gallery scaffolding, was used as a newel post. The stairway into the galleries would have spiralled round it. Thus audiences entering the outer lobby would have either gone to the left of the angle and passed through the passageway into the yard, or have gone right and up the stairs into one of the galleries. This entrance-way would have given access to the yard and galleries on the right-hand side facing the stage. The other entranceway, shown in Wenceslas Hollar's picture of the second Globe as a stair turret, was positioned symmetrically on the other flank of the yard and would have given access to the left side of the auditorium. This evidence for the admission system at the Globe is a clear indication of the improved design of the later generation of amphitheatres compared with the Rose generation.

The archaeological evidence tells us more about the auditorium than it does about the stage at the Rose and the Globe. Foundations give little firm information about the details of the timberwork constructed on them, and of the stage and all its furnishings there is little evidence, apart from the outline of the stage's shape at the Rose and a base for one of its stage posts. The Swan drawing is some help, but the best evidence about the stages is still what can be deduced from the plays that were written for specific playhouses. Of these there is more evidence about the Rose and the Globe than any of the others.

The Globe's yard was larger than the Rose's, and its stage may in consequence have had a markedly different configuration. Square, perhaps, it could afford to have a flat-faced *frons scenae*, instead of the three angled faces at the Rose.[36] Its size must have compared with the Fortune's 43 feet wide by 27 deep, probably more if it extended to the middle of the yard. It had a large trap, big enough for two men to descend at once, and two stage pillars supporting the heavens, which were fretted with golden fire according to Hamlet. It had two stage doors (the quarto of *Pericles* has a stage direction speaking of '*one door*' and '*the other*'), flanking a set of hangings across what was probably a central discovery-space recessed into the *frons*. This central space was necessary for bringing on large properties such as the chair of state, or throne, for all court scenes, and the curtained bed for Desdemona in *Othello*. It was probably also used for regal entries, and for the clowns, who usually made their presence known first by sticking their heads through the hangings.

Above the stage level in the *frons* were the lords' rooms, which Guilpin said were 'o're the stage'.[37] One such room, probably the central one, would have been used for balcony scenes, required for rather more than half of the plays written for the Globe between 1599 and 1609.[38] For some of the scenes, a *'window'* above the stage is mentioned in the stage directions or the text, in others players appear *'on the walls'* or above the gates of a besieged town. Other scenes require a non-specific locality above as a place of observation. In Shakespeare, fourteen references indicate the place simply as *'aloft'* or *'above'*. Ten references, not all of them in plays originally written for the Globe, call it *'on the walls'*, four *'the windows'*, one *'the Tarras'*, and others are simply implied in the dialogue.[39] Two references to a place *'on the top'* occur in plays not written specifically for the Globe, though most likely staged there. They seem to refer to places above the upper playing area. These may have been the topmost spectators' galleries, or a place adjacent to the heavens or the huts – possibly even the trumpeter's place, if the Globe had one as in de Witt's sketch. Thirteen scenes in Shakespeare need descents from the upper area to the stage, and five require ascents, three by way of the tiring-house interior.

The action above was usually brief, twenty-eight of Shakespeare's instances averaging only thirty-seven lines there, and a maximum of three players.[40] They use speech rather than movement. From these observations it is easy to deduce that the area available above the stage was limited. Scholars have accordingly been quick to point out that an above-stage gallery area given over to spectators, like the partitioned gallery of the Swan sketch, could easily have accommodated the above-stage requirements of the Globe plays. Therefore it is likely that the upper levels of the Globe tiring-house façade were constructed in a manner not essentially different from those shown at the Swan. Jonson's reference to 'the lords roome over the stage' at the Globe would seem to confirm this. The players could have simply reserved one of the rooms for playing in when a play demanding such an area was to be put on.

One other matter relates to the gallery over the stage. This is the possibility that one of the rooms in the gallery was normally reserved as a 'music-room', and – a further conjecture – that it was this room that doubled as the above-stage playing area. It has even been suggested that the figures in the third and fourth sections of the gallery (the middle two) in de Witt's sketch represent musicians.[41] There certainly was a music-room at the Swan in 1613, when *A Chaste Maid in Cheapside* was performed, because it calls at one point for *'a sad Song in the Musicke-roome'*.[42]

The question is complicated by what appears to have been a change in the function of music in the amphitheatres during the first decade of the seventeenth century. The induction to the version of *The Malcontent* played at the Globe speaks of the 'not received custome of musicke in our Theater'. This presumably means that they lacked concert musicians performing with strings and woodwinds. Drums, trumpets, fiddles and flutes were standard accessories to performances from early in the history of playing. The fashion for string and woodwind chamber-music began in the hall theatres, where it was played as a kind of overture, and between the acts. The Blackfriars musicians had a considerable reputation even in 1602, when the visiting Duke of Stettin-Pomerania heard an hour-long concert before the play by a consort of lutes, mandolins, bandores, violins and flutes.[43] The Blackfriars music-room was probably a curtained room above the stage, like the musicians' gallery in a hall screen. In the public playhouses, on the other hand, at least up to the end of the sixteenth century, music seems always to have sounded from *'within'*, i.e. from the tiring-house, not in a chamber above the stage. This not only makes it unlikely that de Witt's gallery portrays a music-room, but also makes it doubtful whether the Globe tiring-house gallery originally had one either. The Boar's Head was not given a room in the gallery for musicians when it was designed in 1599. Not until some time after 1604 at the Globe, when the players acknowledged that they were still not accustomed to providing music as part of the afternoon's entertainment, would a music-room have been established. Somewhere between 1607 and 1609, at about the time the boys at Blackfriars relinquished their playhouse to the King's Men, is a likely time for the change. We do know that after 1607 the public-playhouse poets began to follow the private-playhouse practice of dividing their plays into acts.[44] This may signal the adoption of the related practice of inter-act music. The *Chaste Maid* was performed at the Swan in 1613, by which time Langley could well have taken over one of the lords' rooms for music. The Red Bull had a music-room 'above' by about 1608, and the second Globe's music-room certainly had fiddlers, in a curtained alcove 'above'[45] as we learn from a passage in *Late Lancashire Witches*, performed at the Globe in 1634:

ARTH[UR]. Play fidlers any thing.
DOUGH[TY]. I, and lets see your faces, that you play fairely with us.
Musitians shew themselves above.

There is a strong possibility that in the hall playhouses it was the musicians' alcove that the players used for action above.[46] The players at the Globe could have done the same, but there is only one slight piece of evidence that they did so before 1609. Jasper Mayne praised Jonson in 1638 for his care in staging, his realism, in that 'Thou laid'st no sieges to the music room'.[47] Sieges of the tiring-house were less fashionable in the seventeenth than the sixteenth century at the Globe, but in any case Mayne's memory could not have stretched back to much before 1609.

The second and more vexed question, of what was below the tiring-house gallery, is less easy to resolve if only because the evidence provided by the plays is difficult to reconcile with any single kind of structure. Twenty-one of the thirty plays known to have been performed at the Globe between 1599 and 1609 need no inner-stage or discovery-space at all.[48] Of the remaining nine, seven use the feature only once. So it was not pressed into use with great enthusiasm. It can hardly have been a really prominent feature, or if it was, then it must have been erected only for those plays needing it – a prominent feature of the stage's structure that rests unused throughout a performance would be a sore distraction to players and audience alike.

There must in fact have been two kinds of feature. One was permanent, a curtained alcove or discovery-space in the tiring-house wall, which served as a shop, tomb, cell, study or closet. The other was a special property, a raised platform, or even a curtained 'booth' set up on stage, of the kind used in the early years by the travelling players as their tiring-house. It seems to have had various shapes. It might be a tent, a canopied 'state' (a regal throne on a dais), or in *Antony and Cleopatra* a 'monument' big enough to hold Antony's body and several women on top, but low enough for the women to lift the body up on to it. Several plays need a raised area like the dais of the 'state', for such actions as the mountebank speeches in *Volpone*. A platform with steps up to it, which could be used as an executioner's scaffold, is needed in *The Fair Maid of Bristow*. These structures could not have been the same thing as the 'discovery-space', unless they were curtained and the discovery-space was the area inside, a kind of discovery-booth. If it were such a structure, it would have had to be attached to the tiring-house in some way, at a door, so that the objects and players to be discovered could be changed without the audience seeing. *The Devil's Charter* uses the discovery-space six times for different tableaux, as well as two 'tents', all requiring changes to be made inside the discovery-space. And as there seem to have been two doors at the Globe, which could be used even when the discovery-space was in service, a discovery-booth can hardly have been set in front of one of the doors. In *The Devil's Charter* apparitions enter by one door and leave by the other while the discovery-space is in use. Moreover, one of the same play's stage directions speaks of a discovered player coming *'upon the Stage out of his study'*. This is not the kind of terminology likely to be used if the discovery-space study were really a booth already set up on the stage.[49] If the platform or booth construction were put up only for plays needing

27.   The hall screen in the Middle Temple, constructed in 1574.

it, and the discovery-space was simply a curtained alcove in the tiring-house wall, neither feature would have been obtrusive when all the plays not using them were performed.

With a repertory that demanded a different play every afternoon, it is unlikely that the players made much use of elaborate booths or demountable constructions that took a long time to set up. Such constructions would have to be simple enough to be erected on the morning of the performance and removed the same evening or early the next morning before the players came to start rehearsals for that day's play. Large structures would also get the players into difficulties when they had to transfer their play for an evening show at a private house or at venues like the Middle Temple Hall, as Shakespeare's company did with *Twelfth Night* in February 1602. Even their largest properties, the chair of state on its dais, the double bed, had to be readily transportable. Desdemona did not die on the floor when *Othello* was performed at Oxford in 1610.[50]

There was certainly some sort of enclosed space at the back of the stage, which could be pressed into use for the Globe plays. Its use seems to have been essentially for static tableaux, in accordance with a long-established theatrical tradition. The *'brazen Head'* that was revealed *'in the middle of the place behind the Stage'* in *Alphonsus of Aragon* (c. 1587) is echoed in *Volpone's* unveiling of his gold. The players who are 'discovered' in the Globe plays are almost all single figures who do not usually move, unless to step out on to the stage. They are almost all studying, sleeping or dead. In Shakespeare's plays seven are studiers, six sleepers and five corpses.[51] This kind of static display is the clearest distinguishing feature of the discovery scenes. Recognition that they are designed as tableaux can save us from thinking of all scenes that are said in the dialogue to be in bedchambers or other interiors as being tucked away at the back of the stage.

The discovery-space seems to have had a number of lesser uses, some of which can explain other details about the staging. Most importantly it probably made a third entry-point. In *The Devil's Charter* IV.v, the leading character enters *'out of his studie'*, and later exits *'into his studie'*, which we might suppose to be through one of the normal entry doors if it were not that in two other scenes he is discovered in his study and speaks six or eight lines there before moving out onto the stage. Secondly, the curtain or hangings of the discovery-space could also be used for concealment, for Polonius's arras in *Hamlet*, or Galatea in *Philaster*, who eavesdrops from *'behind the Hangings'*. Volpone peers over a curtain to watch his gulls ('Ile get up / Behind the Curtain, on a stool, and hearken; / Some time peep over'). And of course noises off or music *'within'* could most easily be heard from behind a curtain. All three extant illustrations of stages in use between de Witt's Swan and 1642 (*Roxana* (1632), see p. 5; *Messallina* (1640), see p. 163; Kirkman's *The Wits*)[52] show the whole tiring-house façade curtained off. This practice, which must have derived from the curtained booth of the street theatres, was probably fairly general. Possibly de Witt failed to show hangings because his main concern was with structural features. Hangings would have been the most readily modifiable features, of course.

The raised platform, canopied 'state' or curtained booth was a more variable feature. It was usually employed for animated action, as would befit a construction set up on the stage proper. It or they might have been portable enough to be brought in for a particular scene – certainly substantial properties such as canopied beds as well as tables were pushed or carried on and off the stage, and Volpone's rostrum is explicitly said to be carried out on stage. They were less common than discoveries, but they certainly were used. They took the form of tents (*The Devil's Charter, Richard III* and *Troilus and Cressida*), a dais, 'state' or scaffold (*The Fair Maid of Bristow*, and the rostrums in *Volpone* and *Julius*

Caesar), or a raised monument as in *Antony and Cleopatra*. All in all, the various possible features that the tiring-house may have presented to the stage could be said to be like a good nose in a face, flexible and not obtrusive.

Only one other public playhouse, the Red Bull, has been granted the kind of detailed analysis of the staging of its repertory that Shakespeare's playhouse has received. As with the Globe, the conclusion to be drawn from the analysis is that the Red Bull plays 'could be given on a stage structurally like that of the Swan, with the single important addition of a third stage door'.[53] The Red Bull was square in shape, like its near neighbour the Fortune. As we learn from a petition by Martin Slater, a player involved in the enterprise, the builder

altered some stables and other rooms, being before a square court in an inn, to turn them into galleries, with the consent of the parish.[54]

Like the Fortune it was probably similar to the round Globe and Swan in its stage fittings. It had stage posts, a heaven and a large trap. It offered only a small upper playing area, normally reached by stairs in the tiring-house. It had a fair number of discovery-scenes, and possibly a removable curtained booth, as well as a dais for the 'state', or throne, which was also removable. The Red Bull was more inclined to favour spectacle than Shakespeare was, so the Red Bull plays contain a greater use of properties of all kinds amongst their stage effects. But there is nothing that indicates any significant structural differences in the design of the stage area from the Globe, nor of the other amphitheatres.

The evidence for the playhouses as a whole, both amphitheatre and hall, supports this analysis of the Globe and Red Bull plays. T. J. King has examined very carefully the evidence, mainly in stage directions, of 276 plays performed between 1599 and 1642, and found no significant variations in the requirements for staging them.[55] As many as 87 of the plays need only the minimal two doors and floor space, with large properties 'thrust out' as they are required. Of these plays 30 were in the King's Men's repertoire. Only 45 of the 276 need a playing space 'above'; 42 need a trap, and 102 need a discovery-space, half of them King's Men's plays. Everything else that was needed was portable.

One other fairly substantial piece of evidence about the amphitheatres remains to be considered: a contract for building the Hope, similar to Streete's contract for the Fortune. The Hope was erected in 1613–14 by Henslowe and Alleyn, primarily out of their interest in bull- and bear-baiting. It replaced the old Beargarden (also known as Paris Garden), though that place of entertainment had provided only baitings with occasional jigs as interludes.[56] Alleyn and Henslowe planned a regular alternation of baiting and playing. The contract stipulates the usual timber construction on a brick foundation, with three galleries of the same height as the Fortune's, tile roofing, and two external staircases. Its other fittings were to be like those of its neighbour the Swan, except that it was to have boxes in the lowest gallery level, and the stage had to be removable and therefore without pillars to support the heavens. The contractor was to

not onlie take downe or pull downe all that same place or house wherein Beares and Bulls have been heretofore usuallie bayted, and also one other house or staple wherin Bulls and horsses did usuallie stande, sett, lyinge, and beinge uppon or neere the Banksyde in the saide parish of St Saviour in Sowthworke, commonlie called or knowne by the name of the Beare garden, but shall also at his or theire owne proper costes and charges uppon or before the saide laste daie of November newly erect, builde, and sett upp one other same place or Plaiehouse fitt & convenient in all thinges, bothe for players to playe in, and for the game of Beares and Bulls to be bayted in the same, and also a fitt and convenient Tyre house and a stage to be carryed or taken awaie, and to stande uppon tressells good, substanciall, and sufficient for the carryinge and bearinge of suche a stage; And shall new builde, erect, and sett up againe the saide plaie house or game place neere or uppon the saide place, where the saide game place did heretofore stande; And to builde the same of suche large compasse, fforme, widenes, and height as the Plaie house called the Swan in the libertie of Parris garden in the saide parishe of St Saviour now is; And shall also builde two stearecasses without and adjoyninge to the saide Playe house in suche convenient places, as shalbe moste fitt and convenient for the same to stande uppon, and of such largnes and height as the stearecasses of the saide playehouse called the Swan nowe are or bee; And shall also builde the Heavens all over the saide stage, to be borne or carryed without any postes or supporters to be fixed or sett uppon the saide stage, and all gutters of leade needfull for the carryage of all suche raine water as shall fall uppon the same; And shall also make two Boxes in the lowermost storie fitt and decent for gentlemen to sitt in; And shall make the particions betwne the Rommes as they are at the saide Plaie House called the Swan; And to make turned cullumes uppon and over the stage; And shall make the principalls and fore fronte of the saide Plaie house of good and sufficient oken tymber, and no furr tymber to be putt or used in the lower most, or midell stories, except the upright postes on the backparte of the saide stories (all the byndinge joystes to be of oken tymber); the inner principall postes of the first storie to be twelve footes in height and tenn ynches square, the inner principall postes in the midell storie to be eight ynches square, the inner most postes in the upper storie to be seaven ynches square; The prick postes in the first storie to be eight ynches square, in the seconde storie seaven ynches square, and in the upper most storie six ynches square; Also the brest sommers in the lower moste storie to be nyne ynches depe, and seaven ynches in thicknes, and in the midell storie to be eight ynches depe and six ynches in thicknes; The byndinge jostes of the firste storie to be nyne and eight ynches in depthe and thicknes, and in the midell storie to be viii an vii ynches in depthe and thicknes. Item to make a good, sure, and sufficient foundacion of brickes for the saide Play house or game place, and to make it xiiiteene ynches at the leaste above the grounde.[57]

It was a polygonal building, like its predecessor.[58]

Jonson's *Bartholomew Fair* was one of the first plays written for the new Hope, and was played there by the reconstituted Lady Elizabeth's Men in 1614. Not surprisingly, Jonson put in a number of pointed references to the dual-purpose nature of the playhouse. The play begins with a stage-keeper coming out to beg the audience's patience for a delay while one of the players' costumes is sewn up, and is later accused of collecting the apples thrown by the impatient audience to feed 'the bears within'. Jonson claims to have kept a 'special decorum' in the depiction of his Fairground, since the playhouse is 'as durty as *Smithfield* [the real venue of the fair], and as stinking every whit'. He also speaks of a spectator paying 6*d* at the door – a further hint that the old system of paying out penny by penny may have been dropped for the second generation of playhouses.

It is usually thought to be an indication of the reduced status of the public playhouses that the last of them should have been built as a dual-purpose place of entertainment. It should be noted, though, that the building it replaced was solely a baiting-house, and to add playing to its bill of fare actually gave the players an extra venue that they had not had before. Since baiting could not be provided every day (for the animals' sake), it was a sound commercial device for Alleyn and Henslowe to combine their two interests at the one house in this way. None the less, it was not a happy notion. The players and the playhouse owners quarrelled frequently over the priorities the owners gave to baiting over playing, and after 1620 the Hope was hardly used by players at all. By the 1630s it had reverted to the old name of Beargarden. There were enough public playhouses then – the Globe and Fortune were both rebuilt more lavishly after their fires, and substantial improvements seem also to have been made to the Red Bull in the 1620s, if we can trust William Prynne's claim that it was 'reedified' and 'enlarged' somewhere near the time the Fortune was rebuilt.

5. THE HALL PLAYHOUSES

With possibly one striking exception, the other main venues, the hall playhouses, are less well documented. Two fairly general initial presumptions are all that we can make with any confidence: first, that the auditorium area probably differed markedly from those of the public playhouses, in view of the different origins of each kind of structure; secondly, that the actual playing areas of the two kinds of playhouse are less likely to have differed, if only because the builder of the most important of them was James Burbage, and because the King's Men had so little apparent trouble after 1608 in switching themselves and their repertory between the Globe and Blackfriars. Queen Anne's Men also passed from the Red Bull to the Cockpit and back again in 1616.

Of the first commercial indoor playhouse, Richard Farrant's first Blackfriars, we know very little. It had an advantage enjoyed only by its later namesake, of being located inside the City walls and yet free of the city's jurisdiction. As a former monastic precinct the five acres of Blackfriars were technically a 'liberty', with a vague form of local self-government like that of a rural parish. Its independence was a continued irritation to the Lord Mayor of the City, and the City Charter of 1608 finally abolished all the liberties and brought them under City govern-ment. By that time, of course, the playhouses were not only long established but under the royal protection.[59] Farrant leased property there late in 1576, in order to obtain a room for his Chapel Children to perform in. The room he used was the frater of the original monastery. When Farrant rented it, it was divided into smaller rooms by partitions, which Farrant promptly pulled down. William More, the owner of the building, liked neither Farrant's pulling down of the partitions nor his use of the room as a playhouse. After Farrant's death in 1580 his successor as company manager kept the lease from More by various dodges, but More none the less repossessed the building and turned the players out in 1584, after only eight years.

A similar attitude to playing in the precinct showed up amongst the residents when James Burbage tried to set up his new playhouse there in 1596. He bought a considerable property from the same William More who had closed the first playhouse, and converted it into the famous Blackfriars for the sum of £600.[60] It did in the end prove to be a splendid investment, but Burbage himself did not live to see it. He bought the property, so it could not be taken from him as Farrant's property had been, and as the Theatre was about to be. None the less, he could be stopped from using it as a playhouse, and a petition of Blackfriars residents promptly made sure he was stopped, though not until after he had made all the alterations to turn the building into a playhouse. The petition told the Privy Council that

one Burbage hath lately bought certaine roomes in the . . . precinct neere adjoyning unto the dwelling houses of the right honorable the Lord Chamber-laine and the Lord of Hunsdon, which romes the said Burbage is now altering and meaneth very shortly to convert and turne the same into a comon playhouse, which will grow to be a very great annoyance and trouble, not only to all the noblemen and gentlemen thereabout inhabiting but allso a generall inconvenience to all the inhabitants of the same precinct, both by reason of the great resort and gathering togeather of all manner of vagrant and lewde persons that, under cullor of resorting to the playes, will come thither and worke all manner of mischeefe, and allso to the great pestring and filling up of the same precinct, yf it should please God to send any visitation of sicknesse as heretofore hath been, for that the same precinct is allready growne very populous; and besides, that the same playhouse is so neere the Church that the noyse of the drummes and trumpetts will greatly disturbe and hinder both the ministers and parishioners in tyme of devine service and sermons; – In tender consideracion whereof, as allso for that there hath not at any tyme heretofore been used any comon playhouse within the same precinct, but that now all players being banished by the Lord Mayor from playing within the Cittie by reason of the great inconveniences and ill rule that followeth them, they now thincke to plant them selves in liberties.[61]

The Mayor's success in 1595 with his ban on playing at inns inside the City had been noted by the writers of the petition. Burbage's plan for the Blackfriars was clearly seen as an attempt to circumvent the ban. Moreover no hall playhouses were operating in 1596, and the petition-ers' objection to the 'noyse of the drummes and trumpetts' makes it evident that part of their complaint was to the loud instruments common at the amphitheatres being sounded in an enclosed space. The boy company which opened there three years later used no drums or fireworks, and played woodwinds instead of brass horns and trumpets for their music. Eventually Shakespeare's company was to do the same. Where the Globe might have used a trumpet fanfare to herald the visit of foreign dignitaries such as Aragon and Morocco in *The Merchant of Venice*, the Folio text, prepared for the Blackfriars, specifies a cornet. The dumb-show in *Hamlet* is heralded in the 1604 quarto by trumpet-calls, but in the Folio text of 1623 by hautboys, the indoor equivalent.

The Blackfriars property included the paved hall of the old Priory, and a great chamber above it, sometimes called the Upper Frater. Like Farrant's property it was subdivided, and consisted of:

All those Seaven greate upper Romes as they are nowe devided being all upon one flower and sometyme beinge one greate and entire room wth the roufe over the same covered wth Leade . . . And also all that greate paire of wyndinge staires wth the staire case thereunto belonginge wch leadeth upp unto the same seaven greate upper Romes oute of the greate yarde.[62]

It was probably this hall of seven rooms rather than the low-ceilinged one in the old Priory that Burbage made into his theatre. The 'greate paire of wyndinge staires' is implied in various references to the entry being 'below', and to the theatre being up a set of stairs. The total dimensions of the Upper Frater were 110 feet (33.5 metres) by 46 feet (14 metres), though the actual dimensions of the theatre are stated to have been 66 feet (20.1 metres) north to south and 46 feet (14 metres) east to west.[63] The stairway, and, as we know from other evidence,[64] the playhouse entrance, were to the north. It was grand enough to have once been used for meetings of Parliament. Clearly it was beautifully convenient in its geographical and social location, and in its inward dimensions and appearance, for a 'private' playhouse.

The interior dimensions of 66 feet (20.1 metres) by 46 feet (14 metres) compare with the external dimensions of 72 feet (22 metres) for the Rose and 80 feet (24.4 metres) for the Fortune. The auditorium was paved, with benches in the pit and degrees for sitting on in the galleries. The galleries, probably with three levels above the pit, were curved or polygonal timber structures arranged around the three sides in front of the stage.[65] The line of the Blackfriars roof shown in Hollar's 'Long View' shows that the rectangle was aligned with the longer sides roughly north–south. A reference to the eastern end of the stage indicates that it was aligned east–west, which would put it across one of the shorter sides, probably the southern one, since the great staircase was at the northern end.

The stage end had at its rear the tiring-house. It provided separate access for those privileged gallants who paid extra for a stool to view the play from the stage itself, and who reached the stage through the hangings like the players. The stage itself was small, the width of the hall being reduced by the boxes which flanked the stage on either side.[66] These would have taken at least 20 of the available 46 feet. Shirley claimed in 1640 in the prologue to *The Doubtful Heir* that the Globe's stage was 'vast' in comparison with the Blackfriars.[67] The contrast in the known measurements of 25 feet or so of width against the 43 of the Fortune and a similar space at the Globe, makes that a reasonable statement. And with the well-dressed feathered gallants occupying stools on the stage itself, the acting space was certainly cramped. It is hardly surprising that after the adults took it over in 1608 swordplay was confined to the occasional fencing bout and that battles and what Shirley called 'target fighting' were never tried there.

There was room for three ranges of galleries in the auditorium, but it is not certain how many there actually were. They are referred to in a lawsuit in the plural, which implies at least two levels. References to 'the middle region' possibly apply to the middle gallery of a range of three, but might also apply to the pit.[68] I suspect it is the former. One reference specifies an ex-soldier as positioned there, the kind of man with little money but too high a social status to join the 'sixpenny mechanicks' in the topmost gallery. The galleries were curved round the rectilinear auditorium, giving them some kinship to the polygonal amphitheatres.

Admission prices at Blackfriars began at a basic 6*d.*, which gained entry to the galleries. A further 1*s.* provided a bench in the pit. As many as ten gallants, who wished to display themselves at the same time as they got a close view of the play, could pass through the tiring-

Paulis wharfe

28. A detail from Hollar's 'Long View' of London. It shows the tower of St Bride's on the left. Below and to the right, a long steep-pitched roof with two tall lanterns or chimneys protruding from the centre is thought to be the Blackfriars roof.

house and hire a stool to sit on the stage itself, for a total of 2s.[69] A box cost half-a-crown.

The location of the boxes is open to some question. A reference to a tiff between two spectators at the playhouse in 1632 proves that boxes were close enough to the stage for a spectator standing on the stage to obscure a box-holder's view, and for the standing spectator to lunge with his sword at the box-holder when told to move out of the way. That they were at the side rather than the back of the stage is a matter of conjecture, but it seems more likely. It accords with the location of the 'two Boxes in the lowermost storie' of the galleries in the Hope contract. It allows the 'discovery-space' more room at the back of the stage.

Boxes flanking the stage, because they gave a view of the discovery-space in the tiring-house wall, must have made a preferable viewing-place compared with the equivalent lords' rooms in the amphitheatres. There were 'degrees' for spectators in the gallery flanking the central upper-stage music-room of the theatre that Inigo Jones designed to copy the Blackfriars (see Illustration 29), and there was certainly space for seating on the balcony where the lords' rooms were positioned at the Globe. But they did not give a view of the discovery-space, and it is likely that the Blackfriars boxes were set up at the sides of the stage to satisfy that need.

The evidence from plays performed at the Blackfriars suggests that the stage fittings were basically similar to those of public playhouses. There are no references to stage posts, though there must have been a 'heaven', because flights were not unusual. There was a mid-stage trap, according to *Poetaster*, which begins with '*Envie. Arising in the midst of the stage*'. There was a playing area above, which Chapman in *May-Day* several times calls a '*tarras*', and which is used as a window or balcony. Jonson in *Poetaster*, IV. ix, shaped his stage directions ambiguously, as in '*Shee appeareth above, as at her chamber window*'; but in *The Devil is an Ass*, II.vi, he noted in the margin of the text '*This* Scene *is acted at two windo's, as out of two contiguous buildings*'. Elizabethan windows were not necessarily glazed, of course, nor necessarily even papered, and it need not be assumed that more than two adjacent apertures, possibly curtained like the musicians' alcoves, were called for.

What may have been below the tarras or windows is as much a matter of conjecture as it is in the amphitheatres. There is much less evidence for large constructions than in amphitheatre plays, and not much more for a curtained discovery-space. The opening stage direction of *Eastward Ho!* is as explicit as one could hope for:

Enter Maister Touchstone, and Quicksilver at several dores . . . At the middle dore, Enter Golding discovering a Goldsmiths shoppe, and walking short turnes before it.

This implies three doors, the central one large enough to conceal a shop. It suggests the possibility of an arrangement of central double doors flanked by single doorways. Some authors evidently expected one of the doors, presumably the middle one if it was used for discoveries, to be curtained. Davenant's prologue to *The Unfortunate Lovers* speaks of a half-dressed player peeping through the hangings before the play starts, to see how the playhouse is filling up. The 'silke cortaine, come to hang the stage here', mentioned in the induction to *Cynthia's Revels*, would have hung in the doorway or a similar place. It was not hung around the edge of the stage to conceal the understage area, because the Citizen and Wife who sit on the stage in *The Knight of the Burning Pestle* comment on stage hangings within their view. Understage hangings would have been out of sight for them. Either the double doors or the hangings could have opened for discoveries like the one in *A Staple of News*, when '*The study is open'd where she sit in state*'.

Evidence about the other hall playhouses is more fragmentary, but presents a picture largely consistent with that of the Blackfriars. The playhouse used by Paul's Boys, and particularly the stage area, seems to have been even smaller, since the stage was not large enough to allow gallants to sit on stools on it. Admission charges there may have been lower too at one time, perhaps no more than 2*d.* when they first reopened. The space above had a balcony or window, which included a place for musicians. There were two entry doors probably flanking a discovery-space. A structure called a 'canopy' in two of the plays[70] was big enough to seat five boys holding books.

The Whitefriars theatre, which came into being in 1608 after Paul's had closed down, and its abortive successor, Porter's Hall, are almost totally obscure. Whitefriars was built in the former monks' refectory, measuring approximately 85 feet (26 metres) by 35 feet (10.7 metres), longer and narrower than Blackfriars, which almost certainly means that its stage would have been set across one of the shorter sides of the hall. Of Porter's Hall we cannot even be sure that it was private, though the fact that it was intended for use by children and that all the urban playhouses were indoors makes it more than likely.

We know more, conceivably a great deal more, about the Cockpit or Phoenix, which Beeston built in 1616. A plan for a theatre drawn up by Inigo Jones in 1616–18 has features which suggest that it was intended for Beeston. It is a curious shape, round at the auditorium

---

29.   Inigo Jones's drawings for a hall playhouse, probably made for the Cockpit in 1616, sheets 1/7 B and C, Worcester College, Oxford. See John Orrell, *The Theatres of Inigo Jones and John Webb*, Chapter 3, and (with Andrew Gurr) *Rebuilding Shakespeare's Globe*, Chapter 4.

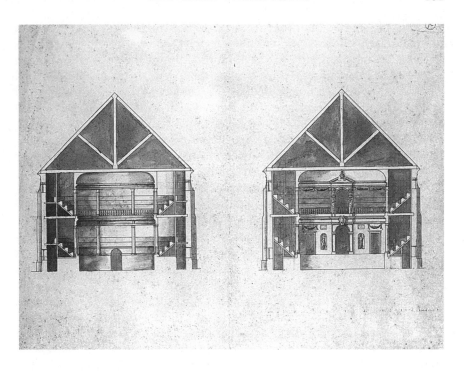

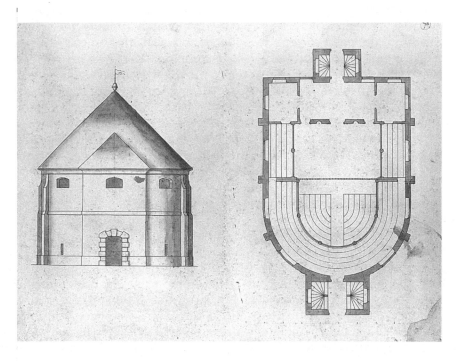

end and squared at the other, in a form that might well have been an adaptation of an existing circular cockpit enlarged for playing. A restraint on new building at the time did permit the reconstruction of old buildings up to one-third bigger than the original foundations. Jones was the King's Surveyor by 1616, and would have known what could and could not be done with the old structure Beeston had leased for his players.[71]

Jones's plan is not perfect. Some confusion between levels in the drawings has led at least one scholar to conclude that it could never have been built.[72] But it would not be the first architectural design requiring modification in practice, and the circumstantial evidence linking it to Beeston's Cockpit is plausible enough to warrant taking the plan seriously as at least a possible model for that playhouse.

Judging from measurements on the plan itself (no scale is given), the interior dimensions were 52 feet (15.8 metres) by 37 feet (11.3 metres), noticeably smaller than the Blackfriars. James Wright, who reported from near the end of the seventeenth century that the Blackfriars, the Cockpit and Salisbury Court built in 1629 were almost exactly the same size,[73] might have been misled by the similarity of the Blackfriars curve within the rectangle and the Cockpit's elongated circle. The stage area of Jones's plan is 23 feet 6 inches (7.2 metres) by 15 feet (4.6 metres), which cannot have been very different from the Blackfriars dimensions. The stage is 4 feet (1.2 metres) high, and the tiring-house behind it 10 feet (3 metres) in depth running the whole breadth of the playhouse at the squared end. Galleries on each side of the stage are a little under 7 feet (2.1 metres) wide. There are two ranges of galleries, the first 11 feet (3.3 metres) above stage level and the second 7 feet (2.1 metres) above that. Each has four degrees, or steps for sitting on, and a passageway at the back. There are three degrees of seats above the stage, except in the centre where an ornamental window 4 feet (1.2 metres) wide dominates the tiring-house façade. At stage level in the façade is a central arched door of the same width as the window above it, 8 feet high (2.4 metres) at the apogee of the arch. On each side of it is a rectangular door 2 feet 6 inches (0.7 metres) wide and 6 feet (1.8 metres) high. There is no sign of a trap door.

The evidence from plays staged at the Cockpit does not contradict this layout. They suggest that its tiring-house had at least two doors, a gallery or 'Balcone', capable of holding a maximum of three players, and that a curtained booth was available for some plays.[74] None·of this of course is out of step with the evidence for all the other venues.

Jones's plan is a handsome one, which the customary painting, marbling and gilding would have made splendid. It is a practical design, too, far less ruled by the classical requirements of the Vitruvian theatre

30 The stage of a hall playhouse, a vignette from the title-page of Nathanael Richards's *Messallina* (1640). Like the *Roxana* vignette p. 5), it shows stage rails and hangings across the tiring-house façade. It has no gallery for spectators, unlike Inigo Jones's design (p. 161), and the curtained window in the centre would have been a musicians' gallery. The hangings are decorated with allegorical figures, including Cupid on the right-hand side. A stage trap is clearly marked. The play was first performed at the Salisbury Court at some time between 1634 and 1636. The vignette is, however, unlikely to be a very accurate depiction of the playhouse stage. See John H. Astington. The Origins of the *Roxana* and *Messallina* Illustrations', *ShS* 43 (1991), pp. 149–69.

that he obeyed for the Cockpit-in-Court in 1629. Beeston ought to have been pleased with it.

One feature that we might have expected to see at the Cockpit, but which is missing from Jones's drawing, is a set of low rails surrounding the stage. These are shown in all three illustrations of indoor stages (see *Roxana*, p. 5 and *Messallina*, p. 163). There are none in the Swan drawing, and it would be tempting to see them as a feature only of the indoor playhouses – a consequence of a more crowded auditorium, and a lower stage height, and there also perhaps for the safety of the peacocks on their stools – if Jones's drawing had included them. Evidently, as with traps and other devices, some playhouses had them and some did not.

One more playhouse was successfully completed and used before the closure in 1642: the Salisbury Court, built by Richard Gunnell and William Blagrave in Whitefriars in 1629. Based on a barn with walls largely of brick, it was most likely rectangular like the Blackfriars, at least on the outside. The conversion probably cost £600.[75] A specification that has survived, for the construction of a dancing-school room 40 feet (12.2 metres) square over the stage, suggests that the width of the hall was 40 feet, a little less than the Blackfriars. It probably also means that the stage was built on one of the narrow sides of the rectangle.

6. COURT THEATRES

We should not pass from considering the playhouses without a look at the third major venue for the plays, the halls at Court. One company or another performed at Court in the festivities almost every Christmas throughout the period. Used in the murk of winter, indoors, with stages and 'degrees' or tiers of seating set up for the occasion, the Court venues resembled hall playhouses rather than the amphitheatres. Under Elizabeth most performances were held in the old Banqueting House in Whitehall, a substantial building in the shape of a 'long square', measuring 332 feet (101.2 metres) in circumference, 40 feet (12.2 metres) high, and fitted with 292 glass windows. In 1607 under James it was pulled down and rebuilt on a rather larger scale, 120 feet by 53 feet (36.6 metres by 16.2 metres). Pillars supported galleries along the east, north and west sides, under which scaffolding for the 'degrees' or tiers was installed by the Revels Office when a play was to be put on. The seating was partitioned into boxes, and the stage was set at one end. It was at first used only for masques, matters of spectacle rather than story, which were no doubt felt to be more suitable for a lavishly equipped new building. It opened with Jonson's *Masque of Beauty* in 1608. Plays were put on there from 1610, though usually they were assigned to the Hall or Great Chamber, or the Cockpit, an enclosed wooden amphitheatre built under Henry VIII for cockfighting, which James's son Prince Henry paid to have altered for playing in 1611. The Revels men were paid in January 1618 for six days' work preparing 'the Banquetting-house the Cockpitt and the Hall . . . for three severall plaies'.[76] Masques and plays of course were by no means the only form of entertainment for royalty. Baiting, which normally took place in the adjacent tiltyard, and cockfighting (in the royal Cockpit even after its conversion for playing) were still regularly on the festive programme. Occasionally baitings were held in the Banqueting House itself (certainly in 1611–12, 1612–13 and 1628–9).[77] Players summoned to perform before royalty in the seventeenth century faced the same kind of competition from animals as they faced through the sixteenth century in the common amphitheatres.

There is little evidence for the design of any of these buildings, let alone the temporary structures put up inside them by the Revels Office for the festivities.[78] Only one out of all the buildings used to stage plays before royalty is well documented.

Just after the 1618–19 Christmas season, on 12 January 1619, the Banqueting House burned to the ground. It was replaced by a building that has rightly been called the most substantial architectural project of the whole early Stuart period. This was Inigo Jones's Banqueting House in Whitehall, a building so valued by Wren that when the rest of Whitehall went up in flames in 1698 he directed the fire-fighters to save Jones's building at all costs, even at the cost of his own designs. Its survival into this century is rather like George Washington's axe, but it is still an impressive monument to its time. It was finished in 1622 at a cost of £9,850. The basic shape is a double cube measuring 110 feet by 55 feet (33.6 metres by 16.8 metres), and 55 feet in height. Magnificently decorated, it attracted masques more than plays, beginning with Jonson's *Masque of Augurs* on Twelfth Night, 1622. The stage was set at the north or lower end, in front of the entrance screen, across the whole width of the hall, a matter of 40 feet (12.2 metres) once allowance is made for the flanking galleries. The depth of the stage varied for different occasions between 27 feet and 40 feet (9.2 metres and 12.2 metres), and it was usually set up at about 6 feet (1.8 metres) high.[79]

Some of the Court stages of the last years were complex affairs. One, designed by Jones for the Queen's pastoral *Florimène* in 1635, which was staged in Whitehall's Great Hall, and for which the groundplan has survived, had a rear stage closed off by shutters with, in front of it, a stage proper, flanked on each side by wings in perspective, and finally a shallow forestage framed by a proscenium arch, with steps at each side for the final descent of the masquers on to the floor for dancing. It must be remembered that this was a royal spectacle, put on by the

31.　The interior of Inigo Jones's Banqueting House, Whitehall, showing the Rubens ceiling installed in the 1630s, after which it was banned from use for plays because of the candle smoke. This setting is for a twentieth-century entertainment.

Queen herself and her French ladies-in-waiting, not a professional theatrical performance.

For the presentation of masques in the Banqueting House an empty space was left in front of the stage for the dancing that concluded each masque. This space ended at the King's 'State', his dais and throne, to which all the sight-lines of the perspective scenery were drawn. For all this the Revels Office was responsible. Perspective staging was too costly a business for the professional players.

In 1635 the Rubens ceiling-paintings arrived at the Banqueting House, and the King put a ban on performing there, for fear of damage to the paintings by candle-smoke. A new masquing-house was built in its place, of wood. As Davenant, whose *Britannia Triumphans* was the first masque to open the new house in January 1638, recorded,

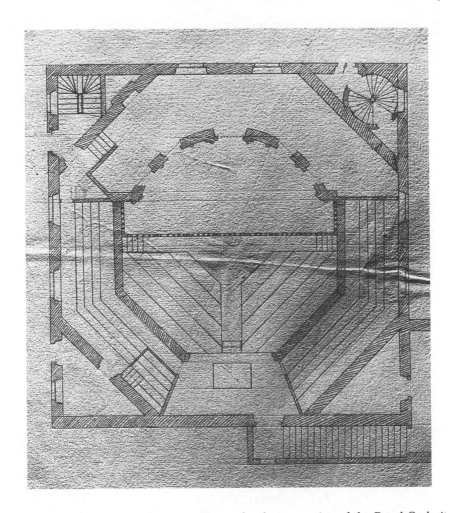

32. John Webb's copy of Jones's designs for the conversion of the Royal Cockpit into a permanent playhouse, the Cockpit-in-Court. The drawings are in Worcester College, Oxford. The plan exploits the octagonal plan of the original gamehouse. See John Orrell, *The Theatres of Inigo Jones and John Webb*, Chapter 5.

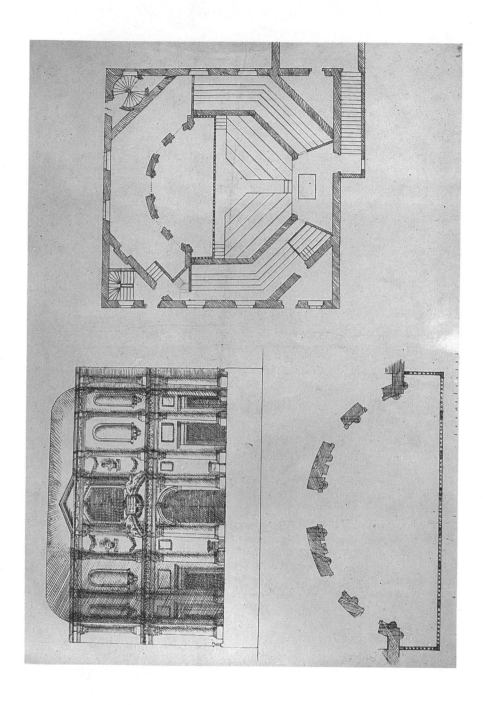

There being now past three yeers of Intermission, that the King and Queenes Majesties have not made Masques with shewes and Intermedii, by reason the roome where formerly they were presented, having the seeling since richly adorn'd with peeces of painting of great value, figuring the acts of King *James* of happy memory, and other inrichments: lest this might suffer by the smoake of many lights, his Majestie commanded the Surveyor of his workes, that a new temporary roome of Timber, both for strength and capacitie of spectators, should bee suddenly built for that use; which being performed in two moneths, the Scenes for this Masque were prepared.[80]

It cost £2,500, the walls being of fir weather-board cladding, and it was set on the Whitehall 'tarras' next to the Banqueting House, which it resembled in size.[81]

Plays had already been found a venue of their own at the Cockpit-in-Court. This was another of Inigo Jones's buildings, replacing Henry VIII's old gamehouse, and set on the same foundation, octagonal internally like the old building but square externally. It was built during 1629–30. For this building not only have detailed accounts of the interior decoration survived, but drawings of the groundplan probably made in 1660 by Jones's assistant John Webb.[82] They show a building about 57 feet (17.7 metres) square, with an octagonal auditorium, each side about 28 feet (8.5 metres) across the gallery rear. One side of the octagon is the entrance, and four sides, two to the left and two to the right of the entrance, make up the galleries. The stage occupies the space of the sixth, seventh and eighth sides, extending almost to the middle of the building. It is shaped like a shallow apron, about 35 feet by 5 feet (10.7 metres by 1.5 metres), with the tiring-house front as a concave bay behind it, giving a maximum stage depth at the centre of the tiring-house front of about 16 feet (4.9 metres). The tiring-house is lavishly pilastered, and pierced by a large central doorway and four smaller doorways arranged symmetrically. Above the central opening is an equally wide 'window' or balcony. The small, shallow stage would prohibit anything at all elaborate in the way of spectacle. It is clearly designed purely for playing.

Not that the theatre was bare. It was lit by iron candelabra, two large and ten small ones around the stage, and three others in the auditorium. The stage was covered in green cloth, the rest in matting. The whole stage area was painted, and its pilasters were gilded. The cover over the stage was made of calico painted blue with silver stars, and fitted on a roller to allow it to be drawn back when the folding throne had to be lowered to the stage. It was royally finished. As the Office of the Works accounts show,

for pryminge stoppinge and payntinge stone Cullor in oyle divers Cornishes pendaunt[es] and mouldings in the viii^t Cant[es] of the Cockepitt wth the postes both belowe and in the gallery above in the insyde all Cont: in measure ccclvi ya^{ds} did at xvi^d the yarde £xxiii xv^s iiii^d, for new Couleringe over wth fayre blewe the viii^t upper squares on the wall three of them beinge wholy shaddowed and the rest mended xl^s, for pryminge and payntinge like glasse xx^{ty} panes wch had bin Lightes xxx^s and for Clenzinge and washinge the gold of the pendaunt[es] and Cornishes and mendinge the same in divers places wth gold Cullor in oyle and mendinge the blew of the same in sondry places 1^s . . .

Carvers for moulding and clensinge of twoe great Statuaes of Plaster of Parris for the Cockpitt mouldinge and castinge three Ballastleavo^{rs} and cuttinge and flutinge the Bodies of twoe Corinthian Columnes ciiii^s . . .

Candlestickes of Iron beautified wth branches Leaves and garnished wth other ornament[es] to beare Lights in the Cockpitt x^{en} at xxx^s the peece £xv . . .

John Walker Property maker viz:^{t} for hanging the Throne and Chaire in the Cockpit wth cloth bound about wth whalebone packthred and wyer for the better foulding of the same to come downe from the Cloud[es] to the Stage cutting fitting and soweing of Callicoe to cover all the roome over head wth in the Cockpitt cutting a great number of Starres of Assidue and setting them one the Blew Callicoe to garnish the cloath there setting one a great number of Coppring[es] to drawe the cloth to and fro . . . for divers times Cullouring in Gould cullo^r the Braunches of xv^e Candlesticks in the Cockpitt whereof tenn smaller and twoe greater then thother about and before the Stage and for Hatching and Guilding them wth fine gould cullouring the great Braunches in the front of the stage and Hatching and Guilding all the ptes to be seene forwards allowed by agrem^t £x in all.[83]

At least some of the playhouses went out in a blaze of glory.

5. The Staging

1. MOBILE STAGING

WE HAVE ALREADY LOOKED at the quality of the players and the structure of the stages. The next matter for consideration is the product of the two put together, the staging. If there were a suitable plural to use for the singular word 'staging', I would use it, because syncretism is misleading in this section more than any other. The classification into the public and private, or amphitheatre and hall, which serves as at least a basic division for the playhouse structures, is not very accurate for categorising the staging, and in some respects it may be actively misleading. At first sight there is some justification for following the division. It is easy to see the staging as chiefly done on a bare stage with portable properties in the public playhouses on the one hand, and according to more modern practices with pictorial scenery and set-pieces in the indoor venues on the other, as in the Restoration theatres, which resemble them much more than they do the public amphitheatres. The boy companies that first occupied the private playhouses had stability of tenure as well as a roof over their heads, some of them had access to the resources of the Revels Office, and their early repertory, especially under John Lyly, shows the kind of sophistication that could well have found the Italian influence of Vitruvian perspective scene-presentation agreeable. Perspective staging was certainly entirely predominant on the Restoration stages. The adult companies by contrast might be seen reflecting their different origins and their susceptibility to the travelling sickness in their preference for representing bedchambers simply by the presence of a bed, and battlefields by the flourishing of swords. Such a division would be quite misleading. The evidence for the staging of plays at the hall playhouses shows if anything that even the plays staged with the most elaborate of Inigo Jones's Vitruvian scenery at Court in Caroline times were put on without it when they returned to the hall playhouses.[1] T. J. King's examination of the Cockpit repertory draws the conclusion that 'in usual practice the playwrights for the [Cockpit] were following the conventions of the earlier Elizabethan "open stage" rather than anticipating the modes of presentation usually associated with the Restoration period'.[2]

Differences in the staging at the different playhouses were dictated by a variety of factors. Each company and each playhouse had a distinct reputation, reflecting the preferences of the audiences who went to them. On the whole the companies and their different kinds of play were a much stronger factor than the different venues. Through the early years the amphitheatres and the shifting adult companies developed the fashion for noisy plays and extravagant verse. In the last thirty years the Blackfriars became the predominant fashionable resort. Its repertoire of Shakespeare and Beaumont and Fletcher plays, supplemented in the 1630s by the courtier poets Davenant and Carew, made it the venue for the rich and fashionable. Its small enclosed shape and half-sized stage also helped to make it more a place of witplay than swordplay, which prevailed at the Globe and the other amphitheatres. The northern amphitheatres, the Fortune and the Red Bull, maintained a repertoire of the older plays that first established the Rose's reputation in the 1590s, including the battle plays of that militant decade. But in the 1620s and 1630s Beeston regularly took the Red Bull plays and players from the amphitheatre playhouse to his Cockpit hall, and their traditions of staging must have gone with them. The King's Men's regular transfer of their Globe plays to the Blackfriars and back again also indicates the durability of staging traditions at the different venues. The Blackfriars consort added music to the King's Men's resources from 1609 onwards, but there are few other signs of substantial changes in staging.

The contrast between the attractions of witplay and swordplay is part of the larger story of the conflict between stage verse and stage spectacle, and the priority that the poets fought the players for, of hearing or beholding. The poets wanted audiences, hearers, to use their ears for the words, while the players went for spectators and spectacle, the pleasures of the eye.[3] Spectacle was a notable excitement for playgoers from the early days. Jonson, to whom the phrase 'judicious spectator' was a contradiction in terms, fought unavailingly for the priority of his words, even though in the masques that he wrote for the Court he made full use of potent visual symbols. When he first wrote for the amphitheatres, near the turn of the century, new tastes in staging were beginning to assert themselves. The revived boy companies were offering more words than spectacle, and there were Hamlets in the audiences to offset Polonius, who preferred 'a jig or a tale of bawdry, or he sleeps'. The clown's jig provided the standard end-piece for an adult company play in the early years. It offers a clear if possibly oversimplified means of distinguishing the trends of the different companies in the years before and after 1600.[4]

The dance that we now think of as the jig is related to the stage jig of Elizabethan times, but the stage versions usually involved song as much as dance, and relate most closely of all to the popular ballads. In their fullest form they were offered as end-pieces after the plays were finished, an item of entertainment quite separate from the play. Short songs or dances might be used as interludes in the course of a play, as in Peele's *James IV*, but the full-scale jigs led an independent existence. The most popular were bawdy knockabout song-and-dance farces, though extempore rhyming on given themes and various forms of dance were equally common, so far as we can judge. John Harington in *Metamorphosis of Ajax* (1596) mentions '*Machachinas*', or sword dances.

Jigs not infrequently resembled the popular ballads in their function as commentaries on topical matters, political, religious or personal. Will Kemp has a hostile word at the end of his *Nine Days' Wonder* for the 'Jig-monger' who manufactured ballads about his morris-dance to Norwich in 1599, and Tarlton involved himself in the Marprelate controversy ten years before that, most probably in his jigs and extemporising. The author of the tract *Mar-Martine* claimed that the violence of abuse that was a feature of the controversy began with the clown:

> These tinkers termes, and barbers jestes first *Tarleton* on the stage,
> Then *Martin* in his bookes of lies, hath put in every page.[5]

Tarlton was the first of the famous jigging clowns. He had parts to perform in the plays his company presented, but he was renowned above all for his comedy as a country clown in jigs, and as an extemporising ballad-maker. One of the *Jests* describes how, when travelling with a company of players, 'Tarlton's use was, the play being done, everyone so pleased to throw up his theame.'[6] He seems to have worn a standard country garb for his end-piece, 'his sute of russet, his buttond cap', and to have entered beating a tabor or drum, which was slung around his neck.

After Tarlton's death in 1588 the famous clowns were Will Kemp and the Admiral's George Attewell. One jig performed by each of them found its way into print, and the two, the rhyming ballad known as 'Attewell's Jig' and the ballad of 'Singing Simkin', are the best examples we have of the kind.[7] The second is not specifically named as Kemp's, though if it is not it must have borne a very close resemblance to 'Kemps newe jygge betwixt, a souldiour and a Miser and Sym the clown'. 'Singing Simkin' is a rhyming farce for four players, a house-wife, the clown, who appears as the housewife's first lover, a soldier, her second lover, whose arrival causes the clown to hide in a chest, and the old husband, who is told when he enters that the soldier is hunting for a thief. The wife and husband persuade the soldier to leave, and let Simkin out of the chest. The husband leaves, Simkin makes up to the wife, the husband catches him at it, and wife and husband together beat the clown off the stage.

The jig reached the height of its fame with Tarlton and Kemp. In the seventeenth century the word became conspicuous chiefly as a term of contempt used by one type of playgoer against another. In the eyes of the satirists it epitomised all that was disgusting in popular entertainment. Jonson in the Epistle to *The Alchemist* and the induction to *Bartholomew Fair* disowned 'the concupiscence of jigs and dances'. Hamlet speaks dismissingly of Polonius's taste in light entertainment linking a jig with a 'tale of bawdry'. Massinger's dedication to *The Roman Actor* (1626) specifically rejects the censure of those who prefer 'jigs and ribaldry'. Mostly it was the obscenity that drew the attacks of the satirists. In 1612 the jigs at the Fortune even drew the official displeasure of the Middlesex magistrates, for the disturbances they caused and the kind of audience they attracted:

Complaynte have beene made at this last Generall Sessions that by reason of certayne lewde Jigges songes and daunces used and accustomed at the play-house called the Fortune in Goulding-lane divers cutt-purses and other lewde and ill disposed persons in great multitudes doe resorte thither at th' end of everye playe many tymes causinge tumultes and outrages wherebye His Majesties peace is often broke and much mischiefe like to ensue thereby.[8]

Some such picture is painted by Dekker in his *Strange Horse-Race* (1613), where he testifies,

I have often seene, after the finishing of some worthy Tragedy, or Catastrophe in the open Theaters, that the Sceane after the Epilogue hath beene more blacke (about a nasty bawdy Jigge) then the most horrid Sceane in the Play was.

The audience at such a time are in commotion, he says, 'the stinkards speaking all things, yet no man understanding any thing' (C4v).

It is probably significant of the divergence in taste and fashion that after 1600 (or to be precise, after Kemp left the Chamberlain's Men in 1599) the only playhouses that were named as presenting jigs were the three to the north of the city, the Fortune, Curtain and Red Bull.[9] These were the playhouses covered by the Middlesex County Order of 1612 suppressing jigs. William Turner's *Dish of Lenten Stuffe* (1613) seems to contrast the northern playhouses against the two Bankside playhouses so far as the performing of jigs went:

> That's the fat foole of the Curtin,
>   and the leane foole of the Bull:
> Since *Shanke* did leave to sing his rimes,
>   he is counted but a gull.
> The players of the Banke side,
>   the round Globe and the Swan,
> Will teach you idle trickes of love,
>   but the Bull will play the man.[10]

If we discount the contrived word-play of the last line, we can read this as meaning that Shank has left the Fortune and jig-making to join the Globe company (which he in fact did in 1613), a change for the worse so far as Turner is concerned. The contrast is between the romantic love offered by the Bankside playhouses and the bawdy jigs of the northern playhouses.

Jigs certainly did persist, in spite of the voice of official displeasure, through to the closure, though their history is obscure. Some jigs, including 'Singing Simkin', were printed with the prose farces and drolls that the playhouses continued furtively and fugitively to offer during the Commonwealth. Their persistence is a sign of how the fashion in plays that they accompanied survived in the northern suburbs after it had been supplanted on the Bankside.

2.   HALL AND AMPHITHEATRE STAGING

The differences in fashion that went with the different repertories are complicated by a number of further variations that did grow out of the differences between the public and private playhouses. The fact that the private playhouses were roofed, for instance, inevitably created variations in what was done at each kind of playhouse. The consort of musicians with their room in the gallery of the private houses has been mentioned already. There was not nearly as much song and music at the amphitheatres as in the halls, even when the latter were occupied by the boys who were supposed to be choristers.[11] The difference lay in the concert overtures at the indoor playhouse, and the use in the open air of instruments the volume of which might have been painful indoors. When the Grocer in *The Knight of the Burning Pestle* demands to hear music, his familiarity with the open-air playhouses leads him to ask for shawms, a hautboy sometimes used as a kind of bagpipe. The hall playhouse boy diplomatically tells him the company only has recorders. War trumpets and military drums, designed to be heard in the uproar of a battlefield, were also instruments more fit for the public amphitheatres than a 60-foot (18-metre) hall.

Only one boy company play, Marston's *Sophonisba*, has battles in it, with trumpet-calls. The stage directions specify not the brass instruments used to convey orders to cavalry on the battlefield and to summon latecomers to the amphitheatres but cornets, a woodwind which gave a similar but quieter sound compared with a trumpet. Only one boy play calls for a brass hunting horn, and that is Jonson's *Epicene, or The Silent Woman*, where it is used to torment the hypersensitive gull Morose.

Other noisy devices must also have needed to be scaled down. The firing of cannon and the use of fireworks were neither of them pleasant devices indoors. The cannon that fired at the Globe for the death of Hamlet and burned it for *Henry VIII* obviously had to be reproduced for similar performances at the Blackfriars. They were, however, reduced in scale. In *Love's Pilgrimage*, played at the Blackfriars in 1635, an order is given to shoot off a cannon (IV.i); the Folio text of the play accordingly has a book-holder's direction *'Joh. Bacon ready to shoot off a Pistol'*.[12] Besides the volume of noise, there was the smell, an objection that also applied in an enclosed space to the fireworks essential to *Faustus* and other plays with devils in them. Marston's *The Fawn* (1605) has the following passage (I.ii):

PAGE. There be squibs sir, which squibs running upon lines like some of our gawdie Gallants sir, keepe a smother sir, with flishing and flashing, and in the end sir, they do sir, –
NYMPHADORO. What sir?
PAGE. Stink sir.

One important change in staging, which does seem to have been universal, may also have been brought about by the influence of the indoor playhouses. This was the practice of breaking off the performance between each act, which spread from the private to the public repertories after about 1607. In the hall playhouses pauses were necessary, if only to keep the candles that lit the stage trimmed.

Jonson's Induction to *A Staple of News* has a stage direction *'The Tiremen enter to mend the lights'*, and the Book-holder instructs them *'Mend your lights, Gentlemen'* in preparation for the Prologue's entry to start the play. All the early public-theatre plays seem to have run continuously; the incidental entertainment being confined to before and after the performance. Beer and bread were sold during the performance, so unless the play itself actually called for a pause, there was little need. Some plays do contain a few hints of pauses, but they are slight. The lovers in *A Midsummer Night's Dream 'sleep all the Act'*, that is, between the end of Act III and the beginning of IV; but that direction is to be found in the Folio text printed in 1623, and might have found its way there at any time up to 1622. *James IV* (1590) has songs or dances, including a hornpipe and a jig, after Acts I, II and IV, to mark pauses in the story, and the plot of the Admiral's *Dead Man's Fortune*, which dates from about 1590, has a line of crosses drawn at each act break, with a note *'musique'* alongside. The manuscript also has lines drawn at each scene-end, however, which were certainly not marked by pauses in the staging even in the private playhouses. They may be simply scribal markings, or relics of the authorial manuscript. I would be inclined to believe that some authors in the 1590s acknowledged act breaks by inserting song-interludes or by placing their mid-play choruses at them, but not that they necessarily expected the players to mark them with the kind of pause that appears in later staging.

The significance of act breaks, which were usually occupied with music and dancing,[13] is that they altered the practice of continuous staging traditional on the amphitheatre stages. Scene divisions in the earlier plays are identifiable only by the departure of one group of players as another group enters. Act divisions were probably treated similarly, except when the chorus, or in the early academic plays like *Gorboduc* a plot-foreshadowing dumb-show, came to herald the next act. Speech was almost non-stop. The only silences were for heavy breathing in the formal pauses during hand-to-hand fights (in *Orlando Furioso*, 'they fight a good while and then breath'), or in the voiceless uproar of battles. Real silences are truly noteworthy, as in Tamburlaine's exit after he has caught Agydas denigrating him to Zenocrate (1 *Tamburlaine*, III.ii):

Tamburlaine goes to her, & takes her away lovingly by the hand, looking wrathfully on Agidas, and sayes nothing.

There are only three such eloquent silences in Shakespeare.[14]

With the players accustomed to holding the attention of audiences many of whom were on their feet closest to the stage, the words must have been rattled off at speeds markedly higher than modern armchair audiences are now used to. The absence of formal intervals on the amphitheatre stages would have helped. In the hall theatres the act-breaks seem to have been designed to last the length of no more than thirty lines of verse.[15] Through the 1590s contemporary accounts claimed that performances of plays of average length, 2,500 lines, took no more than two hours. That was for plays that take three now, even with cuts. Plays grew longer in the seventeenth century, to an average nearer 2,900 lines, though the evidence about performance times does not vary. The prologue to Shirley's *The Duke's Mistress*, a play of roughly 3,000 lines, refers to its time in 1636 as 'but two howers'. Even *Bartholomew Fair*, an exceptionally long play for its time at over 4,000 lines, was said by its author to take 'the space of two houres and a half, and somewhat more.'[16] Possibly, however, Jonson was mocking the official line about the permitted length for the performance of plays. The Lord Chamberlain had laid down the official length in a letter to the Lord Mayor of London in October 1594, when he declared that his new company, Shakespeare's, had given an undertaking

that where heretofore they began not their Plaies til towardes Fower a clock, they will now begin at two and have done betwene fower and five.

Considering that the jigs took extra time at the end of the play, this undertaking allowed precious little time for the 3,700 lines of *Richard III*, still less the 4,000 or so of *Hamlet*. Possibly the two hours' traffic of the stage that Shakespeare proclaimed in *Romeo and Juliet* was a bit of a fiction too.

Continuous and high-speed staging went hand-in-hand with unlocalised settings. The 'scene' was changed simply by one person departing and another entering. *Catiline* offers as similes for rapid movement 'a veil put off, a visor changed, / Or the scene shifted'.[17] The word 'scene' provides some problems, because it could mean the tiring-house (Florio's dictionary defines it as 'a skaffold, a pavillion, or fore part of a theater where players make them readie, being trimmed with hangings, out of which they enter upon the stage'), or it could mean the fictional localities where the action of a play was supposed to happen. Later it also came to mean the canvas flats or 'scenery' that provided backgrounds for such localities. The use of the word in these three senses has misled some scholars into thinking that scenery was used in the hall theatres. Thomas Nabbes has been cited as using the word to mean scenery in the following passage in the prologue to *Hannibal and Scipio* (1637):

> The places sometimes chang'd too for the Scene
> Which is translated as the musick playes
> Betwixt the acts . . .

but the rest of the passage shows he meant fictional localities:

> . . . wherein [the author] likewise prayes
> You will conceive his battailes done.[18]

The same play specifies all the entries for its characters as 'by the right Scoene', 'by the middle Scoene', and 'by the left Scoene' (using the 'tiring-house' sense of the term), and 'in the Balcone'.

Almost all the action took place on the stage or platform, the only area known at the time as the 'stage' (which is why I have been trying to avoid using the terms 'upper stage' and 'inner stage'). Analyses of staging in the repertoires of the Globe on the one hand and the Cockpit on the other indicate that the stage was almost never empty of characters.[19] There was no separation of players from audience by a proscenium arch, of course,[20] and the crowd of 'understanders' jostling alongside the amphitheatre platforms would have had little patience with players who left them to their own devices for any period. References to audiences showing their impatience by such actions as hurling apples at the hangings in order to get the players to start their play are not unknown. The chief feature of the staging and its interaction with the audience was the intimate connection between them. The spectators were as visible as the players, and even more potently they completely surrounded the players on their platform. Indeed, at the hall playhouses some of the audience shared the stage space itself with the action. So the clown's tricks and Hamlet's soliloquies had both to be aimed at the visible presence around the stage.

With unlocalised staging and freely variable 'scenes' all that the poet had to do was slip in a reference early on in his scene to the locality to be imagined, if he wanted a specific one. Jonson in *Every Man Out of His Humour* went to the length of providing two Presenters who inform the audience of each change of locality. At the beginning of Act III, for instance, one says 'we must desire you to presuppose the stage, the middle isle in *Paules*; and that, [*pointing to the tiring-house?*] the west end of it'. Occasionally the stage doors might be called on to serve as specifically separate locations, as in the Globe's *Merry Devil of Edmonton* (1607), where a group of characters are tricked about the names of two inns by a switch of signboards – presumably one over each stage door. Title-boards were occasionally hung by the boys in the private play-houses. *Wily Beguiled* at Paul's and *The Knight of the Burning Pestle* at Blackfriars in 1607 both begin with some by-play about changing their play's title-boards, and *Cynthia's Revels* at Blackfriars in 1601 mentions them. Some sixteenth-century Court plays appear to have used both title- and locality boards. Locality boards were on the whole an early phenomenon, a cumbersome way of locating scenes.

3.   STAGE REALISM

The details of amphitheatre and hall staging can conveniently be divided into a number of categories: stage realism, stage business and effects, properties, costumes (known as apparel) and perspective scenery. By far the most awkward of these to assess is realism. Without the proscenium arch to separate players from audience, as it has generally done since the Restoration, the presentation of illusion as reality was inevitably more complicated. The players were closer for one thing, in the midst of the audience, and lacked the facilities for presenting the pictorial aspects of illusion because they were appearing in three dimensions, not the two that the proscenium-arch picture-frame estab-lishes. Awareness of the illusion as illusion was therefore much closer to the surface all the time. It is presumably because of this that so many of the plays begin with prologues and inductions openly acknowledging that the play which follows is a fiction.

Both poets and players were often reminded that their business was a cheat – either illusion or delusion. In numerous plays a masque or a play within the play (*The Spanish Tragedy*, *The Revenger's Tragedy*, *The Maid's Tragedy*) serves as an emblem of deceit. Playing is counterfeiting, a continual pretence. So the illusion is acknowledged to be illusion. From there it was a slight further twist to develop inductions in which the players come on stage to talk about their play and in so doing actually play themselves, performing what the playwright has written for them to speak in their own personality, as if reality and illusion were the same. *Cynthia's Revels*, the 1604 *Malcontent*, *Bartholomew Fair*, and other Jonson plays, all use such realistic fictions. Playwrights such as Beaumont in *The Knight of the Burning Pestle* bring players disguised as audience on stage to comment on the play they are seeing, confusing the illusion/reality borderline with a sophistication rarely matched in any drama at any time. *Twelfth Night* is crammed with jokes about the stage illusion. At III.iv.131–2, for instance, Fabian watches Malvolio making a gull of himself and says, 'If this were played upon a stage now, I could condemn it as an improbable fiction.' In *The Malcontent's* induction Will Sly comes on stage pretending to be a gallant looking for a stool, and accuses the stage attendant 'Ile hold my life thou took'st me for one of the plaiers.' Later he asks to see 'Harry Cundele, D: Burbidge and W: Sly', and begins to flourish his hat like Osric in *Hamlet*, presumably in imitation of his own playing of the part. The fictional reality was a running paradox, a matter of 'Tragedy / Played in jest, by counterfeiting actors', as Shakespeare put it in 3 *Henry VI*.

Such interplay between illusion and reality went easily with the conventions of continuous staging and unlocalised settings. Sidney's mockery of the playwrights and players who failed to remember that their reality was illusion stayed in the minds of at least some of the dramatists. In his *Defence of Poesy* (c. 1583) Sidney wrote

you shal have *Asia* of the one side, and *Affrick* of the other, and so many other under-kingdoms, that the Player, when he commeth in, must ever begin with telling where he is, or els the tale wil not be conceived. Now ye shal have three ladies walke to gather flowers, and then we must beleeve the stage to be a Garden. By and by, we heare newes of shipwracke in the same place, and then wee are to blame if we accept it not for a Rock. Upon the backe of that, comes out a hidious Monster, with fire and smoke, and then the miserable beholders are bounde to take it for a Cave. While in the meantime two Armies flye in, represented with foure swords and bucklers, and then what harde heart will not receive it for a pitched fielde?[21]

Shakespeare used a presenter as chorus in the last of his history plays in 1599, and acknowledged the inadequacy of his illusion by asking the audience to 'piece out our imperfections with your thoughts'. Jonson echoed Sidney in a prologue to *Every Man in his Humour*, published in the Folio version in 1616, when he claimed that:

> he himselfe must justly hate,
> To make a child, now swadled, to proceede
> Man, and then shoote up, in one beard, and weede,
> Past threescore yeeres: or, with three rustie swords,

And helpe of some few foot-and-a-halfe-foote words,
Fight over *Yorke*, and *Lancasters* long jarres:
And in the tyring-house bring wounds, to scarres.
He rather prayes, you will be pleas'd to see
One such, to day, as other playes should be.
Where neither *Chorus* wafts you ore the seas;
Nor creaking throne comes downe, the boyes to please;
Nor nimble squibbe is seene, to make afear'd
The Gentlewomen; nor roul'd bullet heard
To say, it thunders; nor tempestuous drumme
Rumbles, to tell you when the storme doth come.

Jonson is echoing Sidney in his contempt not for realism in itself, but for a too literal-minded use of mechanical devices, and for the simple-minded belief that illusion can successfully become delusion. It was a matter on which he tended to face both ways, especially while composing his masques.[22]

The painted heavens covering the stage in the amphitheatres provided an automatic visual signal for one stage locality, of course. The trap provided another, its position under the stage surface offering a hell for Marlowe's Barabbas and Faustus to sink into, for devils to spring from, and for the ghost of Hamlet's father to descend into before he speaks from his purgatorial grave under the earth of the stage floor. Painted skies on ceilings were a familiar sight. The Oxford antiquary Brian Twyne described the stage set up for James's visit at Christ Church in 1605 as having 'over all, delicate payntinge resembling ye Cloudes & Sky cullur &c'.[23] Tiring-house fronts were used when town walls were to be besieged, and the central doorway made the town gate, as in *Henry V*'s Harfleur scenes. It served as the Capulet house when Romeo climbed to its balcony. The stage hangings might similarly be used to give signals to the audience. Dekker has an induction in which an observer comments that 'the stage is hung with black, and I perceive / The auditors prepared for a tragedy'. Not much effort was given to catering for the literal-minded realism of localities that Sidney made fun of, but the structural iconography of the stage heaven and hell and the attendant architectural features were fully exploited.

Stage realism did have its simpler levels, of course. Bladders or sponges of vinegar concealed in the armpit and squeezed to produce the semblance of blood were not unknown, and many other realistic details testify to the esteem the players had for realism on this level. In the plot of the Admiral's *Battle of Alcazar* three characters are executed and disembowelled on stage. The appropriate book-holder's instruction is '3 violls of blood & a sheeps gather', that is, a bladder holding liver, heart and lungs. The annotator calls blandly for 'raw flesh' a little earlier in the same plot. It may even have been real blood; calves' or sheep's

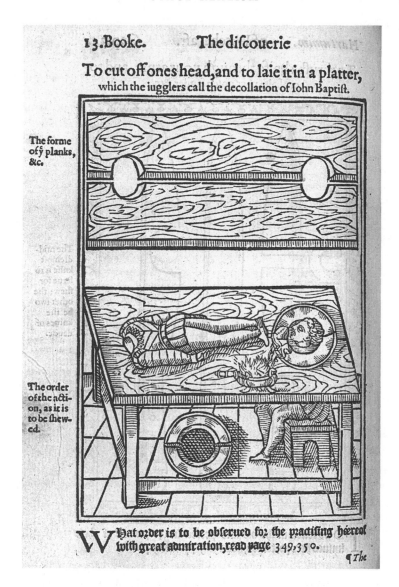

13. Booke. The diſcouerie

To cut off ones head, and to laie it in a platter,
which the iugglers call the decollation of Iohn Baptiſt.

The forme
of ẏ planks,
&c.

The order
of the acti-
on, as it is
to be ſhew-
ed.

What order is to be obſerued foꝛ the practiſing héereof
with great admiration, read page 349, 350.

¶ The

33. A device for displaying decapitated bodies. The original woodcut is in Reginald Scot's *Discoverie of Witchcraft* (1584). Described as a 'juggler's' trick for deceiving the ignorant, it may resemble the kind of device used to display decapitated bodies on stage.

blood does not usually congeal. In *The Spanish Tragedy*, though, a letter said to be written in blood is accompanied by a marginal note *'red ink'*. Some plays had execution scenes involving decapitation. A late anonymous play printed in 1649, *The Rebellion of Naples*, has a stage direction for such an execution, *'He thrusts out his head, and they cut off a false head made of a bladder fill'd with bloud. Exeunt with his body'*. The odds are that this was fanciful, since the play was written during the closure of the theatres, but it might explain how the decapitations in plays like *Faustus*, *The Insatiate Countess* and *Sir John Van Olden Barnavelt* were done.[24] In the 1616 text of *Faustus* the decapitation is preceded by a direction *'Enter Faustus with the false head'*. A list of other realistic devices in staging might include the appearance of the mariners *'wet'* after the shipwreck in *The Tempest*, a device used also in the horse-courser scene of *Faustus*. Smoke was provided to make mists and fog, as in the masque in Act 1 of *The Maid's Tragedy*, which starts with Night coming up through the trap *'in mists'*.

Realism could easily be supplied by means of noises off, and was. Marston in *The Insatiate Countess*, II.vi, ordered *'a trampling of Horses heard'*, and Fletcher in *The Chances*, III.iv, similarly asked for *'A noise within like horses'*. Massinger's *The Guardian* has *'a noyse within, as the fall of a Horse'* (IV.i), after which a character enters and shouts 'Hell take the stumbling Jade.' The firing of cannon and peals of bells were other means of producing noises off, especially in the public playhouses, and the private playhouses seem to have been able to produce bird-song when required. Dekker's *Blurt Master Constable*, a Paul's play of 1601, has the stage direction *'Musicke sodainly plaies and Birds sing'*, and Marston's *Dutch Courtesan* at the Blackfriars in 1603 has *'the Nittingalls sing'*. *The Pilgrim*, performed by the King's Men in 1621, has two stage directions, one simply *'Musicke and birds'*, the other *'Musick afar off. Pot birds.'* The last reference is probably not to capons but to the Elizabethan device of producing a warbling note by blowing through a pipe into a pot of water.[25]

Realism of this kind was by no means uniform, of course. It appears usually as a special effect designed to intensify the inherent comedy or tragedy of its occasion. 'When the bad bleedes,' as Vindice says in *The Revenger's Tragedy*, 'then is the Tragedie good.' We must measure such effects against totally non-realistic conventions of the kind suggested by Henslowe's note of a 'robe for to goo invisibell' (*Diary*, p. 325). In the anonymous *Two Noble Ladies*, a Red Bull play of 1619–23, two soldiers are drowned on stage, in the following passage:

1ST [SOLDIER]. what strange noise is this?
2ND [SOLDIER]. dispatch, the tide swells high. what feind is this?
1ST. what furie ceazes me?

2ND. Alas, I'm hurried headlong to the streame.
1ST. And so am I, wee both must drowne and die.

The accompanying stage directions show how the players managed to drown themselves. Opposite 'what strange noise is this?' is written *'Thunder. Enter 2 Tritons with silver trumpets'*, and after 'what feind is this?' *'This tritons ceaz the souldiers.'* They drown as *'The Tritons dragge them in sounding their trumpets.'*[26]

Realism is closely linked with spectacle, and with stage business and effects, which themselves were likely to vary according to the nature of each playing company's repertory. Here the distinction drawn earlier, between on the one hand the plays dating before about 1600 and the plays at the northern playhouses after that and on the other the private-theatre plays and Globe plays, once again crops up. Some general impression of the former can be found in the English Wagner Book of 1594, a fantasy on the life and death of Faustus strongly coloured by memories of the play in performance:

there might you see the ground-worke at the one end of the Stage whereout the personated divels should enter in their fiery ornaments, made like the broad wide mouth of an huge Dragon . . . the teeth of this Hels-mouth far out stretching.[27]

The hell-mouth that is 'discovered' in the 1616 text of *Faustus* has usually been identified with the 'i Hell mought' in Henslowe's inventory of the Rose's properties. The Fortune players offered *Faustus* up in the same way in 1620, when, as a contemporary witnessed,

a man may behold shagg-hayr'd Devills runne roaring over the Stage with Squibs in their mouthes, while Drummers make Thunder in the Tyring-house, and the twelve-penny Hirelings make artificiall Lightning in their Heavens.[28]

The public-theatre players had considerable resources, and resourcefulness, for this kind of staging. A foreign visitor wrote this account of what he saw at the first Beargarden in 1584:

There is a round building three storeys high, in which are kept about a hundred large English dogs, with separate wooden kennels for each of them. These dogs were made to fight singly with three bears, the second bear being larger than the first and the third larger than the second. After this a horse was brought in and chased by the dogs, and at last a bull, who defended himself bravely. The next was that a number of men and women came forward from a separate compartment, dancing, conversing and fighting with each other: also a man who threw some white bread among the crowd, that scrambled for it. Right over the middle of the place a rose was fixed, this rose being set on fire by a rocket: suddenly lots of apples and pears fell out of it down upon the people standing below. Whilst the people were scrambling for the apples, some rockets were made to fall down upon them out of the rose, which caused a great fright but amused the spectators. After this, rockets and other fireworks came flying out of all corners, and that was the end of the play.[29]

There is a suggestion of the traveller's tale about this, though the baiting and the jig that followed it are easily enough authenticated, and fireworks were freely used. The pyrotechnics in Heywood's *Ages* plays at the Red Bull in 1610–12 involved some extraordinary feats. In *The Silver Age*, for instance, 'Enter Pluto *with a club of fire, a burning crowne . . . and a guard of Divels, all with burning weapons*'; '*Jupiter appeares in his glory under a Raine-bow*'; '*Thunder, lightnings*, Jupiter *descends in his majesty, his Thunderbolt burning . . . As he toucheth the bed it fires, and all flyes up.*' One stage direction in *The Silver Age* concludes '*fire-workes all over the house*'. The hall playhouses, and on the whole the Globe, made less use of such spectacular resources.

The fact that the amphitheatres used daylight and the halls relied on candles seems to have made surprisingly little difference to the means of presenting night scenes. In plays written for both kinds of playhouse night scenes are signified in words and by the players or stage hands bringing on flaming torches. Since the hall performances were in daylight like the amphitheatres, their windows must have helped the candles in providing general illumination. Other atmosphere effects, thunder, lightning and mists, noises off and mood music of various kinds, all occur in plays put on at all the playhouses. Thunder came from the 'roul'd bullet' on a sheet of metal, or a 'tempestuous drum', as Jonson said, lightning from squibs, and mists from smoke. There are even some hints that the heavens were not beyond dropping a gentle rain upon the earth beneath in *The Brazen Age* and in Dekker's *If It Be Not Good, the Devil is in It*, both at the Red Bull. Atmospherics in a metaphorical sense appeared in the stage hangings, which might be black for a tragedy,[30] and in off-stage music. The Blackfriars, with its famous consort of musicians, made this readily available in plays like *The Duchess of Malfi*, where the Madmen sing '*to a dismall kind of Musique*'. In Marston's *Sophonisba* there is a stage direction '*Infernall Musicke plaies softly whilst Erictho enters and when she speakes ceaseth.*' Martin Peerson, who had a financial interest in the second Blackfriars boys, was a professional musician. He left the Blackfriars to become singing master at Paul's School. Phillip Rosseter, who started the abortive Porter's Hall playhouse in 1615, was another professional musician. Music in the amphitheatres was commonly introduced as song, with or without accompaniment, and the usual musical atmospherics were supplied in the form of a sennet or flourish of trumpets of the kind that heralded the commencement of a play. Drums provided martial music as well as thunder, and accompanied battle scenes in consort with the trumpets. The equipment of the Admiral's Men in 1598 included three trumpets, one drum, a treble and bass viol, a bandore, a sackbut, 'iii tymbrells' and 'i chyme of bells'.

4. STAGE PROPERTIES

Displays and discoveries were matters of stage business as spectacle, besides their function in the dramatic action. The early playhouses offered displays of special properties, like the brazen head in *Friar Bacon and Friar Bungay* and in *Alphonsus of Aragon*, the hell-mouth of *Faustus* or the cauldron for the finale of *The Jew of Malta*. The Globe displayed Volpone's gold, while the revelations of the Red Bull included a Trojan Horse. On the whole the hall playhouses went in for more functional displays. Shops, studies and cells in all the playhouses appeared furnished to show what they were, as in the Red Bull's *If It Be Not Good*, where a cell has '*A table . . . set out with a candle burning, a deaths head* [i.e. a skull] *a cloke and a cross'*. *The Devil's Law-case* at the same playhouse discovered a table with '*two Tapers, a Deaths head, a Booke'*. The study in the Globe's *Devil's Charter* is equipped for one discovery with '*books, coffers, [a] triple Crowne upon a cushion . . .'* and in another a player is '*beholding a Magicall glasse with other observations'*.

Properties were tangible assets to a play-acting company, and the list of properties that Henslowe compiled in March 1598 is a businessman's inventory of his stock. It is also the most precise indication we have of a company's normal resources in time of prosperity. The full list is as follows:

Item, i rocke, i cage, i tombe, i Hell mought.
Item, i tome of Guido, i tome of Dido, i bedsteade.
Item, viii lances, i payer of stayers for Fayeton.
Item, ii stepells, & i chyme of belles, & i beacon.
Item, i hecfor for the playe of Faeton, the limes dead [a heifer for the sacrifice?]
Item, i globe, & i golden scepter, iii clobes.
Item, ii marchepanes, & the sittie of Rome.
Item, i gowlden flece; ii rackets; i baye tree.
Item, i wooden hatchett; i lether hatchete.
Item, i wooden canepie; owld Mahemetes head.
Item, i lyone skin; i beares skyne; & Faetones lymes, & Faeton charete; & Argosse heade.
Item, Nepun forcke & garland.
Item, i crosers stafe; Kentes woden leage.
Item, Jerosses head & raynbowe; i littel alter.
Item, viii viserdes; Tamberlyne brydell; i wooden matook.
Item, Cupedes bowe, & quiver; the clothe of the Sone & Mone.
Item, i bores heade & Serberosse iii heads.
Item, i Cadeseus; ii mose banckes, & i snake.

Item, ii fanes of feathers; Belendon stable; i tree of gowlden apelles; Tantelouse tre; ix eyorn targates.

Item, i copper targate, & xvii foyles.

Item, iii wooden targates; i greve armer.

Item, i syne for Mother Readcap; i buckler.

Item, Mercures wings; Tasso picter; i helmet with a dragon, i shelde, with iii lyones; i elme bowle.

Item, i chayne of dragons; i gylte speare.

Item, ii coffenes; i bulles head; and i vylter.

Item, iii tymbrells; i dragon in fostes.

Item, i lyone; ii lyone heades; i great horse with his leages; i sack-bute.

Item, i whell and frame in the Sege of London.

Item, i paire of rowghte gloves.

Item, i poopes miter.

Item, iii Imperial crownes; i playne crowne.

Item, i gostes crown; i crowne with a sone.

Item, i frame for the heading in Black Jone.

Item, i black dogge.

Item, i cauderm for the Jewe.

The lists of Revels Office properties for Court performances of about the same time as this inventory are broadly similar.

A few of these properties were evidently designed for display but the majority are portable, equipment rather than set-pieces.[31] The portable nature of most properties means that somebody or some bodies had to be employed to bring on those properties that were not actually worn or carried on and off the stage by players. *King Lear*'s direction at II.ii, '*Stocks brought out*', means that a pair of anonymous hirelings carried the required object on and set it down at a suitably conspicuous place. There is an elaborate stage direction in the Blackfriars play *Bussy D'Ambois*, V.i,

Montsurry bare, unbrac't, pulling Tamyra in, . . . one bearing light, a standish, and paper, which sets a Table.

This requires an entry by a hatless Montsurry (we have to remember that hats were worn indoors and therefore on stage), with his doublet unlaced, dragging the boy playing Tamyra in, followed by an invisible boy (a which not a who), with a candle, an inkstand and a sheet of paper, which he sets out on a table already in position on stage.

So far as the evidence of stage directions enables us to judge, even the most substantial properties were likely to be carried onto the stage more often than they were discovered. The terminology is ambiguous, though, and a stage direction like '*Enter X upon a bed*' may mean either that the bed was pushed out onto the stage or that it was discovered, and the term '*set out*' seems sometimes to mean 'carried on to the stage', and sometimes 'discovered'.[32]

It seems logical to assume that a four-poster bed 'put out' for a bedroom scene would be put back again afterwards. But would the same thing have happened to trees, mossy banks and similar less obtrusive objects? Some scholars think they could have been on stage throughout the play.[33] I should think the stage-keepers were kept busier than that. The three trees listed in Henslowe's inventory are all designed for specific purposes: one of golden apples, one for Tantalus and one bay-tree. There is no hint that he bothered at all about undifferentiated trees for forest scenes, and he might not even have supplied rose bushes for the rose garden scenes in Shakespeare's history plays. A special tree like the one for Tantalus would hardly have been left on stage throughout the play. In *A Warning for Fair Women*, performed by Shakespeare's company, there is a dumb-show in which the trap-door is used to spectacular effect: '*suddenly riseth up a great tree*'. It is subsequently felled and, I would expect, dragged off. There is little justification for the view that all such devices needed for a play were left on stage throughout the performance.[34] If tables, chairs, benches, beds and thrones could be shifted, so could every other object.

One very spectacular form of display utilising only portable properties was of course the procession. Like a mannequin parade it showed off costumes and accessories to advantage, and as in mannequin parades its members 'passed over the stage' in solemn march, probably out on to the stage by one door and into the tiring-house again by the other. It has been conjectured that 'passing over the stage' meant exactly that – climbing onto the stage from the yard on one side and descending to the yard again on the other.[35] I find this doubtful, if only because the stage doors leading straight from the tiring-house were already in existence, and because there is no evidence that steps ever existed from the yard up to the stage. Certainly at the Blackfriars, with its rail surmounting the low stage rim, there was no easy way up onto the stage for the Citizen's wife in *The Knight of the Burning Pestle*. An archetype for stage processions can be found in the several stately pomps of *Tamburlaine*, like the one at the death of Zenocrate:

Tamburlaine, with Usumcasane, and his three sons, foure bearing the hearse of Zenocrate; and the drums sounding a dolefull martch; the Towne burning.

All the companies liked processions, though the earlier companies and those playing at the Fortune and Red Bull made more of the martial and pompous aspects, and the hall playhouses more of the sumptuous and elegant. Both kinds of venue not infrequently joined processions to dumb-shows, or at the hall playhouses to masques. Nathanael Richards, in his tragedy *Messallina*, written for the King's Revels at Salisbury Court in 1635, appended this hopeful direction:

Cornets sound a Flourish, Enter Senate who placed by Sulpilius, cornets cease, and the Antique maske consisting of eight Bachinalians, enter guirt with vine leaves, and shap'd in the middle with Tunne Vessells, each bearing a Cup in their hands, who during the first straine of Musick playd foure times over, enter two at a time, at the tune's end, make stand; draw wine and carouse, then dance all: the antimasque gone off, and solemne musicke playing; Messallina and Silius gloriously crown'd in an Arch-glittering Cloud aloft, court each other.

Descents and ascents of deities from the stage heavens were matters of spectacle, too. The earlier plays tended to allow their gods to walk on like any mortal; the first of Shakespeare's gods to fly in was Jupiter on his eagle in *Cymbeline*. Flights were more favoured by the boy companies than the adults; they had a weight advantage, of course. The ingenuities of Inigo Jones in the Court spectacles of later years, which allowed boys to fly in not only vertically but at a slant, may have encouraged imitation in the commercial venues.

Dumb-shows were affairs of pure spectacle, and employed relatively far more properties than the plays in which they were incorporated. At their simplest they were parades of spectacle, formal processions using all the most gorgeous apparel, with crowns, sceptres, torches and swords, in the company's possession. State occasions like the coronation in *The Devil's Charter* or the funeral at the beginning of Act II in *Antonio's Revenge* were characteristic of this kind. The stage direction for the latter gives a hint of what they were like:

The Cornets sound a cynet.
Enter two mourners with torches, two with streamers; Castilio & Forobosco, with torches: a Heralde bearing Andrugio's helme & sword: the coffin: Maria supported by Lucio and Alberto, Antonio by himselfe: Piero, and Strozzo talking: Galeatzo and Matzagente, Balurdo & Pandulfo: the coffin set downe: helme, sworde and streamers hung up, placed by the Herald: whil'st Antonio and Maria wet their handkerchers with their teares, kisse them, and lay them on the hearse, kneeling: all goe out but Piero. Cornets cease, and he speakes.

The earlier classical plays such as *Gorboduc* and *Jocasta* used dumb-shows at the end of each act to summarise the plot of the following act. Some later plays of the boy companies also filled some of their inter-acts with dumb-shows, as in *Histriomastix*, III, *Antonio and Mellida*, III, at Paul's and *The Malcontent*, II, at Blackfriars. By the turn of the century, though, dumb-shows that mimed a plot-story were seen by some of the more acid playwrights as laughably archaic, to judge by their contempt for 'pantomimick action'. Dumb-shows were deliberately used as old-fashioned devices in *Hamlet* and Middleton's *Your Five Gallants*. They became fashionable again for some years after *Pericles* in 1607, and regularly appeared in the King's Men's repertoire of plays, inset as tableaux or spectacles like the show of madmen in *The Duchess of Malfi*.

Heywood, in a prologue to a Red Bull play printed in 1615, *The Four Prentices of London*, still insisted on their value for abridging a story

in dumbe shewes, which were they writ at large,
Would aske a long and tedious circumstance.

and as late as 1634 a Cockpit play by the same author, *A Maidenhead Well Lost*, had a dumb-show as plot-thickened as this:

Musicke. A Dumbe Shew. Enter Millaine, to him Storza, and brings in Lauretta masked. The Duke takes her and puts her into Bed, and Exit. Enter both the Dukes and Julia, they make signes to her and Exit; Storza hides Julia in a corner, and stands before her. Enter againe with the Prince to bring him to bed: They cheere him on, and others snatch his points, and so Exit. The Dukes Imbrace and Exeunt.[36]

Stage business and spectacle of this kind should not be allowed to obscure the fact that the stages themselves were colourful but essentially bare, and that as a general rule the better the playwright the less spectacle there was likely to be in his plays. Of all Shakespeare's scenes written for the Globe, 80 per cent, it has been estimated, could have been performed on a completely bare stage platform.[37] The one play of Shakespeare's that makes great use of stage spectacle and business is *The Tempest*, a play in which Shakespeare seems almost to have been mocking his own art by the closeness with which he observed the neo-classical unities of time and place. The contrast with *The Tempest*'s immediate predecessor, *The Winter's Tale*, which swings in time through a whole generation and in place between Sicily and the sea-coast of Bohemia, is as complete as it well could be. The stage business in *The Tempest* operates as a metaphor of Prospero's and Shakespeare's arts, of course, and is closed to our questions for that reason.[38] But it does raise a suspicion about how deeply Shakespeare's tongue was embedded in his cheek in the last plays.

The relative frequency with which properties were discovered for display rather than brought on is hard to tell, because the stage directions are ambiguous. The Globe, Red Bull and Cockpit, the three playhouses whose plays have been most closely scrutinised for the evidence of their stage directions, all seem to have favoured either method without much consistency. In any case, the occupants of beds, the most substantial properties of all, usually emerged from them onto the stage fairly promptly. The Swan's doorways may not have provided a large enough discovery-space for such properties, since *The Chaste Maid*, III.ii opens with a bed being '*thrust out*'; but this is no evidence to draw general conclusions from. Tables and chairs, more easily portable than beds, were revealed in the discovery-space when they represented a study or a cell, but were equally often carried on. Benches and stools, the 'state' or throne, a 'bar' for judgement scenes, trees and arbours,

Abbildung der Session des Parlaments zu Londen vber den Sententz des Grafen von Stafford.

34.   Hollar's engraving of the scene in Westminster Hall at the trial of the Earl of Strafford, 1641, showing a canopied throne on its dais. This is the kind of canopied 'state' commonly 'put out' for court scenes, whether royal or judicial.

and a mossy or flowery bank could all be carried on. Hirelings always brought banquets on, sometimes already set out on a table. The 'quaint device' by which Ariel makes the banquet vanish in *The Tempest* was, I would think, a kind of reversible table-top with dishes fastened to one surface and the other bare – in which case the banquet would certainly have been brought out already fastened to the table.

Even a property as heavy as a regal throne with its pedestal or dais, the 'state', would have been carried or trundled on. The 'throne' that descends from the heavens in *Faustus* and *A Looking-Glass for London and England*, the 'creaking throne' scorned by Jonson, which Henslowe notes as being stored in the heavens, was a chair for flights and nothing else, quite distinct from the 'state'.[39] Hirelings would have brought out the throne from which Claudius conducts the business of Denmark in I.ii of *Hamlet*, and over which he makes his little joke about how Fortinbras wrongly assumes 'our state to be disjoint and out of frame' as a result of its previous occupant's sudden death. It was a solid piece of furniture. The dais on which the 'state' throne usually rested was as much as four steps high, to judge by the counting of Mariana in II.i of *The Dumb Knight*. She ascends it to be executed, saying

> this first step lower,
> Mounts to this next; this, thus and thus hath brought
> My bodies frame unto its highest throne.

This dais or scaffold was also carried on by stage hands, to judge by the stage direction in the same play, '*Enter Chyp, Shaveing and others with a Scaffold.*'[40]

Given storage space, the wealthier and longer-lived companies could accumulate a good many standard properties. Some of course had to be custom-built for particular plays in the repertory. William Percy's curious plays, which seem to have been written for Paul's in the years after 1599, contain lists of the properties needed for performing them. *Cuckqueans and Cuckolds Errant* needed two inn-signs specially painted, besides a title-board, a rope-ladder and a bench:

The Properties
Harwich, In Middle of the Stage Colchester with Image of Tarlton, Signe and Ghirlond under him also. The Raungers Lodge, Maldon, A Ladder of Roapes trussed up neare Harwich and Aloft the Title The CuckQueanes and Cuckolds Errants. A Long Fourme.

The Faery Pastorall was more demanding:

The Properties
Highest, aloft, and on the Top of the Musick Tree the Title The Faery Pastorall, Beneath him pind on Post of the Tree The Scene Elvida Forrest. Lowest of all over the Canopie ΝΑΠΑΙΤΒΟΔΔΑΙΟΝ or Faery Chappell. A kiln of Brick. A Fowen Cott. A Hollowe Oake with vice of wood to shutt to. A Lowe well with Roape and Pullye. A Fourme of Turves. A greene Bank being Pillowe to the Hed but. Lastly A Hole to creepe in and out.

Pretty well all of these properties, with the exception of the 'greene Bank' and possibly the enigmatic 'Fowen Cott' would have had to be constructed for the performance. They might well merely be the poet's wishful thinking, and may never have been staged. The modesty of Shakespeare's demands for his plays probably reflects his financial interests as well as his dramatic sophistication.

5. STAGE COSTUMES

Colour was a major source of stage symbolism. The decorums of social status were rigidly marked by dress and its colours in accordance with the Tudor sumptuary laws. Hamlet's 'nighted colour' and Malvolio's yellow garters stood out as conspicuously discordant elements in a tradition of dress that everyone knew in detail. Such colours were an advertisement, a flaunted message. Costume was an instrument of meaning as well as spectacle and colour. Henslowe's 'tyer man' at the Rose, Steven Magett, was as vital a member of the playhouse operation as the book-keeper.[41] Apparel and playbooks were the company's two vital resources. Henslowe invested rather more money in apparel for the players than in playbooks, and far more than in stage properties. When the Globe and the Fortune were burnt, and when Beeston forsook Queen Anne's Men for his own enterprises, it was the loss of playbooks and apparel that the players bewailed, not the properties. Alleyn's accounts list some quite startling totals for clothing by present-day priorities: £20 10s. 6d. for a 'black velvet cloak with sleeves embrodered all with silver and gold', more than a third of Shakespeare's price for a house in Stratford. No wonder Henslowe had a rule against players leaving the playhouse wearing his apparel.

It was the magnificence of playing apparel that made the players common symbols of the distance between appearances and reality in Elizabethan society. Greene in *A Quip for an Upstart Courtier* (1592) wrote of a player wearing a

murrey cloth gowne . . . faced down before with gray conny, and laide thick on the sleeves with lace, which he quaintly bare up to shew his white Taffata hose, and black silk stockings. A huge ruffe about his necke wrapt in his great head like a wicker cage, a little Hat with brims like the wings of a doublet, wherein he wore a Jewel of Glasse, as broad as a chancery seale.

The image of the player jetting it in borrowed apparel is given point by the custom that Thomas Platter noted in 1599:

it is the English usage for eminent lords or knights at their decease to bequeath and leave almost the best of their clothes to their serving men, which it is unseemly for the latter to wear, so that they offer them then for sale for a small sum to the actors.[42]

The colours of the costumes matched the spectacular painting of the playhouses. Henslowe's and Alleyn's papers list cloaks in scarlet with gold laces and buttons, and in purple satin adorned with silver; a doublet in copper lace (for Tamburlaine), carnation velvet, flame, ginger, red and green; and women's gowns of white satin and cloth of gold. There is one complete inventory of apparel in Alleyn's hand, undated but probably of the same time as Henslowe's list of properties made in March 1598 (*Diary*, pp. 291–4). It speaks for itself.

Clokes

1 A scarlett cloke wth ii brode gould Laces: w^t gould buttens of the sam downe the sids

2 A black velvett cloke
3 A scarlett cloke Layd downe wth silver Lace and silver buttens
4 A short velvett cap clok embroydered w^t gould and gould spangles
5 A watshod sattin clok w^t v gould laces
6 A purpell sattin welted w^t velvett and silver twist
7 A black tufted cloke
8 A damask cloke garded w^t velvett
9 A longe blak tafata cloke
10 A colored bugell for a boye
11 A scarlett w^t buttens of gould fact w^t blew velvett
12 A scarlett fact w^t blak velvett
13 A stamell cloke w^t gould lace
14 blak bugell cloke

Gownes

1 hary ye viii gowne
2 the blak velvett gowne w^t wight fure
3 A crimosin Robe strypt w^t gould fact w^t ermin
4 on of wrought cloth of gould
5 on of red silk w^t gould buttens
6 a cardinalls gowne
7 wemens gowns
8, 9 i blak velvett embroyde^d w^t gould
10 i cloth of gould candish his stuf
11 i blak velvett lact and drawne out w^t wight sarsnett
12 A black silk w^t red flush
13 A cloth of silver for pan
14 A yelow silk gowne
15 a red silk gowne
16 angels silk
17 ii blew calico gowns

Antik sutes

1 a cote of crimosen velvett cutt in payns and embrydered in gould
2 i cloth of gould cote w^t grene bases
3 i cloth of gould cote w^t oraing tawny bases
4 i cloth of silver cott w^t blewe silk & tinsell bases
5 i blew damask cote the more
6 a red velvett horsmans cote
7 A yelow tafata pd
8 cloth of gould horsmans cote
9 cloth of bodkin horsmans cote
10 orayng tany horsmans cot of cloth lact
11 daniels gowne
12 blew embroyderde bases
13 will somers cote
14 wight embroyd^r bases

15 gilt lether cot
16 ii hedtirs sett w^t stons

Jerkings and dublets

 1 A crymosin velvett pe^s w^t gould buttens & lace
 2 a crymasin sattin case lact w^t gould lace all over
 3 A velvett dublett cut dimond lact w^t gould lace and spang^s
 4 A dublett of blak velvett cut on sillver tinsell
 5 A ginger colored dublett
 6 i wight sattin cute on wight
 7 blak velvett w^t goul^d lace
 8 green velvett
 9 blak tafata cut on blak velvett lacte w^t bugell
10 blak velvett playne
11 ould wight sattin
12 red velvett for a boye
13 A carnation velvett lact w^t silver
14 A yelow spangled case
15 red velvett w^t blew sattin sleves & case
16 cloth of silver Jerkin
17 faustus Jerkin his clok

frenchose

 1 blew velvett embr^d w^t gould paynes blew sattin scalin
 2 silver paynes lact w^t carnation satins lact over w^t silver
 3 the guises
 4 Rich payns w^t long stokins
 5 gould payns w^t blak stript scalings of canish
 6 gould payns w^t velvett scalings
 7 gould payns w^t red strypt scaling
 8 blak bugell
 9 red payns for a boy w^t yelo scalins
10 pryams hoes
11 spangled hoes

venetians

 1 A purpell velvett cut in dimonds lact & spangels
 2 red velved lact w^t gould spanish
 3 A purpell vellvett emproydored w^t silver cut on tinsell
 4 green velvett lact w^t gould spanish

---

35. An Elizabethan gallant. A miniature by Nicholas Hilliard, painted in about 1590, of a young man. The original is in the Victoria and Albert Museum. It is inscribed *Dat poenas laudata fides* ('my praised faith causes my sufferings'), a quotation from Lucan's *De Bello Civili*. It has been rather too confidently identified as the Earl of Essex registering his love for the Queen. It shows a lover, and the lover's standard gesture, hand on heart. The symbolism of the crossed legs is rather less obvious.

5 blake velvett
6 cloth of silver
7 gren strypt sattin
8 cloth of gould for a boye

The age was not only colourful but also intensely fashion-conscious. The range of available fabrics was enormous, and the turnover of fashionable fabrics and cuts was enormous too, which probably helped the players a little in acquiring lordly cast-offs. It was an age of glorious variety, in which, as always in the world of fashion, new names had constantly to be chosen as new shades of colour were invented. Pepper, tobacco, sea-water and puke (a dark brown) were a few of the many Elizabethan inventions.[43]

Colour symbolism was inevitable and universal throughout the Renaissance, though the range of possible interpretations of the significances of colours was almost as wide as the range of colours. Red for blood, yellow for the sun, white for purity, black for gloom or evil and death were all traditional. Tamburlaine's famous degrees of mercy, signified by his white, red and black tents, and on stage by the changing colours of his robes, reflect a set of values for colours that can still be recognised. Other significances were more local. When Malvolio in *Twelfth Night* is gulled into appearing cross-gartered, like a lover, his yellow hose as well as his crossed garters indicate his new role. When he says he is 'not black in my mind, though yellow in my legs', he means that his yellow stockings show him to be a lover, but that he is not a melancholy (black-minded) one. The black of a Hamlet and a Bosola, and the yellow of a Malvolio, Parolles or Iachimo, were standard signals.

There were costumes to match vocations, of course: doctors' gowns of scarlet, lawyers' gowns in black, blue coats for serving-men, a 'friars gown of gray', a 'cardinalls gowne' in scarlet, shepherds' coats, fools' coats with cap and bauble, and of course soldiers' coats. These were worn with little concern for historical accuracy, if Henry Peacham's drawing of a scene from *Titus Andronicus* made in about 1595, is any indication. In the drawing the leading character is in a form of Roman dress reasonably like a toga, but the men flanking him are clearly dressed as Elizabethan soldiers. 'Turkish bonnets' get a mention in *Soliman and Perseda*, and Henslowe's lists include 'ii Danes sutes', 'i mores cote', four 'Turkes heds' and 'the suit of motley for the Scotchman', which sounds suspiciously like a plaid.

Some costumes gave information about locality or setting. Nightcaps and candles signified night scenes and bedrooms, riding boots signified travel. Hats were used to signal status, and for gestures of respect. The higher the hat the higher the social status. A workman or servant wore a flat cap or bonnet, a citizen a taller hat with a small feather, a gallant

36. A drawing, attributed to Henry Peacham, of a performance of *Titus Andronicus*,
c. 1595, in the collection of the Marquess of Bath. The drawing is accompanied by
thirty lines of text from the play.

or courtier a high hat and a long plume. All hats were doffed as a mark
of respect in the presence of a lord or ruler. Anyone addressing the
king knelt hat in hand while speaking. The story of King James in 1600,
when he was threatened by the assassins of the Gowry conspiracy, tells
that the assassin holding a dagger to James's heart had some trouble
with his own headgear:

having such crueltie in his lookes, and standing so irreverently covered with his
Hat on, which forme of rygorous behaviour, could prognosticat nothing to his
majestie, but present extremitie. But at his majesties perswasive language, he
appeared to be somewhat amazed, and discovering his head againe, swore and
protested that his majesties life should be safe.[44]

The games played in *Richard II* over Bullingbrook kneeling to York and
Northumberland to the king are another indication of how potent were
the decorums of costume and behaviour.

Mad women, such as Cassandra in *Troilus and Cressida* or Queen
Elizabeth in *Richard III*, wore long-haired wigs, a fairly realistic symbol
of their condition. Costumes for 'Negro Moors', as Peele called them,
were spectacular rather than realistic.[45] None the less, considerable
efforts were made on occasions to simulate dark skin and curly hair.
Face masks and elbow gloves of velvet, and black leather leggings were
topped with 'Corled hed Sculles of blacke Laune' in early Court
performances. Paint superseded masks in the seventeenth century, on
the initiative of Queen Anne herself, who appeared with eleven of her

ladies in blackface for the *Masque of Blackness* in 1605. Sir Dudley Carleton acidly reported that

instead of Vizzards [i.e. masks], their Faces and Arms up to the Elbows, were painted black, which was Disguise sufficient, for they were hard to be known; but it became them nothing so well as their red and white, and you cannot imagine a more ugly Sight, then a Troop of lean-cheek'd Moors.[46]

Exotic costumes existed for various gods: for Juno, Phaeton, Neptune and Iris in Henslowe's lists, together with an intriguing 'Eves bodice'. He also had a 'fairys gown of buckram', 'a pair of gyants hose', and 'coats for giants', and a ghost's suit and bodice. From his function as bear-ward he could no doubt have imitated *The Winter's Tale* by introducing a real bear on stage, but his players, perhaps understandably, seem to have preferred doing it themselves, and his lists accordingly show 'i bears head' and 'i bears skin', as well as a bull's head and a head of Cerberus, 'i lions skin' and 'ii lions heads'.

In the later years, under the lavish Stuarts, the players collected the cast-offs from Court shows of plays and masques, for which costumes were made specially. Suckling paid out several hundred pounds to stage his play *Aglaura* at Court over Christmas 1637, and afterwards passed the costumes on with the play to the King's Men, who put it on at Blackfriars. In the words of a contemporary:

Two of the King's Servants, Privy-Chamber Men both, have writ each of them a play, Sir *John Sutlin* and *Will. Barclay*, which have been acted in Court, and at the *Black Friars*, with much Applause. *Sutlin's* Play cost three or four hundred Pounds setting out, eight or ten Suits of new Cloaths he gave the Players; an unheard of Prodigality.[47]

Several other plays, similarly produced, benefited the professional players who took them back to their own playhouses.

6. COURT STAGING

It has been argued that in Caroline times the players also took with them from Court the elaborate perspective 'scenes' that Inigo Jones gave to such plays.[48] I think it has been fairly conclusively proved that they did not. Scenic apparatus was less costly, less portable and less readily re-usable than apparel. Furthermore the Court stages, which used perspectives regularly for masques and plays, always took several days to prepare. The commercial playhouses could not have afforded the loss of playing-time involved in setting up such non-traditional

---

37. A design by Inigo Jones for a Daughter of Niger in *The Masque of Blackness* (1605), in the collection of the Duke of Devonshire, the Chatsworth Settlement.

devices. Still less could they have spent time and money making their own scenery. There are occasional references to pieces of scenery being employed in the private playhouses from the earliest days, but they cannot ever have been a prominent feature of the staging, or they would have drawn more comment. *Periaktoi*, great prisms with a different scene painted on each of the three faces, set on a pivot to revolve when required, are mentioned in connection with the first Blackfriars,[49] and Jonson speaks of a 'piece of *perspective*' in the induction to *Cynthia's Revels*, but there are few other references except to Court staging. The bare stage backed with a curtain on which the Tudor moralities and farces were played forms the basis of the Elizabethan staging tradition, and seems to have remained firmly entrenched at all the Stuart playhouses up to the closure. The Court, largely through the person of Jones, the English Bernini, was converted to the Italian perspective staging early on, but tradition and commerce combined to keep it off the common stages.

The Court masques were intricate affairs combining music and dance with verse-speaking in visually gorgeous settings designed as banquets for all the senses. They were also much more of a participation sport than the purely spectator sport of the professionals. The plot or allegory and the words belonged in a form quite distinct from the drama. The professional players could never match what were in effect the most lavish family charades England has ever seen. As Bentley has said, scenery was conceived of as 'a special display exhibition'.[50] It seems to have been a feature reserved for special occasions, rather than for particular plays, as an extra adornment, a garnish to the entertainment.

Scenery was not a necessary feature of any play, to judge by the frequency with which the players seized on plays that had been staged at Court with scenery, in order to perform them without scenery on the commercial stages. They did participate in performances at Court using scenery, however, and it may be worth looking at a contemporary description of one such Court spectacle if only to see what the players were familiar with. The best description by far is of a show at Court in 1618, reported by Orazio Busino, chaplain to the Venetian Embassy, with all the frankness of a homesick expatriate writing in confidence about his outlandish hosts. I make no apology for quoting it at length.

In London, as the capital of a most flourishing kingdom, there are theatrical performances throughout the entire year in various parts of the city, and these are always frequented by many people devoted to pleasure, who, for the most part, dress grandly and colourfully, so that they appear, if possible, more than princes, or rather they appear actors. Similarly in the King's court after

Christmas day begins a series of sumptuous banquets, well performed plays, and very graceful masques of knights and ladies. The most distinguished of the masques is performed on the day after the feast of the three wise men, in accordance with an ancient custom of this royal palace, where in a large hall arranged like a theatre, with well-secured boxes all around, the stage is placed at one end, and facing it at the other end, his majesty's chair under a large canopy, and near him stools for the foreign ambassadors. On the 16th of this month of January [i.e. 6th January English style] his excellency was invited to see this performance and masque, prepared with extraordinary care and elegance, in which the chief performer was the only son and honoured heir of his majesty, the Prince of Wales, seventeen years of age, a lively youth, handsome and very graceful. At the fourth hour of the night we went to court privately, through the park, and entered the royal apartments. His excellency was entertained awhile by a principal courtier until everything was prepared, and we others of his retinue, all perfumed, escorted by the master of ceremonies, entered the usual box of the Venetian embassy, where, unfortunately, we were so crowded and uncomfortable that had it not been for our curiosity we would have given up or expired. Moreover we had the additional curse of a Spaniard who came into our box by courtesy of the master of ceremonies, asking for only two fingers of room, though we had no space to run around in, and by God, he placed himself more comfortably than all of us. In short, I have no patience with these crows; it was observed that they had settled in all the best locations. The ambassador was near the King; others with gold chains round their necks sat with the lords of the Council; others were in their own box attending the ambassadress; and this fellow comes into our place! While waiting for the King we took pleasure in admiring the decorations, in observing the beauty of the hall, with two orders of columns one on top of the other, their distance from the wall the full width of the passage, the upper gallery supported by Doric columns, and above these the Ionic, which hold up the roof of the hall. It is all of wood, including even the pillars, carved and gilded with great skill. From the roof hang garlands and angels in relief. There were two rows of lights, which were to be lit at the proper time.

Then there was such a crowd; for though they claim to admit only those favoured with invitations, nevertheless every box was full, especially with most noble and richly dressed ladies, 600 and more in number, according to the general opinion; their clothes of such various styles and colours as to be indescribable; the most delicate plumes on their hats, and in their hands as fans; and on their foreheads strings of jewels, and on their necks and bosoms and in their girdles, and on their garments in such quantity that they appeared so many queens; so that at first, when there was little light, as if it were the twilight of dusk or dawn, the splendour of the diamonds and other jewels was so brilliant that they appeared so many stars. During the two hours' wait, we had time to admire them again and again; because of my poor vision, I could not form an accurate judgement from afar, and I referred myself in everything to my colleagues, who reported to me that they discerned beautiful and delightful faces, and at every moment they would say, 'Oh look at this one, oh

38. (a) A painting of Lucy, Countess of Bedford, in masque costume, by Marcus
Gheerhardts, from the collection of the Marquess of Tavistock at Woburn Abbey.
(b) A drawing by Inigo Jones for a lady's masque costume, from the collection of
the Duke of Devonshire, the Chatsworth Settlement.
Except where a particular symbolism was intended, masquing costumes seem
generally to have been elaborate versions of currently fashionable dress, usually
with gauze draperies added to enhance the movements of the dance.

see that one; whose wife is that one in the third row, and whose daughter is that pretty one nearby?' However, they concluded that among much grain there were also husks and straw mixed in, that is to say, some withered ladies, and some votaries of San Carlo; but that the beauties were of superlative quality. Even though I am old and half blind, I can testify to the accuracy of this account. The dress worn by these ladies is very beautiful, for those who like it, and for some of them it serves to hide the defects of nature, because in the back it hangs almost from the neck to the ground, with long, tight sleeves, and no waist, and without folds; so that any deformity, however monstrous, remains hidden. The farthingale also plays its part. The plump and buxom show their bosoms very openly, and the lean go muffled up to the throat, all of them with men's shoes, or at least with very low slippers. Face masks are as important to them as bread at table, but for these public spectacles they put them aside willingly.

At about the 6th hour of the night his majesty appeared with his court, having passed through the apartments where the ambassadors were waiting, and he graciously brought them along with him, that is to say, the Spanish and Venetian ambassadors, it not being the turn of the French ambassador, because of his and the Spaniard's disputes over precedence. As he entered the hall fifteen or twenty cornets and trumpets began to play, antiphonally and very well. After his majesty had been seated under the canopy alone, the Queen not being present because of some indisposition, he had the ambassadors sit on two stools, and the great officers and magistrates sat on benches. The Lord Chamberlain then had the way cleared, and in the middle of the room there appeared a fine and spacious area all covered with green cloth. A large curtain – painted to represent a tent of gold with a broad fringe, the background of blue canvas flecked all over with golden stars – was made to fall in an instant. This concealed the stage at the beginning; on its being removed there appeared first of all Mount Atlas, and one saw only his huge head at the peak, right under the very roof of the hall; it rolled its eyes and moved itself with wonderful cunning. To make the main ballet and masque seem more light and elegant, they had some mummers in the first scene, for example a very fat Bacchus in a car drawn by four men in long robes, who sang *sotto voce* before his majesty. There was another fat man on foot, dressed in a short red costume, who spoke, and during the speech went reeling about like a drunkard, cup in hand, so that he seemed to be Bacchus' cupbearer; this first scene was very light and funny. Then followed twelve extravagant masquers, one with a barrel round his middle, the others in great wicker flasks very well made; and they danced for a while to the sound of the cornets and trumpets with various and most extravagant movements. Then came a huge man in the shape of Hercules with his club, who wrestled with Antaeus, etc.; and then appeared twelve masked boys, like so many frogs, who danced together with various grotesque gestures. All at once they fell to earth, and were quickly driven off by Hercules. The mountain then opened by the turning of two doors, and from behind the low hills of a distant landscape one saw day break, some gilded columns being placed along the sides to make the distance seem greater. Next Mercury appeared before the King and made a speech, and then came a musician with a guitar, dressed in a long robe, who played and sang some trills, implying that he was some deity; and then came a number of musicians dressed in the long red robes of high priests, with golden mitres, and in their midst was a goddess in a long white costume. They sang some short pieces that we did not understand; it is true that this performance was not much to our taste, accustomed as we are to the elegant and harmonious music of Italy.

Finally six [i.e. twelve] masked knights appeared, dressed as if in livery, six having full hose and breeches with slashes or folds of white silk trimmed with gold and silver, and the other six with their breeches below the knee, their half hose also crimson, and white shoes. Their doublets went well with this, cut in the manner of ancient Roman corslets; and on their heads they had long hair, crowns, and very large white feathers, and on their faces black masks. These all descended from the scene together in the figure of a pyramid, with the Prince alone always at the apex. When they reached the ground one suddenly heard the music of violins, to the number of more than twenty-five or thirty, all in a box. When the knights had made their bows to his majesty they began to dance in tempo and with a variety of steps, keeping the same figure for awhile, and then changing places with each other in divers ways, always ending their leaps together. When this was finished, each one took his lady, the Prince accompanying the principal lady among those who were standing ready to dance, and the others doing the same in succession, making bows first to his majesty and then to each other. They did all sorts of ballets and dances of every country, such as passemeasures, corantos, canaries, Spanish dances, and a hundred other beautiful turns to delight the fancy. Finally they danced the Spanish dance once more with their ladies, and because they were tired began to lag; and the King, who is by nature choleric, grew impatient and shouted loudly, 'Why don't they dance? What did you make me come here for? Devil take all of you, dance!' At once the Marquis of Buckingham, his majesty's favourite minion, sprang forward, and danced a number of high and very tiny capers with such grace and lightness that he made everyone admire and love him, and also managed to calm the rage of his angry lord. Inspired by this, the other masquers continued to display their powers one after another, with different ladies, concluding with capers, and lifting their goddesses from the ground. We counted 34 capers in succession cut by one knight, but none matched the splendid technique of the Marquis. The Prince, however, surpassed them all in his bows, being very formal in doing his obeisance both to his majesty and to the lady with whom he was dancing, nor was he seen to dance once out of step, which cannot perhaps be said for the others. Because of his youth, he does not yet have much breath; nevertheless he cut some capers with considerable grace. When the performance of these twelve accomplished knights was completed, after they had overcome the sloth and drunkenness of Bacchus with their prowess, the Prince went in triumph to kiss his royal father's hands, by whom he was embraced and warmly kissed. The King then honoured the Marquis with extraordinary signs of affection, touching his face. His majesty rose from his chair, and taking the ambassadors along with him, passed through a number of rooms and galleries and came to a hall where the usual supper was prepared for the performers, a light being carried before him. He glanced round the table and departed, and at once like so many harpies the company fell on their prey. The table was almost entirely covered with sweetmeats, with all kinds of sugar confections. There were some large figures, but they were of painted cardboard, for decoration. The meal was served in bowls or plates of glass; the first assault threw the table to the ground, and the crash of glass platters reminded me exactly of the windows breaking in a great midsummer storm. The story ended at two hours after midnight, and half disgusted and exhausted we returned home.[51]

The masque Busino saw was Jonson's *Pleasure Reconciled to Virtue*, performed at the first Banqueting House. It is our loss that Busino gave no comparable account of any of the occasions when the King's Men or Cockpit company performed plays at Court on stages designed by Jones, as they did during the Christmas festivities in some years.

In Caroline times, of twelve plays that we know were performed for the Court with scenery, three were put on privately by the Queen's ladies, two privately by the Earl of Pembroke's household, three at Oxford by the university, three at Court by the King's Men, and one at Court by the Cockpit company of 1634.[52] All but two or three used Jones's designs. The four plays performed by the professional players were all transferred to the private playhouses, some with the costumes used in the Court performance, but none with the scenery. One of the Oxford plays went to London for a second performance before the Court, this time by the King's Men, at the instigation of the Chancellor, Archbishop Laud (who, incidentally, claimed that the professionals performed the play less well than the students). It cost £100 just to make the costumes and scenery ready again for the second performance. Laud showed an understandable anxiety about the university's property that he had committed to London, and the Queen had to assure him

you may be confident that no Part of these things yᵗ are come to our hands, shall be suffered to bee prostituted upon any Mercenary Stage, but shall bee carefully Reserv'd for our owne Occasions and particular Entertainments att Court.

The mercenary players on the whole probably expected little else, though they were obviously known to be waiting for any scraps that might fall from the royal stage.

7. DIRECTING PERFORMANCES

A large part of the business of staging must have depended on the amount of time available for rehearsals, and the related question whether anyone may have served as co-ordinator or stage director of performances. Henslowe's records for the Rose indicate that on average mounting a new play took three weeks from delivery of the completed playbook to the first performance. Since the company was playing every afternoon, and probably spent part of each morning running through that day's play, the company cannot have had much free time for full rehearsals of the new plays. Moreover in that three weeks the scribe still needed time to copy out all the major speaking parts, and they had to be learned. And there was the risk that the new play might not succeed on stage. Quite a few of the seventeen or more plays taken on each year at the Rose appear in the performance lists only once.[53] So the temptation must have been great not to put too much effort into a new play until its success on stage and its retention in the repertory were assured. Only then, perhaps, would much effort be put into polishing the production. With such large and rapidly changing repertoires of plays, no company could afford to spend much time on the niceties of staging. The players must have been left largely to their own devices. Such a high-speed repertory system put a premium on traditional practices.

The manipulation of the business, the stage-management side, fell naturally into the hands of the only member of the company who had to be reasonably familiar with the whole text of the play, the book-holder or book-keeper. He was responsible for seeing that players were ready on their cues, and for having properties to hand for carrying on or being discovered as and when they might be needed. He had several 'stage-keepers' to help him, who also served as supernumeraries. A marginal note in Heywood's *The Captives* orders '*stage keepers as a guard*'. He lurked in the tiring-house, as we learn from such references as the one in *The Maid in the Mill*, a King's Men's play of 1623, where a woman's screams are heard '*within*', and a character says 'they are out of their parts sure: it may be 'tis the Book-holder's fault: I'll go see'. Ben Jonson, probably with an excess of modesty, disclaimed any direct responsibility for the staging of *Cynthia's Revels* by getting one of the boys in the induction to say

wee are not so officiously befriended by him, as to have his presence in the tiring-house, to prompt us aloud, stampe at the booke-holder, sweare for our properties, curse the poore tire-man, raile the musicke out of tune, and sweat for everie veniall trespasse we commit.

In view of the pains Jonson obviously took in preparing this play especially so that the boys could show their paces, it is likely that this denial is another of his minglings of appearance and reality. His direct interest in the production of his plays was to become a byword with theatregoers, one that he himself exploited in the induction to *Barthole-mew Fair*, where the stage-keeper complains aggrievedly that the author has taken no notice of his experienced advice.

It was easier to tell youths how to perform their play than adult sharers, of course, which may be why the only other known statement about a supervising or directing hand is about a manager of a young company. William Beeston was commended for training his young players in their trade, in Brome's epilogue to *The Court Beggar*:

But this small Poet vents [no wit] but his own, and his by whose care and directions this Stage is govern'd, who has for many yeares both in his fathers dayes, and since directed Poets to write & Players to speak till he traind up these youths here to what they are now. I some of 'em before they were able to say a grace of two lines long to have more parts in their pates then would fill so many Dry-fats.

This is training in playing, of course, not directing the performance.

Apart from Jonson, the only clear hints I know of to suggest that a poet participated in the staging of his plays come from the first cause of all the attention paid to Shakespearean drama in the last four centuries. The couplet quoted on page 114 about Burbage's mannerism in playing Richard III with 'his hand continuall on his dagger' refers to a gesture for which there is some historical justification. Holinshed's account of Richard reads in part

When he stood musing, he would bite and chaw busilie his nether lip; as who said, that his fierce nature in his cruell bodie alwaies chafed, stirred, and was ever unquiet: beside that, the dagger which he ware, he would (when he studied) with his hand plucke up & downe in the sheath to the midst, never drawing it fullie out.[54]

There was at least one fellow of Burbage who knew Holinshed and could have told him of that mannerism. The same author would most likely have been the one to elaborate on the bare stage direction '*Enter Clifford wounded*' in the Folio text of *3 Henry VI*, and to tell the player or tire-man what to do. The equivalent stage direction in the reported text reads '*Enter Clifford wounded, with an arrow in his necke*', the correct place for the wound according to the sources of the play. And thirdly, another reported text, of *2 Henry VI*, tells us that the stage direction '*Enter Richard, and Somerset to fight*', was also amplified in the staging by reference to the play's source. Somerset was said to have died at St Albans under an inn-sign, and the play follows that report, as the stage direction in the reported text says: '. . . *enter the Duke of* Somerset, *and* Richard *fighting and Richard kils him under the signe of the Castle in saint Albones.*' These three instances of authorial intervention in the staging, incidentally, confirm that Shakespeare must have been a fellow with Burbage and the others in the 1592 Pembroke's company, some members of which made up the reported texts of the two *Henry VI* plays, and were familiar with *Richard III*.

6. The Audiences

1. SOCIAL ATTITUDES TO PLAYGOING

A CATHOLIC ARCHPRIEST named William Harison discovered in 1623
that some of his priests were in the habit of seeing plays at the
amphitheatres. With pained understanding he pointed out to them that

such playes are made to sport, and delight the auditorie, which consisting most
of young gallants, and Protestants (for no true Puritanes will endure to bee
present at playes) how unlikely is it, but that there are, and must bee, at least
some passages in the playes, which may relish, and tickle the humor of such
persons, or else good night to the players.[1]

Similar presumptions and similar deductions about the relationship
between Shakespearean plays and their audiences have been made for
the last 370 years. Working in the reverse direction to Harison and
noting that events shown in the plays were bloody and bawdy, scholars
have found it easy to assume that the audiences to whom such plays
were fed were correspondingly riotous and self-willed. The trouble is
that this kind of presumption has no particular validity. One might look
at twentieth-century television and by the same presumption conclude
that audiences now are quite as lecherous and disorderly in their living
rooms as those of Shakespeare's day are thought to have been in their
playhouses.

It may for all we know be true that the basic mentality of the
Elizabethan and early Stuart audiences is not essentially different from
that of the majority audiences of today, and that in consequence we do
not need to look very deeply into their composition. It is knowing even
that much that is difficult. Of course the returns on the labour of
summarising and generalising about such intangibles are likely to be
small. There was on average over that seventy years or so of London
commercial theatre as many as a million visits to the playhouse a year.
Any generalisation covering that number would have to be stretched
thinly. Three of the four estates of the theatre, the playhouses, staging
and even the playing, can evoke generalisations with far more strength.
None the less, the audiences were there, and our picture of the
Shakespearean stage is incomplete without some impression of them as

one of the factors conditioning performances. Unless we make Harison's kind of presumption we cannot really draw firm conclusions about their mentality or their influence on playwriting. But there is evidence about their constituent members, those sections of society that did help the players to stay prosperous, their behaviour, their favourite habits and tastes, and we can draw from these things a recognisable if impressionistic picture of the theatre's fourth estate.

To take the broad perspective first: from 1574 to 1642 the London playhouses found their audiences amongst a population which grew from about 200,000 to nearly 400,000 people. In 1595 the estimates suggest that the two acting companies were visited by about 15,000 people weekly. In 1620 when six playhouses were open, three of them the smaller private houses, the weekly total was probably nearer 25,000.[2] Perhaps about 15 or 20 per cent of all the people living within reach of Shoreditch and Southwark were regular playgoers. Modern estimates of the capacities of the amphitheatres converge on about 2,500 as a maximum figure (de Witt estimated 3,000 for the Swan).[3] According to Henslowe, the only impresario whose accounts we have in any detail, the largest audiences attended for new plays and on public holidays, the average attendance being more like half of the capacity. Seasonal variation was less than might be expected, Henslowe's daily receipts dropping from £44 19s. in May to £37 11s. in January.[4] The auditorium area in hall playhouses such as Blackfriars seems to have been much less than half that of the amphitheatres, to judge by Beaumont's description in 1609 of the Blackfriars as a place where 'a·thousand men in judgement sit'. But of course their admission charges were much higher. The Blackfriars seems consistently to have made more money for the King's Men than the Globe.

Figures such as these, rough estimates as they are, do not say much about the more revealing but less tangible matters, like the place playgoing occupied in Shakespearean society, how largely it figured in the flood of contemporary social life, or what image it offered the public. Shakespearean London more than most conurbations had a many-headed public divided against itself, and the images its members painted of playhouses and playgoing were highly variable and of very doubtful reliability, particularly from the non-playgoing 80 per cent. The spokesmen for Puritan London described playhouse audiences as riotous and immoral; the poets described them as ignorant and wilful; the City Fathers regarded them as riotous and seditious. If any of these images had been in any large degree true the playhouses would have been closed much earlier than 1642. As it was, on the one distressing occasion when officialdom did investigate the playhouses – in 1602 on the instructions of the Privy Council to clear places of resort of idle and disorderly persons and press them for the army – it found the image

had misled them. According to contemporary gossip the City Fathers
chose to clear the playhouses first, even before the taverns and brothels,
and found 'not only . . . Gentlemen, and servingmen, but Lawyers,
Clarkes, country men that had lawe cawses, aye the Quens men,
knightes, and as it was credibly reported one Earle'.[5]

Any general picture based on contemporary evidence has to be built
up piecemeal. It will rather be a series of pictures, changing in space
and time as the audiences changed, varying from playhouse to playhouse, from the audiences for Marlowe to the audiences for Davenant.
Even contemporary generalisations of acknowledged impartiality need
qualifying when the 'contemporary' label covers seventy years of rapid
social and cultural change.

One of the more reliable types of witness here as elsewhere was the
traveller from abroad. The Elizabethan players were famous across
Europe and many of the foreigners who passed through London took
care to see them. As tourists they also not infrequently recorded what
they saw for the benefit of their fellow-countrymen with the kind of
detail that the Londoner, to whom such things were automatic knowledge, usually omitted. Thomas Platter, a young Swiss who travelled
widely in England in 1599, told of seeing a play at the Curtain:

in conclusion they danced very charmingly in English and Irish fashion. Thus
daily at two in the afternoon, London has two, sometimes three plays running
in different places, competing with each other, and those which play best obtain
most spectators. The playhouses are so constructed that they play on a raised
platform, so that everyone has a good view. There are different galleries and
places, however, where the seating is better and more comfortable and therefore
more expensive. For whoever cares to stand below only pays one English
penny, but if he wishes to sit he enters by another door, and pays another
penny, while if he desires to sit in the most comfortable seats which are
cushioned, where he not only sees everything well, but can also be seen, then
he pays yet another English penny at another door. And during the performance food and drink are carried round the audience, so that for what one cares
to pay one may also have refreshment.[6]

This is a typical (if minimal) portrait of a public-theatre scene on the
eve of the rebirth of the private theatres. Platter's admission prices are
confirmed by Lambarde. There were, in addition to the standing room
in the yard and the penny and twopenny galleries, in all the amphitheatres one or more lords' rooms, where the charge was 6d. (half a
shilling in the old currency). There is no positive evidence that these
prices altered at any time in the period. In the hall playhouses, as
we have noted, the basic admission was 6d., and a stool on the stage
itself cost a further 6d. The boxes at the side of the stage cost half-a-
crown.[7]

2. SOCIAL DIVISIONS IN THE PLAYHOUSES

These prices understandably tended to shape the distribution of social classes in the playhouses. The basic penny at the Globe in 1600 was cheap by the standards of most forms of entertainment at the time, though the hall playhouses' basic 6d., one-twelfth of the London artisan's weekly wage,[8] was by amphitheatre standards truly a lord's price for the two hours of stage traffic. The other major pastimes available, however, gambling, whoring and drinking, were all by that standard lordly sports. Tobacco was 3d. for a small pipeful, and even the nuts that spectators commonly chewed during performances cost up to 6d. Only bear-baiting was as cheap as the yard of the public playhouses. The working classes seem to have paid up to 2d. for their plays according to the author of *Father Hubburd's Tales* (1603), who writes of 'a dull Audience of Stinkards sitting in the Penny Galleries of a Theater, and yawning upon the Players'. Sir Humphrey Mildmay, a landed gentleman about town in the 1630s, used to pay for a twelve-penny room at the hall playhouse, and paid a similar price, presumably for a lord's room, when he went to the Globe in the summer months.[9] The amphitheatre's shilling may have been made up to that total in his accounts by a boatman's fee of sixpence.

The different pricing did apparently make a difference in the audiences. The praeludium to Goffe's *Careless Shepherdess*, played at a hall playhouse in 1629, has a Citizen say

> I will hasten to the money Box,
> And to take my shilling out again, for now
> I have considered that it is too much;
> I'll go to th'Bull, or Fortune, and there see
> A Play for two pense, with a Jig to boot.

If a merchant or craftsman found the shilling too much, it is not likely that apprentices would have been tempted.

One of the fundamental differences between all the various audiences must have existed between the social classes, in simple financial terms of those who could not afford the hall playhouse charges and those who could. It is easy to exaggerate the difference, and certainly the Globe, at least after 1609 as the King's Men's summer resort, attracted the playgoers used to seeing them at the Blackfriars. Mildmay's diary records several plays seen at Court, eighteen visits to Blackfriars and four to the Cockpit, but also four to the Globe. The Globe company, even in the decade before 1609, was summoned to play at Court twice as often as any other company, in fact as often as all the other companies put together. It is unlikely that those who favoured them so much at Court would have ignored them at the Globe. The rich and the poor audiences were not mutually exclusive; rather the rich went to hall and amphitheatre playhouse alike, the poor more exclusively to the amphitheatres.

Looking back from 1699 the antiquary James Wright summed up the general impressions of the different Caroline playhouses as they evolved after 1609 as follows:

Before the Wars, there were in being all these Playhouses at the same time. The *Black-friars*, and *Globe* on the *Bankside*, a Winter and Summer House, belonging to the same Company called the King's Servants; the *Cockpit* or *Phoenix*, in *Drury-Lane*, called the Queen's Servants; the private House in *Salisbury-court*, called the Prince's Servants; the Fortune near *White-cross-street*, and the Red Bull at the upper end of St. *John's-street*: The two last were mostly frequented by Citizens, and the meaner sort of People. All these Companies got Money, and Liv'd in Reputation, especially those of the *Black-friers*, who were Men of grave and sober Behaviour.[10]

Most of the evidence for the composition of audiences at these various playhouses supports Wright's description, though by no means straightforwardly. The boy companies at the new hall theatres in 1600 seem not so much to have drawn wealthy audiences away from the amphitheatres as, for a time and in ways that changed, to have excluded the poorer patrons. Marston, writing about St Paul's Boys in 1600, in *Jack Drum's Entertainment*, V.i, told his listeners

> I like the Audience that frequenteth there
> With much applause: A man shall not be choakte
> With the stench of Garlicke, nor be pasted
> To the barmy Jacket of a Beer-brewer.

and called them 'a good gentle Audience'. It was a hopeful pronouncement, and probably meant more that the stinkard was banished from the yard to the top gallery than that he was totally excluded. By 1609 Jonson was writing of 'six-penny mechanicks' and the 'shop's foreman . . . that may judge for his sixpence' at Blackfriars. It is also worth bearing in mind that the first performance of Beaumont's *Knight of the Burning Pestle* at the Blackfriars in 1607 was a total flop because, as the publisher of the First Quarto (1613) said, the audience missed 'the privie mark of irony about it'. That a burlesque of citizen plays should be construed by the audience as a straight citizen play rather implies that the citizen element in the audience was stronger than Beaumont bargained for.

The wealthy and especially the young had patronised the amphitheatres readily enough up to the reopening of the halls in 1599. In the 1580s city apprentices and the Inns-of-Court law students were equally notorious for their behaviour in such public places. In the 1590s, with only the amphitheatres open to all Londoners, people from the whole social gamut, male and female, attended plays. As the law student John Davies put it, citizens and artisans joined with gentlemen and prostitutes, porters and household servants.

> For as we see at all the playhouse dores,
> When ended is the play, the daunce, and song,
> A thousand townsemen, gentlemen, and whores,
> Porters and serving-men together throng . . . [11]

There was of course more comment on the higher social levels attending than on the lower classes. Nashe in 1592 listed the classes with conspicuous leisure who became 'afternoon's men' (a euphemism for drunkards): 'Gentlemen of the Court, the Innes of the Courte, and the number of Captaines and Souldiers about London': gallants, lawyers and soldiers on leave. Foreign tourists also normally visited the theatres, since they were counted as one of the famous sights of London.

Foreign ambassadors in particular made their presence known by visits to the amphitheatres. The French ambassador and his wife went to the Globe to see *Pericles* in 1608. At a time of considerable hostility to Spain in 1621, the Spanish ambassador and his train saw a play at the Fortune, and afterwards treated the players to a banquet. The scandal over the performances of the anti-Spanish *A Game at Chess* at the Globe in 1624 produced the following note from a contemporary observer:

I doubt not but you have heard of our famous play of Gondomar, which hath been followed with extraordinary concourse, and frequented by all sorts of people old and younge, rich and poore, masters and servants, papists and puritans, wise men *et. ct.*, churchmen and statesmen, as Sir Henry Wotton, Sir Albert Morton, Sir Benjamin Ruddier, Sir Thomas Lake, and a world besides; the Lady Smith would have gon yf she could have persuaded me to go with her. I am not so sowre nor severe but I could not sit so long, for we must have been there before one a clocke at farthest to find any roome.[12]

The concourse at such a scandalous play was not extraordinary for its social altitude but for its wide range. A more run-of-the-mill occasion was reported by Busino, the wide-eyed Venetian, who visited the Fortune in 1617, and was impressed

to see such a crowd of nobility, so very well arrayed that they looked like so many princes, listening as silently and soberly as possible. These theatres are frequented by a number of respectable and handsome ladies, who come freely and seat themselves among the men without the slightest hesitation.[13]

He goes on to describe being accosted by one such masked gentlewoman, in two languages; she was probably set on him as a joke by his ambassador.

John Earle, writing of a leading actor in 1628, coupled gentlewomen

and law students as the most frequent playgoers, claiming with characteristic malice that both types went for the pleasure the leading player
gave them:

The waiting-women Spectators are over-eares in love with him, and Ladies
send for him to act in their Chambers. Your Innes of Court men were undone
but for him, hee is their chiefe guest and imployment, and the sole businesse
that makes them Afternoones men.[14]

A more detailed, though not necessarily more typical, catalogue of a
Blackfriars audience under the Stuarts was given in 1617 by the Inns-of-
Court student Henry Fitzgeoffrey, in a book of verses called *Satyres and
Satyricall Epigrams: with Certaine Observations at Black-Fryers*. In a looser
version of the Theophrastan 'Characters' manner he describes a *'Captain
Martio*, he ith' *Renounce Me* Band, / That in the middle Region doth
stand', *'Sir Iland Hunt*, a Travailer that will tell / Of stranger Things then
Tatterd Tom ere li't of', 'A *Cheapside* Dame' (i.e. a Citizen's wife), a high-
heeled 'world of fashions' (male), 'A *Woman* of the *masculine Gender*', a
'plumed *Dandebrat*, / Yon Ladyes *Shittle-cocke*', and a 'misshappen
Prodigall' who passes on to the stage from the tiring-house as if he had
not a debt in the world. Later, and perhaps a little inconsistently, the
audience is described as 'this *Microcosme*, Man's societie'.

Both Earle's and Fitzgeoffrey's descriptions are of the Blackfriars,
unquestionably the most reputable playhouse of the whole later period.
In 1630 it was the focus of a literary quarrel that in a small way illustrates
the differences between the playhouses at that time. Davenant's second
commercial-theatre play, *The Just Italian*, failed when put on by the
King's Men. His friends promptly supplied him with sympathetic
prefatory verses for the publication of the play early in 1630. One of
them was Thomas Carew, who wrote of the audience:

> they'l still slight
> All that exceeds Red Bull, and Cockpit flight.
> These are the men in crowded heapes that throng
> To that adulterate stage, where not a tong
> Of th'untun'd Kennell, can a line repeat
> Of serious sence: but like lips, meet like meat;
> Whilst the true brood of Actors, that alone
> Keepe naturall unstrayn'd Action in her throne
> Behold their benches bare, though they rehearse
> The tearser *Beaumonts*, or great *Johnsons* verse.

This slur, linking Beeston's company at the Cockpit with the tear-throat
citizen fare of the Red Bull, found a prompt reply in verses attached to
Shirley's *Grateful Servant*, one of the only two plays by Shirley to be
printed with prefatory verses. One defender of Shirley and the Cockpit

repertory, for which Shirley was the leading poet, called Carew's poem a cock and bull story:

>   I must
> Be to my conscience and thy Poem just,
> Which grac'd with comely action, did appeare
> The full delight of every eye and eare,
> And had that stage no other play, it might
> Have made the critticke blushe at cock-pit flight,
> Who not discovering what pitch it flies
> His wit came down in pitty to his eyes
> And lent him a discourse of cock and bull
> To make his other commendations full:
> But let such Momi passe, and give applause
> Among the brood of actors, in whose cause,
> As Champion he hath sweat, let their stale pride
> Finde some excuse in being magnified,
> Thy Muse will live, and no adulterate pen
> Shall wound her, through the sides of common men
> Let 'em unkennell malice, yet thy praise
> Shall mount secure, hell cannot blast thy bayes.[15]

Others of Shirley's sympathisers upheld his 'So smooth, so sweet' verse against the 'mighty rimes, / Audacious metaphors' of Davenant at the Blackfriars. Shirley himself defended his actors – 'the most of them deserving a name in the file of those that are eminent for gracefull and unaffected action'. It has been suggested that what gave Shirley's supporters so much exercise was not only the 'untun'd Kennell' charge but more particularly the 'cock and bull' association of the 'Cocke-pit flight' with that of the Red Bull. It is more likely to be a slur associating the indoor Cockpit's repertoire of plays with the amphitheatre Red Bull's. Several Red Bull plays, including Heywood's *Rape of Lucrece* and Marlowe's *Jew of Malta*, had found their way into the Cockpit repertoire by the late 1620s.[16] Heywood in fact later answered the slur on behalf of both playhouses. In Book IV of his religious poem *The Hierarchy of the Blessed Angels* (1635), he broke out against Carew and Davenant in righteous if postponed indignation:

> Whence growes this Innovation? How comes it
> Some dare to measure mouthes for every bit
> The Muse shall tast? And those Approv'd Tongues call
> Which have pleased Court and City, indeed All;
> An untuned Kennel: when the populous Throng
> Of Auditors have thought the Muses sung,
> When they but spake? How comes it (ere he know it)
> A puny shall assume the name of poet,
> And in a Tympa'nous and Thrasonicke stile

> (Words at which th'Ignorant laugh but the learn'd smile
> Because Adulterate and Undenizen'd) he
> Should taske such Artists, as have took Degre
> Before he was a Fresh-man?

It was more a personal quarrel than a war about dramatic standards, since Heywood for one took it personally. But the question of differing standards did exist. Carew's view of the superiority of the Blackfriars repertory was reasserted by Leonard Digges in commendatory verses attached to Shakespeare's *Poems* of 1640. Digges exhorted contemporary scribblers not to pollute Shakespeare's stage:

> But if you needs must write, if poverty
> So pinch, that otherwise you starve and die,
> On Gods name may the Bull or Cockpit have
> Your lame blancke Verse, to keepe you from the grave:
> Or let new Fortunes younger brethren see,
> What they can picke from your lean industry.
> I do not wonder when you offer at
> Black-friers, that you suffer.

This is a celebration of the superior standards offered at the Blackfriars, rather than any essential difference in the repertory. The whole quarrel shows an awareness by the rival poets of the homogeneity of each playhouse's audiences, and their tendency to differ.

The chief problem in differentiating the playhouse audiences is not in fact so much between the citizen and amphitheatre Red Bull and Fortune on the one hand, and the courtier hall Blackfriars on the other, as in locating the place held by the Globe after 1608–9, when the King's Men became hall theatre players as well as amphitheatre, and used the Globe for the summer season from May to September and Blackfriars through the rest of the year. By 1630 the Blackfriars was taking nearly twice as much money as the Globe on the average, and was used for twice as long in the year. The title-pages of play quartos published between 1616 and 1642 mention performances at the Blackfriars alone forty-nine times; ten name both Blackfriars and Globe, and only five give the Globe alone as the venue. It is unlikely that many or even any of these plays had really only been acted at one of the playhouses, because the repertoire of the King's Men seems to have been almost completely interchangeable, at least down to the last decade. The Globe of course was open mainly while the Inns of Court were in vacation and the aristocracy out of town, and it is likely to be this circumstance as much as its more 'popular' amphitheatre image that made it seem less distinguished than the Blackfriars. Henry Glapthorne's *Poems* (1639) contains a prologue 'To a Reviv'd Vacation Play', which puts forward the hope that its wit will find some response from an audience of citizens, but on the other hand Davenant's *News from Plymouth*, acted at the Globe in vacation, has a prologue expressing joy at the appearance there of a Blackfriars audience:

> A Noble Company! for we can spy
> Beside rich gawdy Sirs, some that rely
> More on their Judgments, then their Cloathes, and may
> With wit as well as Pride, rescue our Play:
> And 'tis but just, though each Spectator knows
> This House, and season, does more promise shewes,
> Dancing, and Buckler Fights, then Art, or Witt.

If the prologue was written along with the play, of course, Davenant must have been just making a hopeful prophecy, or preparing a loaded compliment for an audience that he did *not* expect to be keen on wit. His last lines suggest that the Globe provided jigs and spectacles in spite of the success of the musicians at the Blackfriars. The same point appears in the prologue to Shirley's *Doubtful Heir* (1640), which supplies a detailed catalogue of the differences between the two playhouses in a backhanded apology for presenting a play written for the Blackfriars at the Globe:

> Our Author did not calculate this Play
> For this Meridian; the Bankside, he knows,
> Are far more skilfull at the Ebbes and flows
> Of water, than of wit, he did not mean
> For the elevation of your poles, this scene.
> No shews, no dance and what you most delight in,
> Grave understanders, here's no target fighting.

The catalogue goes on at some length.

The trappings of hall and amphitheatre performance evidently remained at each theatre, and the repertories of plays were possibly in the later years also divided, though not as much as some poets wished. On Davenant's testimony and evidence such as Mildmay's diary it also appears that in summer the Blackfriars audiences did not altogether forsake the King's Men just because they moved to the Globe and were producing their plays with public theatre appurtenances. In these later years both audiences were socially mixed, to judge by Lovelace's epilogue to his lost play *The Scholars*, published in 1649. The difference at Blackfriars between the gallery and the pit required two plays in one:

> His *Schollars* school'd, sayd if he had been wise
> He should have wove in one two comedies.
> The first for th'gallery, in which the throne
> To their amazement should descend alone,
> The rosin-lightning flash and monster spire
> Squibs, and words hotter than his fire.

> Th'other for the gentlemen o'th'pit
> Like to themselves all spirit, fancy, wit.

The price differential no doubt reduced the proportion of commoners in the gallery of the Blackfriars in the winter, compared with the numbers standing around the Globe stage. The disappearance of the landed gentry to their estates and of the afternoon men from the Inns of Court no doubt similarly reduced the proportion of gallants at the Globe in summer. But at neither playhouse could the King's Men expect a complete change of audience. The most conspicuous difference was probably the positioning of the audience. At the Globe the spectators surrounding the stage were in the cheapest places. At the Blackfriars the witty and the elegant were closest, the poorer folk furthest from the stage.

The fact that all these references to a difference between the audiences of halls and amphitheatres appeared in Caroline times, from about 1630 on, reflects what is probably one consequence of social polarisation. The sides that were to join battle after 1640 were moving into position. When Prynne was being so savagely punished for his attack on Henrietta Maria's amateur theatricals in 1633, the world of playgoing was for the first time unambiguously identified as the avenue where the world of fashion most loved to stroll. For the first time respectable ladies formed a noticeable proportion of the audience. Poets paid attention to them, giving their plays titles like *The Lady's Privilege* or *The Lady's Trial*, writing flattering prologues and dedicating the published texts to them. Brome's epilogue to *The Court Beggar* (1640) addresses an audience made up of 'Ladyes', 'Cavaliers' and 'generous spirits of the City', in that order. These were all in plays for the hall playhouses, of course, in a repertory that saw the presence of ladies chiefly as a restraining influence. Shirley in his prologue to *The Imposture* (1640) called the 'gentlemen' of his audience the 'commissioners of wit', and the 'ladies' the arbiters of decorum.

> In all his poems you have been his care,
> Nor shall you need to wrinkle now that fair
> Smooth alabaster of your brow; no fright
> Shall strike chaste ears, or dye the harmless white
> Of any cheek with blushes: by this pen,
> No innocence shall bleed in any scene.

No bawdy, pure poetic justice and no fireworks in a playhouse where ladies are present.

3.   AUDIENCE BEHAVIOUR

Evidence for the behaviour of Shakespearean audiences is much more plentiful than for their constitution; rather too plentiful in fact. As

Alfred Harbage puts it, most of the testimony for audience behaviour 'expresses a social attitude or comes from disappointed poets, disgruntled preachers, wary politicians, or spokesmen for threatened commercial interests'.[17] Harbage makes the point that the bulk of the unfavourable testimony can be discounted by analogy with the similar body of testimony against the depraved and corrupted nature of plays. Since the one set of testimonies can be proved false by reference to the plays accused of corruption, the equivalent testimonies for riotous behaviour among the audiences can similarly be distrusted. The inclination to do so is strengthened on finding that Stephen Gosson, once a player and writer of plays, and later one of the most eloquent writers of testimonies against the playhouses, took his descriptions of Elizabethan audiences from Ovid's accounts of Roman audiences in the *Amores*.[18] Harison's cautious and not implausible deduction about the nature of plays, quoted at the beginning of this chapter, was a safer argument for a non-playgoer to use than the accusations levelled by the non-playgoing Puritans and City Fathers. One might expect the poets to carry more weight with their condemnations, and they were certainly more eloquent: Nashe attacked audiences in 1592, Heywood in 1595, Marston in 1597, 1603 and 1604, Chapman in 1599, Beaumont in 1607 and 1609, Fletcher in 1609 and 1613, Dekker in 1609 and 1610, Webster in 1611, Middleton in 1613, Carew in 1630, and Jonson at frequent intervals throughout his career.[19] But all their attacks were against bad judgement rather than bad behaviour, and can therefore hardly be disinterested. A few poets sometimes went to the other extreme of flattery, but with no more sign of disinterest than when they condemned.

There is some evidence of violence and lawlessness in the playhouses between 1574 and 1642, but there is nothing to show that it was more than the occasional consequence of large crowds gathering together for a length of time. Chambers[20] lists instances of lawlessness in playhouses including a case of stealing at the Red Bull in 1613, a stabbing (the Fortune in the same year), fighting (the Red Bull in 1610), and receiving a stolen diamond (the Curtain in 1594). There were also such minor consequences of ill manners as the lawsuit brought in Star Chamber by a Captain Essex against the Irish Lord Thurles (a few weeks later to be the Duke of Ormond) in 1632, resulting from a brawl with swords when Thurles took up a position on the stage at the Blackfriars and obstructed the view of Captain Essex and the Earl of Essex's new wife, whom the Captain was escorting, in their box.[21]

As in any crowd of course pickpockets and prostitutes were to be found at work, but even for them the taverns were better employment. A pickpocket caught in 1600 at one of the Middlesex amphitheatres was the only one, amongst 118 proven cases in that year, to be taken at a playhouse.[22] In all, one pickpocket in seven of those convicted at the Middlesex sessions was caught at a playhouse,[23] which is not a bad record considering the small range of places where crowds might foregather in the northern suburbs and countryside of sixteenth-century Middlesex. In the case of the Fortune, there was even a rather self-conscious pride in the association of cutpurses and similar rogues with the house. Dekker and Middleton wrote a play, *The Roaring Girl*, celebrating one Marion Frith, a well-known female transvestite, who herself favoured the Fortune. In 1611 or 1612 the *Consistory of London Correction Book* recorded Roaring Moll's bad reputation, and especially that

being at a play about three quarters of a yeare since at ye Fortune in man's apparel and in her boots and wth a sword at her syde she told the company then present y[t] she thought many of them were of opinion that she was a man, but if any of them would come to her lodging they should finde she is a woman, and some other immodest and lascivious speaches she also used at y[t] time and also sat upon the stage in the public viewe of all the people there present in man's apparel and played upon her lute and sange a song.[24]

Moll may in fact have sat on stage for a performance of *The Roaring Girl* itself. Certainly in the printed text at V.i, she is utilised to identify her cutpurse associates in the playhouse audience. In I.ii a leading gentle-man character presents a detailed description of the Fortune audience and also identifies a cutpurse amongst them:

> The furniture that doth adorne this roome,
> Cost many a faire gray groat ere it came here,
> But good things are most cheape, when th'are most deere,
> Nay when you looke into my galleries,
> How bravely they are trim'd up, you all shall sweare
> Y'are highly pleasd to see whats set downe there:
> Stories of men and women (mixt together
> Faire ones with foule, like sun-shine in wet wether)
> Within one square a thousand heads are laid
> So close, that all of heads, the roome seemes made,
> As many faces there (fill'd with blith lookes)
> Shew like the promising titles of new bookes,
> (Writ merily) the Readers being their owne eyes,
> Which seeme to move and to give plaudities,
>   And here and there (whilst with obsequious eares,
> Throng'd heapes do listen) a cut purse thrusts and leeres
> With haukes eyes for his prey: I need not shew him,
> By a hanging villanous looke, your selves may know him,
> The face is drawne so rarely. Then sir below,
> The very flowre (as twere) waves to and fro,
> And like a floating Iland, seemes to move,
> Upon a sea bound in with shores above.

In a neat ambiguity, the 'galleries' are described as both full of pictures and of playgoers. The yard is a sea of faces. This compares with the fact that it was the Fortune that was singled out in the Middlesex order of 1612 to suppress its jigs because of the cutpurses they attracted.

The presence of cutpurses and other criminals was a common claim made against the playhouses, although since there were almost no other places besides the churches where large numbers of people assembled we need not take the claims too seriously. There are not many records of criminals being charged with crimes at the playhouses. Accounts of affrays, or fights between apprentices and others, appear more frequently. But the criminal records only show the tip of what was probably a large iceberg of minor disturbances. The apprentices on holiday attacked the Cockpit, as noted above, and a similar display of crowd spirit eager to create a disruption is described by Edmond Gayton in 1654 from his colourful memory:

the players have been appointed, notwithstanding their bills to the contrary, to act what the major part of the company had a mind to. Sometimes *Tamerlane*, sometimes *Jugurtha*, sometimes *The Jew of Malta*, and sometimes parts of all these; and at last, none of the three taking, they were forced to undress and put off their tragick habits, and conclude the day with *The Merry Milkmaides*. And unless this were done, and the popular humour satisfied (as sometimes it so fortun'd that the players were refractory), the benches, the tiles, the laths, the stones, oranges, apples, nuts, flew about most liberally; and as there were mechanicks of all professions, who fell every one to his trade, and dissolved a house in an instant, and made a ruin of a stately fabric.[25]

The plays Gayton mentions were in the Red Bull and Fortune repertoires, and it is understandable that the more riotous happenings, like the lawbreaking, occurred there more than elsewhere. Captain Essex's altercation is the only kind of incident recorded at the Blackfriars.

Riots, brawls and lawbreaking were hardly everyday happenings, and it is impossible to gauge the behaviour of a typical audience by them. Habitual practices tell us more than such exceptions. The most obtrusive habits were to be seen in the hall playhouses in the gallants who sat on stools on the stage, and, in all the playhouses, in the nut-cracking, which was a favourite exercise for everybody. A gallant talking and smoking on a stool on the periphery of the stage was, and meant himself to be, an extremely obtrusive feature of the performance. It was a popular habit from the time the hall playhouses first opened, and however objectionable to the mass of the audience and the players it survived. The preface to the first Shakespeare Folio in 1623 complained of wits sitting 'on the Stage at Black-friers, or the Cock-pit, to arraigne Playes dailie'. The players were similarly unhappy about the noise of nuts being cracked during their performances; nut-cracking in fact was the only regular complaint apart from the prologue's customary plea for silence.[26] Jasper Mayne's prologue to *The City Match* bravely declares that the author has no fear of 'them who sixpence pay and sixpence crack', but according to Thomas Palmer in the 1647 Beaumont and Fletcher Folio it took a Falstaff to keep the audience from their cracking. Bottle ale, which was sold during the performance, was also occasionally remarked on for the potentially misunderstood hiss it gave when opened.

Just as contemporary commentators wrote mostly about the great who attended the playhouses, so they wrote more about exceptional audience behaviour than about ordinary audiences. Stephen Gosson may well have continued to see plays after being paid for his pamphlets attacking the theatre that he wrote in the early 1580s. Even after becoming a cleric he could still use analogies drawn from playgoing. One in particular reflects what was probably a standard practice at the amphitheatres. At a sermon he delivered at the great public venue for preachers, Paul's Cross, on 7 May 1598, called 'The Trumpet of Warre', he said that

in publique Theaters, when any notable shew passeth over the stage, the people arise up out of their seates, & stand upright with delight and eagernesse to view it well.

Such actions today are found at football matches more often than in theatres. It was a consequence of the new delight in spectacle, the press of people in the auditorium, and the informal, crowded seating on wooden benches.

Hisses or 'mewes', as well as applause, were given freely, and not only at the end of the play. Drayton speaks of

> Showts and Claps at ev'ry little pawse,
> When the proud Round on ev'ry side hath rung.[27]

And they were highly responsive in sentiment too. An academic spectator seeing a performance of *Othello* by the King's Men at Oxford in 1610 wrote that

not only by their speech but also by their deeds they drew tears. – But indeed Desdemona, killed by her husband, although she always acted the matter very well, in her death moved us still more greatly; when lying in bed she implored the pity of those watching with her countenance alone.[28]

The famous anecdote of the audience at *Faustus* being startled when the theatre fabric gave a loud crack speaks of the tension that audiences could generate. Not of course that they were often easily satisfied. Middleton echoed several fellow-poets in complaining of the variousness of audience tastes, in the prologue to *No Wit, No Help like a Woman's*:

> How is't possible to suffice
> So many Ears, so many Eyes?
> Some in wit, some in shows
> Take delight, and some in Clothes;
> Some for mirth they chiefly come,
> Some for passion, for both some;
> Some for lascivious meetings, that's their arrant;
> Some to detract and ignorance their warrant.
> How is't possible to please
> Opinion tos'd in such wilde Seas?

The poets' complaints about the intelligence of their audiences sometimes took the form of accusations that they came for the spectacle, not the words, 'only to see men speak'.[29] As Jonson put it, plays should be

> offered, as a Rite,
> To Schollers, *that can judge, and faire report*
> *The sense they heare, above the vulgar sort*
> *Of Nut-crackers, that onely come for sight.*[30]

One can count as many as thirty-four complaints from almost all the dramatists of the time (except Shakespeare) about the kind of reception their plays were given. And yet very few of the plays that failed then, with the sole exceptions of *The Knight of the Burning Pestle* and possibly *The White Devil*, would stand much chance of success now. Where audiences then and now would be more inclined to differ is over the plays that were the greatest successes of the early period. Judging by the number of editions printed, with *Faustus*, *Hamlet* and the *Henry IV* plays, the most popular pieces from the whole seventy years of playing were *The Spanish Tragedy*, *Mucedorus*, *Philaster*, Heywood's *If You Know Not Me*, and *Pericles*. The failures among the better plays of the period might be put down to the fickleness of individual audiences, but the successes among the better plays were made by the consistent judgements of a long series of audiences. They could hardly be called bad judges.

To conclude this section on audience behaviour it is instructive to put beside each other two pieces of evidence that come from the same time and more or less the same place, the Blackfriars at the end of the boy company's tenure in 1608. The first is Dekker's splendidly vivid set of burlesque advice to the ambitious gallant on how to behave in a playhouse. His remarks are meant to apply to any playhouse, but fit best at the leading hall playhouse.

let our Gallant . . . presently advance himselfe up to the Throne of the Stage. I meane not into the Lords roome (which is now but the Stages Suburbs): No, those boxes, by the iniquity of custome, conspiracy of waiting-women and Gentlemen-Ushers, that there sweat together, and the covetousness of Sharers, are contemptibly thrust into the reare, and much new Satten is there dambd, by being smothred to death in darknesse. But on the very Rushes where the Comedy is to daunce, yea, and under the state of *Cambises* himself, must our fethered *Estridge*, like a piece of Ordnance, be planted valiantly (because impudently) beating downe the mewes and hisses of the opposed rascality . . .

Present not your selfe on the Stage (especially at a new play) untill the quaking prologue hath (by rubbing) got culor into his cheekes, and is ready to give the trumpets their Cue, that hees upon point to enter: for then it is time, as though you were one of the *properties*, or that you dropt out of the *Hangings*, to creepe from behind the Arras, with your *Tripos* or three-footed stoole in one hand, and a teston [sixpence] mounted betweene a forefinger and a thumbe in the other: for if you should bestow your person upon the vulgar, when the belly of the house is but halfe full, your apparell is quite eaten up, the fashion lost, and the proportion of your body in more danger to be devoured then if it were served up on the Counter amongst the Powltry: avoid that as you would the Bastome. It shall crowne you with rich commendation, to laugh alowd in the middest of the most serious and saddest scene of the terriblest Tragedy: and let that clapper (your tongue) be tost so high, that all the house may ring of it: your Lords use it; your Knights are Apes to the Lords, and do so too: your Inne-a-court-man is Zany to the Knights, and (mary very scurvily) comes likewise limping after it: bee thou a beagle to them all, and never lin snuffing [lie sniffing], till you have scented them: . . .

Now sir, if the writer be a fellow that hath either epigrammed you, or hath had a flirt at your mistris, or hath brought either your feather, or your red beard, or your little legs &c. on the stage, you shall disgrace him worse then by tossing him in a blancket, or giving him the bastinado in a Taverne, if, in the middle of his play, (bee it Pastoral or Comedy, Morall or Tragedie) you rise with a screwd and discontented face from your stoole to be gone: no matter whether the Scenes be good or no; the better they are the worse do you distast them: and, beeing on your feet, sneake not away like a coward, but salute all your gentle acquaintance, that are spred either on the rushes, or on stooles about you, and draw what troupe you can from the stage after you: the *Mimicks* are beholden to you, for allowing them elbow roome: their Poet cries, perhaps, a pox go with you, but care not for that, theres no musick without frets.

Mary, if either the company, or indisposition of the weather binde you to sit it out, my counsell is then that you turne plain Ape, take up a rush, and tickle the earnest eares of your fellow gallants, to make other fooles fall a laughing: mewe at passionate speeches, blare at merrie, finde fault with the musicke, whew at the childrens Action, whistle at the songs: and above all, curse the sharers, that whereas the same day you had bestowed forty shillings on an embrodered Felt and Feather, (Scotch-fashion) for your mistres in the Court, or your punck in the city, within two houres after, you encounter with the very same block on the stage, when the haberdasher swore to you the impression was extant but that morning.[31]

The advantage to modern actors of keeping their audiences in the dark is obvious. Dekker's satire is of course an exaggeration, but as a burlesque of a gull's actions and motivations it is exactly parallel to other burlesques of gallant behaviour in the induction to *Cynthia's Revels*, one of the earliest boy plays at the Blackfriars in 1601, and *The Isle of Gulls*, another Blackfriars play of 1606.

The other piece of evidence from the Blackfriars in 1608 tells of one effect of the kind of wilfulness described by Dekker. John Fletcher in 1608 wrote a careful and ambitious work, *The Faithful Shepherdess*, essentially an Arcadian pastoral drama of a type previously played only before Court or university audiences. It did not take at all on its first commercial appearance. As Fletcher angrily reported

It is a pastorall Tragic-comedie, which the people seeing when it was plaid, having ever had a singuler guift in defining, concluded to be a play of country hired Shepheards in gray cloakes, with curtaild dogs in strings, sometimes laughing together, and sometimes killing one another: And missing whitsun ales, creame, wassel and morris-dances, began to be angry.

The audience that received Fletcher's play with such lower-class expectation was at the Blackfriars watching a boy company. Shortly afterwards the King's Men took over the theatre and performed Beaumont and Fletcher's *Philaster*, a modified version of the same kind of play, which had an enormous success and created a fashion for tragi-comedy to outlast the Stuart reign. Such apparent inconsistency on the part of the Blackfriars audiences should warn us first of the danger of making too absolute a distinction between the audiences at one kind of playhouse and another. Secondly the success of *Philaster* and the subsequent Beaumont and Fletcher plays should show that the poets were on occasion capable of forcing a new dramatic fashion on their wayward brethren. Catering to existing tastes was not the sole function of the Shakespearean dramatists.

4. CHANGES IN FASHION

The perspective that still remains to be laid down in this portrait of playhouse audiences is the chronological one. Plays such as *Faustus* and *The Spanish Tragedy* were popular at the Fortune until the theatres were closed, but the plays that were written for the Cockpit and Blackfriars in Caroline times were vastly different from the products of Shakespeare's Globe and the playhouses that preceded it. One group of playhouses, the Curtain, Rose and Swan before 1600 and the Red Bull and Fortune afterwards, retained a fairly consistent repertory throughout the whole seventy years. The plays of Shakespeare's company on the whole kept in step with their fellows' amphitheatre plays until some time after 1608,

when the hall playhouses started moving away to end up with the
Caroline fashion. One cannot really speak of a hall playhouse style of
repertory before the King's Men became themselves hall players; it was
rather a boy company repertory before that, one that was not taken up by
the adults. To see the separate repertories in Harbage's term as 'rival
traditions' before 1609, one working-class and the other aristocratic, is
misleading, and even later it would be an over-simplification, though
differences there certainly were. The hall playhouse plays from the start
had music and masquing while the amphitheatres had jigs and thunder.
The hall plays of the later Blackfriars did take over the tradition of wit and
aristocratic pastoral rather than rant and huffing parts, and the boys'
Blackfriars plays had a good deal of sexual licence, which soon returned
under the King's company. But neither tradition was exclusive of features
or even plays belonging to the other, and where Shakespeare's Globe fits
into the picture before 1609 is a still unresolved question. Even after his
company had moved into the Blackfriars they chose to play *Mucedorus*,
perhaps the most popular of all the lower-class plays, and they performed
it before the King. Burbage appears to have played Jeronimo in their
version of *The Spanish Tragedy* until not long before his death in 1619. The
Untuned Kennel debate of 1630 suggests that so much great gulf as there
was had been fixed between individual hall playhouses as well as between
halls and amphitheatres. Not unless we knew the complete repertory of
all the major playhouses for much of the period, which we do not, should
we be able to trace the chronology or even the degree of change with
confidence and precision.

It takes a perspective of forty or fifty years to recognise real changes
in repertories and audience fashions. Differences did undoubtedly grow
in the course of time. It is hard to visualise *Faustus* being staged in the
hall playhouse repertory in 1620 quite as John Melton described it at the
Fortune. By 1632 Jonson was looking back on the fashion still current at
the Fortune as one belonging wholly to former days. In *The Magnetic
Lady* he summarised the plot of an old play that sounds suspiciously
like Beaumont's burlesque of the same fashion for knights errant in *The
Knight of the Burning Pestle* in 1607:

if a Child could be borne, in a Play, and grow up to a man, i' the first Scene,
before hee went off the Stage; and then after to come forth a Squire, and bee
made a Knight: and that Knight to travell betweene the Acts, and doe wonders
i' the holy land, or else where; kill Paynims, wild Boores, dun Cowes, and other
Monsters; beget him a reputation, and marry an Emperours Daughter for his
Mistris; convert her Fathers Countrey; and at last come home, lame . . . These
miracles would please, I assure you.[32]

Sidney and Beaumont had fired first, long before, but it was a still-
living target in the open playhouses. One of Jonson's tribe of followers,

Richard Brome, copied him in *The Antipodes* (1638) with a scene in which a lord reproves an actor for various old-fashioned tricks including extempore clowning:

> when you are
> To speake to your coactors in the Scene,
> You hold interloquutions with the Audients.
> *Bi[play].* That is a way my Lord has bin allow'd
> On elder stages to move mirth and laughter.
> *Letoy.* Yes in the dayes of *Tarlton* and *Kempe*,
> Before the stage was purg'd from barbarisme,
> And brought to the perfection it now shines with.   (II.ii)

What seems to have happened in the twilight of the Stuart Gods is that the amphitheatre playhouses soldiered on with an old repertory while the hall playhouses recruited the new plays. In such circumstances the gulf would inevitably widen. The analogy with the world of fashion in dress, where some keep up to date and others stick to the clothes of their youth, was recognised by Middleton in the epistle to *The Roaring Girl*:

The fashion of play-making, I can properly compare to nothing, so naturally, as the alteration in apparell. For in the time of the Great-crop-doublet, your huge bombasted plaies, quilted with mighty words to leane purpose was onely then in fashion. And as the doublet fell, neater inventions beganne to set up. Now in the time of sprucenes, our plaies followe the nicenes of our Garments, single plots, quaint conceits, letcherous jests, drest up in hanging sleeves, and those are fit for the Times and the Tearmers.

Middleton's analogy was drawn up as early as 1611, and the fact that it was as pertinent in 1642 as in 1611 shows the slowness of the changes being mapped, and perhaps the thoroughness of the split that lasted so many years. The one play that, according to Anthony Scoloker, had managed to 'please all' was *Hamlet*; but that was at the Globe in 1601.[33] When the plays that occupied the stage in the great years that followed fell out of fashion then, by 1642, it was indeed, as Harison put it, good night to the players.

Appendix: A Select List of Plays and their Playhouses

The following list is designed as a basis for reference from specific plays to their company and playhouse. It is arranged in alphabetical order of plays, by the first proper name in the titles, which are given as regularised in *ES* and *JCS*. It only includes those extant plays which can be assigned with reasonable confidence to a particular company and playhouse. The information has been compiled largely from *ES* III–IV, *JCS* III–V and Harbage, *Annals of English Drama 975–1700*, third edition, revised by Sylvia Stoler Wagonheim, 1989, with a few modifications. The entries incorporate, for instance, suggestions about dating Ford's later plays (post-1628) in Andrew Gurr, 'Singing through the Chatter: Ford and Contemporary Theatrical Fashion', in *John Ford: Critical Re-Visions*, ed. Michael Neill (Cambridge 1988), pp. 81–96.

Similar names were sometimes used by different playing companies, chiefly the various Queen's and Prince's companies, and the King's Revels. Queen Elizabeth's is called Queen's, while Anne's and Henrietta's are indicated by the personal name. The first Jacobean Prince's company is called Prince's, and the post-1615 companies are called Prince Charles's. All the boy companies have the name 'Children' in their title. Thus the King's Revels Children of 1607–9 can be distinguished from the Salisbury Court King's Revels company. The company of boys who played at the first Blackfriars are called the Chapel Children, and the company which ran at the second Blackfriars from 1599 to 1608 under a variety of names (Revels Children, Queen's Revels Children, Children of the Chapel) are uniformly called Blackfriars Children, even after their move in 1608 to the Whitefriars playhouse. However, both of the Paul's boy companies are called Paul's Children. Beeston's Boys retain their title because they were not strictly a company of children.

Some of the details in the list, notably those relating to Shakespeare's plays, are subjects for continuing debate. In particular the evidence for the assignment of Chamberlain's Company plays dated between 1597 and 1599 to a particular playhouse and King's Company plays from after 1609 to the Globe or the Blackfriars is inadequate. Where a playhouse is positively assigned it means that the playhouse named has been specifically linked with the play in question. The naming of one playhouse does not mean that a play was necessarily performed only at that playhouse. Where a later performance by a different company or at a different playhouse is known, it is also noted. A play noted as performed by Beeston's Boys in 1639 indicates that it appears on Beeston's list of that year, naming the plays he wanted protected for his company. The dates given for many plays are conjectural. They usually relate to first performance rather than to the time of original composition.

PLAY	AUTHOR	DATE	COMPANY	PLAYHOUSE
Aglaura	Suckling	1637	King's	Blackfriars
Albertus Wallenstein	Glapthorne	1634–9	King's	Globe
The Alchemist	Jonson	1610	King's	Blackfriars
All Fools	Chapman	1601	Blackfriars Children	Blackfriars
All's Lost by Lust	Middleton and Rowley	1617–19 1639	Queen Anne's Beeston's Boys	Red Bull Cockpit
All's Well That Ends Well	Shakespeare	1602?	Chamberlain's	Globe
Amends for Ladies	Field	1610–11	Blackfriars Children	Whitefriars
Amyntas	Randolph	1630	King's Revels	Salisbury Court
The Antipodes	Brome	1636–8	Queen Henrietta's	Salisbury Court
The Antiquary	Marmion	1634–6	Queen Henrietta's	Cockpit
Antonio and Mellida	Marston	1599	Paul's Children	Paul's
Antonio's Revenge	Marston	1600	Paul's Children	Paul's
Antony and Cleopatra	Shakespeare	1608	King's	Globe
Anything for a Quiet Life	Middleton	1620–1	King's	Blackfriars
Argalus and Parthenia	Glapthorne	1637–8	Beeston's Boys	Cockpit
The Arraignment of Paris	Peele	1581–4	Chapel Children	first Blackfriars
As You Like It	Shakespeare	1599	Chamberlain's	Globe
Friar Bacon and Friar Bungay	Greene	1589 1592 1594 1602	Strange's Queen's/Sussex's Admiral's Prince's	Theatre? Rose Rose Fortune
The Ball	Shirley	1632	Queen Henrietta's	Cockpit
Sir John Van Olden Barnavelt	Fletcher	1619	King's	Globe?
Bartholomew Fair	Jonson	1614	Lady Elizabeth's	Hope
The Bashful Lover	Massinger	1636	King's	Blackfriars
The Battle of Alcazar	Peele	c. 1589	Admiral's	Rose?
The Beggar's Bush	Fletcher (and Massinger?)	1615–22	King's	Blackfriars
Believe As You List	Massinger	1631	King's	Blackfriars?
The Bird in a Cage	Shirley	1633	Queen Henrietta's	Cockpit
The Blind Beggar of Alexandria	Chapman	1596	Admiral's	Rose
1 The Blind Beggar of Bednal Green	Chettle and Day	1600 c. 1631 c. 1634	Admiral's Prince Charles's Prince Charles's	Rose Salisbury Court Red Bull
The Bloody Banquet	Drue	1639	Beeston's Boys	Cockpit
The Bloody Brother (Rollo)	Fletcher	1617?	King's	Globe/Blackfriars
Blurt Master Constable	Dekker	1601	Paul's Children	Paul's

PLAY	AUTHOR	DATE	COMPANY	PLAYHOUSE
The Bondman	Massinger	1623	Lady Elizabeth's	Cockpit
		1639	Beeston's Boys	Cockpit
Bonduca	Fletcher	1611–14	King's	Globe?/ Blackfriars?
The Brazen Age	Heywood	1610–13	Queen Anne's	Red Bull
Brennoralt	Suckling	1639–41	King's	Blackfriars
The Bride	Nabbes	1638	Beeston's Boys	Cockpit
The Broken Heart	Ford	1629?	King's	Blackfriars
The Brothers	Shirley	1641?	King's	Blackfriars
Bussy D'Ambois	Chapman	1604	Paul's Children	Paul's
		c. 1606	Blackfriars Children	Blackfriars
		1634	King's	Blackfriars
The Conspiracy and Tragedy of Byron	Chapman	1607–8	Blackfriars Children	Blackfriars
Charles Duke of Byron	Chapman	1608	Blackfriars Children	Blackfriars
The Captain	Fletcher	1609–12	King's	Globe?/ Blackfriars?
The Captives	Heywood	1624	Lady Elizabeth's	Cockpit
The Cardinal	Shirley	1641	King's	Blackfriars
Catiline	Jonson	1611	King's	Globe?/Blackfriars
Chabot	Chapman	c. 1613?	Lady Elizabeth's	Hope?
		1635	Queen Henrietta's	Cockpit
A Challenge for Beauty	Heywood	1635	King's	Globe/Blackfriars
The Chances	Fletcher	1617	King's	Blackfriars
The Changeling	Middleton and Rowley	1622	Lady Elizabeth's	Cockpit
		1639	Beeston's Boys	Cockpit
A Chaste Maid in Cheapside	Middleton	1613	Lady Elizabeth's	Swan
1 The Cid	Rutter	1637–8	Beeston's Boys	Cockpit
The City Madam	Massinger	1632	King's	Blackfriars
The City Match	Mayne	1637–8	King's	Blackfriars
The City Nightcap	Davenport	1624	Lady Elizabeth's	Cockpit
		c. 1639	Beeston's Boys	Cockpit
Claracilla	Killigrew	1635–6	Queen Henrietta's	Cockpit
Coriolanus	Shakespeare	1608	King's	Globe
The Coronation	Shirley	1635	Queen Henrietta's	Cockpit
		1639	Beeston's Boys	Cockpit
The Costly Whore	Anon	1619–32	Red Bull Company	Red Bull
The Country Captain	Cavendish and Shirley	1639–40	King's	Blackfriars
The Court Beggar	Brome	1639–40	Beeston's Boys	Cockpit
Covent Garden	Nabbes	1633	Queen Henrietta's	Cockpit
The Coxcomb	Beaumont and Fletcher	1608–9	Blackfriars Children	Blackfriars?
		c. 1614	Lady Elizabeth's	
		1622	King's	Globe/Blackfriars
The Cruel Brother	Davenant	1627	King's	Blackfriars
The Cunning Lovers	Brome, Alexander(?)	1638	Beeston's Boys	Cockpit

PLAY	AUTHOR	DATE	COMPANY	PLAYHOUSE
Cupid's Revenge	Beaumont and Fletcher	1608	Blackfriars Children	Blackfriars
Cupid's Whirligig	Sharpham	1608	King's Revels Children	Whitefriars
The Custom of the Country	Fletcher and Massinger	1620	King's	Blackfriars
Cymbeline	Shakespeare	1609	King's	Globe
Cynthia's Revels	Jonson	1600	Blackfriars Children	Blackfriars
The Deserving Favourite	Carlell	1629	King's	Blackfriars
The Devil is an Ass	Jonson	1616	King's	Blackfriars
The Devil's Charter	Barnes	1606	King's	Globe
The Devil's Law-Case	Webster	1617	Queen Anne's	Red Bull
The Distresses	Davenant	1639	King's	Blackfriars
The Double Marriage	Fletcher and Massinger	1619–23	King's	Blackfriars
The Duchess of Malfi	Webster	1614	King's	Blackfriars/Globe
The Duchess of Suffolk	Drue	1624	Palsgrave's	Fortune
The Duke of Milan	Massinger	1621–2	King's	Blackfriars
The Duke's Mistress	Shirley	1636	Queen Henrietta's	Cockpit
The Dumb Knight	Markham and Machin	1607–8	King's Revels Children	Whitefriars
The Dutch Courtesan	Marston	1605	Blackfriars Children	Blackfriars
Eastward Ho!	Chapman, Jonson and Marston	1605	Blackfriars Children	Blackfriars
Edward II	Marlowe	1592 *c.* 1617	Pembroke's Queen Anne's	Theatre? Red Bull
The Elder Brother	Fletcher	1625?	King's	Blackfriars
The Emperor of the East	Massinger	1631	King's	Globe/Blackfriars
Endymion	Lyly	1588	Paul's Children	Paul's
Englishmen for my money	Haughton	1598	Admiral's	Rose
The English Moor	Brome	1637	Queen Henrietta's	Salisbury Court
The English Traveller	Heywood	*c.* 1627?	Queen Henrietta's	Cockpit
Epicene	Jonson	1609	Blackfriars Children	Whitefriars
Every Man in his Humour	Jonson	1598 1605	Chamberlain's King's	Curtain? Globe
Every Man out of his Humour	Jonson	1599	Chamberlain's	Globe
The Example	Shirley	1634 1639	Queen Henrietta's Beeston's Boys	Cockpit Cockpit
Fair Em	Anon	*c.* 1590	Strange's	Rose?
The Fair Favourite	Davenant	1638	King's	Blackfriars
The Fair Maid of Bristow	Anon	*c.* 1604	King's	Globe

PLAY	AUTHOR	DATE	COMPANY	PLAYHOUSE
The Fair Maid of the Inn	Fletcher	1625	King's	Blackfriars
2 The Fair Maid of the West	Heywood	1630–1	Queen Henrietta's	Cockpit
A Fair Quarrel	Middleton and Rowley	1615–17 1639	Prince's Beeston's Boys	Red Bull Cockpit
The Faithful Shepherdess	Fletcher	1608	Blackfriars Children	Blackfriars
The False One	Fletcher and Massinger	1619–23	King's	Blackfriars
The Famous Victories of Henry V	Anon	c. 1588?	Queen's	Bull Inn
The Fatal Contract	Heminges	1638–9?	Queen Henrietta's	Salisbury Court
The Fatal Dowry	Field and Massinger	1617–19	King's	Globe/Blackfriars
Dr Faustus	Marlowe	1588? 1619	Strange's? Prince's	Rose? Fortune
The Fawn	Marston	1605	Blackfriars Children	Blackfriars
A Fine Companion	Marmion	1632–3	Prince Charles's	Salisbury Court
The Fleer	Sharpham	1606	Blackfriars Children	Blackfriars
Fortune by Land and Sea	Heywood and Rowley	1607–9	Queen Anne's	Red Bull
The Four Prentices of London	Heywood	c. 1594?	Admiral's Queen Anne's	Rose Red Bull
Gallathea	Lyly	1584–8	Paul's Children	Paul's
A Game at Chess	Middleton	1624	King's	Globe
The Gamester	Shirley	1633	Queen Henrietta's	Cockpit
The Gentleman Usher	Chapman	1602(?)	Blackfriars Children	Blackfriars
Sir Giles Goosecap	Chapman	1602	Blackfriars Children	Blackfriars
The Goblins	Suckling	1637–41	King's	Blackfriars
The Golden Age	Heywood	1610?	Queen Anne's	Red Bull
The Grateful Servant	Shirley	1629 1639	Queen Henrietta's Beeston's Boys	Cockpit Cockpit
The Great Duke of Florence	Massinger	1627 1639	Queen Henrietta's Beeston's Boys	Cockpit Cockpit
Greene's Tu Quoque	Cooke	1611	Queen Anne's	Red Bull
The Guardian	Massinger	1633	King's	Blackfriars
Hamlet	Shakespeare	1601	Chamberlain's	Globe
Hannibal and Scipio	Nabbes	1635	Queen Henrietta's	Cockpit
The Heir	May	1620	Red Bull Company	Red Bull
Hengist (The Mayor of Quinborough)	Middleton	c. 1610? c. 1617?	King's?	Blackfriars?
1 and 2 Henry IV	Shakespeare	1596–7	Chamberlain's	Theatre?
Henry V	Shakespeare	1599	Chamberlain's	Curtain?/Globe

PLAY	AUTHOR	DATE	COMPANY	PLAYHOUSE
1 Henry VI	Shakespeare	1590?	Admiral's/ Strange's?	Rose?
		1594		Rose
2 and 3 Henry VI	Shakespeare	1592–3?	Pembroke's	Theatre?
Henry VIII	Fletcher and Shakespeare	1613	King's	Globe
Herod and Antipater	Markham and Sampson	1619–22	Red Bull Company	Red Bull
Hoffman	Chettle	1602	Admiral's	Fortune
		c. 1630	Queen Henrietta's	Cockpit
The Hollander (Love's Trial)	Glapthorne	1636	Queen Henrietta's	Cockpit
Holland's Leaguer	Marmion	1631	Prince Charles's	Salisbury Court
The Honest Lawyer	S.S.	1614–15	Queen Anne's	Red Bull
1 and 2 The Honest Whore	Dekker and Middleton	1604–5	Prince's	Fortune
		c. 1635	Queen Henrietta's	Cockpit
The Humorous Courtier	Shirley	1631	Queen Henrietta's	Cockpit
An Humorous Day's Mirth	Chapman	1597	Admiral's	Rose
The Humorous Lieutenant	Fletcher	1619(?)	King's	Blackfriars
Humour out of Breath	Day	1608	King's Revels Children	Whitefriars?
Robert Earl of Huntingdon	Chettle and Munday	1598	Admiral's	Rose
Hyde Park	Shirley	1632	Queen Henrietta's	Cockpit
If It Be Not Good, the Devil Is In It	Dekker	1611–12	Queen Anne's	Red Bull
1 and 2 If You Know Not Me, You Know Nobody	Heywood	1604–5 c. 1630	Queen Anne's Queen Henrietta's	Red Bull Cockpit
The Imposture	Shirley	1640	King's	Blackfriars
The Insatiate Countess	Marston and Barksted	1607–8	Blackfriars Children	Whitefriars
The Iron Age	Heywood	1612–13	Queen Anne's	Red Bull
The Island Princess	Fletcher	1619–21	King's	Blackfriars
The Isle of Gulls	Day	1606	Blackfriars Children	Blackfriars
The Jew of Malta	Marlowe	1589	Strange's/ Admiral's	Theatre?
		1594	Admiral's	Rose
		c. 1632	Queen Henrietta's	Cockpit
A Jovial Crew	Brome	1641	Beeston's Boys	Cockpit
Julius Caesar	Shakespeare	1599	Chamberlain's	Globe
The Just Italian	Davenant	1629	King's	Blackfriars
A King and No King	Beaumont and Fletcher	1611	King's	Globe/Blackfriars
King John and Matilda	Davenport	1628–34	Queen Henrietta's	Cockpit
		c. 1640	Beeston's Boys	Cockpit
King Lear	Shakespeare	1605	King's	Globe

PLAY	AUTHOR	DATE	COMPANY	PLAYHOUSE
A Knack to Know a Knave	Anon	1592	Strange's/ Admiral's	Rose
A Knack to Know an Honest Man	Anon	1594	Admiral's	Rose
The Knight of Malta	Fletcher and Field (and Massinger?)	1616–19	King's	Blackfriars
The Knight of the Burning Pestle	Beaumont	1607	Blackfriars Children	Blackfriars
The Lady Mother	Glapthorne	1635	King's Revels	Salisbury Court
The Lady of Pleasure	Shirley	1635	Queen Henrietta's	Cockpit
		1639	Beeston's Boys	Cockpit
The Lady's Privilege	Glapthorne	1637–40	Beeston's Boys	Cockpit
The Lady's Trial	Ford	1638	Beeston's Boys	Cockpit
A Larum for London	Anon	1594–1600	Chamberlain's	Globe
The Late Lancashire Witches	Brome and Heywood	1634	King's	Globe
The Laws of Candy	Fletcher? and Ford?	1619–23	King's	Blackfriars
Law Tricks	Day	1604	Blackfriars Children	Blackfriars
The Little French Lawyer	Fletcher and Massinger	1619–23	King's	Blackfriars
The London Prodigal	Anon	1604	King's	Globe
Look About You	Anon	1599(?)	Admiral's	Rose
The Lost Lady	Berkeley	1637–8	King's	Blackfriars
Love and Honour	Davenant	1634	King's	Blackfriars
Love Tricks (The School of Compliment)	Shirley	1625	Lady Elizabeth's	Cockpit
		1631	Queen Henrietta's	Cockpit
		1639	Beeston's Boys	Cockpit
The Lover's Melancholy	Ford	1628	King's	Globe/Blackfriars
Love's Cruelty	Shirley	1631	Queen Henrietta's	Cockpit
		1639	Beeston's Boys	Cockpit
Love's Labours Lost	Shakespeare	1594?	Chamberlain's	Theatre?/Globe/ Blackfriars
Love's Metamorphosis	Lyly	1589–90	Paul's Children	Paul's
Love's Mistress	Heywood	1634	Queen Henrietta's	Cockpit
Love's Sacrifice	Ford	1631(?)	Queen Henrietta's	Cockpit
		1639	Beeston's Boys	Cockpit
The Loyal Subject	Fletcher	1618	King's	Blackfriars
Macbeth	Shakespeare	1606	King's	Globe
A Mad World, my Masters	Middleton	1605–6	Paul's Children	Paul's
		c. 1640	Queen Henrietta's	Salisbury Court
The Madcap	Heminges	1633	King's Revels	Fortune
The Magnetic Lady	Jonson	1632	King's	Blackfriars

PLAY	AUTHOR	DATE	COMPANY	PLAYHOUSE
The Maid in the Mill	Fletcher and Rowley	1623	King's	Blackfriars?
The Maid of Honour	Massinger	1621–2	Red Bull Company	Red Bull
		1632	Queen Henrietta's	Cockpit
		1639	Beeston's Boys	Cockpit
The Maid's Revenge	Shirley	1626	Queen Henrietta's	Cockpit
		1639	Beeston's Boys	Cockpit
The Maid's Tragedy	Beaumont and Fletcher	1610	King's	Blackfriars
A Maidenhead Well Lost	Heywood	1625–34	Queen Henrietta's	Cockpit
The Malcontent	Marston	1603	Blackfriars Children King's	Blackfriars Globe
The Martyred Soldier	Shirley	1627–35	Queen Henrietta's	Cockpit
A Match at Midnight	Rowley	1621–3	Red Bull Company	Red Bull
Match Me in London	Dekker	1621?	Red Bull Company	Red Bull
		c. 1630	Queen Henrietta's	Cockpit
May-Day	Chapman	1601–2?	Blackfriars Children	Blackfriars
Measure for Measure	Shakespeare	1603	King's	Globe
The Merchant of Venice	Shakespeare	1596?	Chamberlain's	Theatre
The Merry Devil of Edmonton	Anon	c. 1602	Chamberlain's	Globe
The Merry Wives of Windsor	Shakespeare	1597?	Chamberlain's	Theatre?/Globe/ Blackfriars
Messallina	Richards	1634–6	King's Revels	Salisbury Court
Michaelmas Term	Middleton	1606	Paul's Children	Paul's
Microcosmus	Nabbes	1637	Queen Henrietta's	Salisbury Court
Midas	Lyly	1589	Paul's Children	Paul's
A Midsummer Night's Dream	Shakespeare	1595?	Chamberlain's	Theatre
The Miseries of Enforced Marriage	Wilkins	1606	King's	Globe
Monsieur D'Olive	Chapman	1605	Blackfriars Children	Blackfriars
Mother Bombie	Lyly	c. 1589	Paul's Children	Paul's
Much Ado About Nothing	Shakespeare	1598	Chamberlain's	Curtain?
The Muses' Looking Glass	Randolph	1630	King's Revels	Salisbury Court
The New Inn	Jonson	1629	King's	Blackfriars
A New Way to Pay Old Debts	Massinger	1625	Prince Charles's	Cockpit
		c. 1633	Queen Henrietta's	Cockpit
		1639	Beeston's Boys	Cockpit

PLAY	AUTHOR	DATE	COMPANY	PLAYHOUSE
News from Plymouth	Davenant	1635	King's	Globe
The Noble Stranger	Sharpe	1638–40	Queen Henrietta's	Salisbury Court
The Northern Lass	Brome	1629	King's	Globe/Blackfriars
Northward Ho!	Dekker and Webster	1605	Paul's Children	Paul's
The Novella	Brome	1632–3	King's	Blackfriars
1 Sir John Oldcastle	Drayton, Hathway, Munday and Wilson	1599 1602	Admiral's Worcester's	Rose Rose
Old Fortunatus	Dekker	1599	Admiral's	Rose
The Opportunity	Shirley	1634	Queen Henrietta's	Cockpit
Orlando Furioso	Greene	*c.* 1591	Queen's Admiral's	Rose? Rose
Othello	Shakespeare	1603–4	Chamberlain's	Globe/Blackfriars
1 and 2 The Passionate Lovers	Carlell	1638	King's	Blackfriars
Patient Grissil	Chettle, Dekker and Haughton	1600	Admiral's	Fortune
Pericles	Shakespeare	1608	King's	Globe
Perkin Warbeck	Ford	1632	Queen Henrietta's	Cockpit
Philaster	Beaumont and Fletcher	1609	King's	Globe/Blackfriars
Philotas	Daniel	1604	Blackfriars Children	Blackfriars
The Phoenix	Middleton	1603–4	Paul's Children	Paul's
The Picture	Massinger	1629	King's	Globe/Blackfriars
The Pilgrim	Fletcher	1621?	King's	Blackfriars
The Platonic Lovers	Davenant	1635	King's	Blackfriars
Poetaster	Jonson	1601	Blackfriars Children	Blackfriars
The Poor Man's Comfort	Daborne	1610–17	Queen Anne's	Red Bull
The Prisoners	Killigrew	1632–5	Queen Henrietta's	Cockpit
The Prophetess	Fletcher (and Massinger?)	1622	King's	Blackfriars
The Puritan	Middleton	1606	Paul's Children	Paul's
The Queen and Concubine	Brome	1635–9	King's Revels	Salisbury Court
The Queen of Corinth	Fletcher (and Massinger and Field?)	1616–18	King's	Blackfriars
Ram-Alley	Barry	1607–8	King's Revels Children	Whitefriars
The Rape of Lucrece	Heywood	*c.* 1608 1628 1639	Queen Anne's Queen Henrietta's Beeston's Boys	Red Bull Cockpit Cockpit
The Rebellion	Rawlins	1629–39	King's Revels	Salisbury Court
The Renegado	Massinger	1624 1630 1639	Lady Elizabeth's Queen Henrietta's Beeston's Boys	Cockpit Cockpit Cockpit

PLAY	AUTHOR	DATE	COMPANY	PLAYHOUSE
The Revenge of Bussy	Chapman	c. 1610	Blackfriars Children?	Whitefriars?
The Revenger's Tragedy	Middleton?	1606–7	King's	Globe
Richard II	Shakespeare	1595	Chamberlain's	Theatre?/Globe
Richard III	Shakespeare	1593?	Pembroke's	Theatre?
		1594	Chamberlain's	Theatre?/Globe
The Roaring Girl	Dekker and Middleton	1611	Prince's	Fortune
The Roman Actor	Massinger	1626	King's	Blackfriars
Romeo and Juliet	Shakespeare	1594?	Chamberlain's	Theatre?/Globe
The Royal King and the Loyal Subject	Heywood	1602	Worcester's	Curtain
Rule a Wife and Have a Wife	Fletcher	1624	King's	Blackfriars
Sappho and Phao	Lyly	1583	Chapel/Paul's Children	first Blackfriars
Satiromastix	Dekker	1601	Paul's Children Chamberlain's	Paul's Globe
The Sea Voyage	Fletcher (and Massinger?)	1622	King's	Globe
Sejanus	Jonson	1603	King's	Globe
The Shepherd's Holiday	Rutter	1633–5	Queen Henrietta's	Cockpit
The Shoemaker's Holiday	Dekker	1599	Admiral's	Rose
The Silver Age	Heywood	1610–12	Queen Anne's	Red Bull
The Sisters	Shirley	1642	King's	Blackfriars
Sophonisba (Wonder of Women)	Marston	1605	Blackfriars Children	Blackfriars
The Sophy	Denham	1641	King's	Blackfriars
The Spanish Curate	Fletcher (and Massinger?)	1622	King's	Blackfriars
The Spanish Gypsy	Dekker and Ford	1623	Lady Elizabeth's	Cockpit
		1639	Beeston's Boys	Cockpit
The Spanish Tragedy	Kyd	c. 1587		
		1592–3	Strange's	Rose
		1597–1602	Admiral's	Fortune
The Sparagus Garden	Brome	1635	King's Revels	Salisbury Court
The Staple of News	Jonson	1626	King's	Blackfriars
Captain Thomas Stukeley	Anon	1596	Admiral's	Rose
Swetnam the Woman Hater	Anon	1617–18	Queen Anne's	Red Bull
The Swisser	Wilson	1631	King's	Blackfriars
The Tale of a Tub	Jonson	1633	Queen Henrietta's	Cockpit
1 and 2 Tamburlaine	Marlowe	1587–8	Admiral's Queen Anne's	Theatre/Rose Red Bull
The Taming of the Shrew	Shakespeare	1593?	Chamberlain's	Theatre?/Globe/ Blackfriars
The Tempest	Shakespeare	1610	King's	Blackfriars
Thierry and Theodoret	Fletcher	1613–21	King's	Blackfriars

PLAY	AUTHOR	DATE	COMPANY	PLAYHOUSE
The Three Ladies of London	Wilson	1581	Leicester's	Theatre?
The Three Lords and Three Ladies of London	Wilson	1588	Queen's? Admiral's	Rose?
'Tis Pity She's a Whore	Ford	1630?	Queen Henrietta's	Cockpit
		1639	Beeston's Boys	Cockpit
Titus Andronicus	Shakespeare	1591?	Strange's/ Pembroke's/ Sussex's Chamberlain's	Rose?/Theatre? Rose Globe
The Traitor	Shirley	1631	Queen Henrietta's	Cockpit
The Travels of the Three English Brothers	Day, Rowley and Wilkins	1607	Queen Anne's	Red Bull
A Trick to Catch the Old One	Middleton	1605–6 c. 1607	Paul's Children Blackfriars Children	Paul's Blackfriars
The Turk	Mason	1607	King's Revels Children	Whitefriars
Twelfth Night	Shakespeare	1600	Chamberlain's	Globe
1 Two Angry Women of Abingdon	Porter	c. 1597?	Admiral's	Rose
The Two Maids of Moreclacke	Armin	1606–8	King's Revels Children	Whitefriars
The Two Merry Milkmaids	I.C.	1619–20	Red Bull Company	Red Bull
The Two Noble Kinsmen	Fletcher and Shakespeare	1613?	King's	Blackfriars
The Two Noble Ladies	Anon	1619–23	Red Bull Company	Red Bull
The Unfortunate Lovers	Davenant	1638	King's	Blackfriars
The Unnatural Combat	Massinger	1624–5	King's	Globe
Valentinian	Fletcher	1610–14	King's	Globe?/ Blackfriars?
The Variety	Cavendish	1641–2(?)	King's	Blackfriars
The Virgin Martyr	Dekker and Massinger	1620	Red Bull Company	Red Bull
Volpone	Jonson	1605 1635	King's	Globe Blackfriars
A Warning for Fair Women	Anon	c. 1599	Chamberlain's	Curtain?
The Wars of Cyrus	Anon	1576–80	Chapel Children	first Blackfriars
The Wedding	Shirley	1626–9	Queen Henrietta's	Cockpit
		1639	Beeston's Boys	Cockpit
Westward Ho!	Dekker and Webster	1604	Paul's Children	Paul's
What You Will	Marston	1601	Paul's Children	Paul's
When You See Me, You Know Me	Rowley, S.	1604	Prince's	Fortune

PLAY	AUTHOR	DATE	COMPANY	PLAYHOUSE
The White Devil	Webster	1612	Queen Anne's	Red Bull
		c. 1630	Queen Henrietta's	Cockpit
The Whore of Babylon	Dekker	1606	Prince's	Fortune
The Widow	Middleton	1616	King's	Blackfriars
The Widow's Tears	Chapman	*c.* 1605	Blackfriars Children	Blackfriars
A Wife for a Month	Fletcher	1624	King's	Blackfriars
The Wild Goose Chase	Fletcher	1621?	King's	Blackfriars
The Winter's Tale	Shakespeare	*c.* 1610	King's	Globe
The Wisdom of Doctor Dodypoll	Anon	1599	Paul's Children	Paul's
Wit in a Constable	Glapthorne	1636–8 (revised 1639)	Beeston's Boys	Cockpit
The Witch	Middleton	*c.* 1616	King's	Blackfriars
The Witch of Edmonton	Dekker, Ford and Rowley	1621	Prince Charles's	Cockpit
The Wits	Davenant	1634	King's	Blackfriars
The Witty Fair One	Shirley	1628	Queen Henrietta's	Cockpit
The Woman Hater	Beaumont	*c.* 1606	Paul's Children	Paul's
A Woman is a Weathercock	Field	1609?	Blackfriars Children	Whitefriars
A Woman Killed with Kindness	Heywood	1603	Worcester's	Rose
The Wounds of Civil War	Lodge	*c.* 1588	Admiral's	Theatre/Rose?
The Yorkshire Tragedy	Anon	*c.* 1606	King's	Globe
The Young Admiral	Shirley	1633	Queen Henrietta's	Cockpit
		1639	Beeston's Boys	Cockpit

Notes

𝔖𝔶

The following abbreviations have been used in the Notes and the Bibliography:

C.S.P.	*Calendar of State Papers.*
Dramatic Documents	W. W. Greg (ed.), *Dramatic Documents from the Elizabethan Playhouses* (2 vols., Oxford 1931).
EES	Glynne Wickham, *Early English Stages 1300–1660* (4 vols.; Vol.I London 1959; Vol. II, part 1 1963; Vol. II, part 2 1972; Vol. III 1981).
ELR	*English Literary Renaissance.*
ES	E. K. Chambers, *The Elizabethan Stage* (4 vols., Oxford 1923).
ET	*The Elizabethan Theatre.*
Henslowe's Diary	R. A. Foakes and R. T. Rickert (eds.), *Henslowe's Diary* (Cambridge 1961).
Henslowe Papers	W. W. Greg (ed.), *The Henslowe Papers* (London 1907).
Herbert	J. Q. Adams (ed.), *The Dramatic Records of Sir Henry Herbert* (New Haven 1917).
HLQ	*Huntington Library Quarterly.*
JCS	G. E. Bentley, *The Jacobean and Caroline Stage* (7 vols., Oxford 1941–68).
JEGP	*Journal of English and Germanic Philology.*
MLN	*Modern Language Notes.*
MLR	*Modern Language Review.*
MP	*Modern Philology.*
NQ	*Notes and Queries.*
Nungezer	E. Nungezer, *A Dictionary of Actors and of Other Persons Associated with the Public Representation of Plays in England before 1642* (New Haven 1929).
PMLA	*Publications of the Modern Language Association of America.*
RD	*Renaissance Drama.*
RORD	*Research Opportunities in Renaissance Drama.*
RES	*Review of English Studies.*
Revels History	J. Leeds Barroll, Alexander Leggatt, Richard Hosley and Alvin Kernan, *The Revels History of Drama in English*, Vol. III, 1576–1613 (London 1975).
SB	*Studies in Bibliography.*
SEL	*Studies in English Literature.*

ShAB	Shakespeare Association Bulletin.
ShS	Shakespeare Survey.
ShStud	Shakespeare Studies.
SP	Studies in Philology.
SQ	Shakespeare Quarterly.
ThS	Theatre Survey.
TN	Theatre Notebook.
TR/TRI	Theatre Research (to 1974: then Theatre Research International).
WS	E. K. Chambers, William Shakespeare (2 vols., Oxford 1930).

Besides the editions abbreviated as *Henslowe's Diary* and *Henslowe Papers*, there is a facsimile edition of all the papers: R. A. Foakes (ed.), *The Henslowe Papers* (2 vols., London 1978). Vol. I reproduces the Diary and Vol. II the Papers. Texts quoted from either transcription of the Papers have been checked against the facsimile. References to plays of Shakespeare are to the New Cambridge editions, or, where these are not yet available, to the New Shakespeare. References to Jonson are to the edition of C. H. Herford, P. and E. Simpson (11 vols., Oxford 1925–52). References to Massinger are to *The Plays and Poems of Philip Massinger*, edd. Philip Edwards and Colin Gibson (5 vols., Oxford 1976).

1. INTRODUCTION (pp. 1–26)

There are several general works that deal with the background to the Shakespearean stage, including A. M. Nagler's short book, *Shakespeare's Stage* (New Haven 1958), K. J. Holzknecht's *The Backgrounds of Shakespeare's Plays* (New York 1950) and Bernard Beckerman's still unsurpassed *Shakespeare at the Globe 1599–1609* (New York 1962). A series which offers a useful introductory coverage to sections of the period, with special emphasis on the original staging, includes Peter Thomson's *Shakespeare's Theatre* (London 1983) and Michael Hattaway's *Elizabethan Popular Theatre: Plays in Performance* (London 1982). There is no background study of the whole period up to 1642. The four volumes of *ES* contain the bulk of the information that was available up to 1920 on the theatre background from the mid-sixteenth century to about 1616. The first two volumes of *JCS*, published in 1941, give a history of the playing companies and print some important background documents. Vols. III–V list the extant information about the playwrights and their plays, as it was known by 1954. Vol. VI gives the information about the playhouses, correct up to 1966, and Vol. VII supplies an index for all seven volumes. Volumes III and IV of the *Revels History* contain a set of rather disjointed essays on some of the major aspects of the subject, including an essay by Richard Hosley on the playhouses in Vol. III, and good introductory essays about the later period in Vol. IV. A few of the other essays that throw light on particular aspects are noted below, and a fairly comprehensive list of the more useful publications is given in the Bibliography.

1 See George F. Reynolds, '*Hamlet* at the Globe', *ShS* 9 (1956), 50.
2 See Mark C. Pilkinton, 'The Playhouse in Wine Street, Bristol', *TN* 37 (1983), 14–21.

3 *ES* IV, 269.

4 *JCS* VI, 49–50.

5 *ES* IV, 273–4.

6 *JCS* VI, 29.

7 *Shakespeare's Europe: A Survey of the Condition of Europe at the End of the 16th Century, Being Unpublished Chapters of Fynes Moryson's Itinerary (1617)*, ed. Charles Hughes (second edition, New York 1967), p. 476.

  8 *Henslowe Papers*, p. 106. A facsimile is printed in Foakes (ed.) *The Henslowe Papers*, II.2.41.

9 John Burnett, *A History of the Cost of Living* (London 1969), p. 71.

10 L. C. Knights, *Drama and Society in the Age of Jonson* (London 1937), p. 174.

11 Burnett, *Cost of Living*, p. 112.

12 See Laurence Stone, *The Crisis of the Aristocracy 1558–1641* (Oxford 1964), pp. 386–403.

13 *JCS* VI, 54.

14 This question is considered at greater length in Andrew Gurr, *Playgoing in Shakespeare's London* (Cambridge 1987), pp. 170–7.

15 See C. C. Mish, 'Comparative Popularity of Early Fiction and Drama', *NQ* 197 (1952), 269–70.

16 Michael Neill, '"Wits most accomplished Senate": The Audience of the Caroline Private Theatres', *SEL* 18 (1978), 359.

17 Alfred Harbage's *Shakespeare and the Rival Traditions* (New York 1952) analyses the differences between hall and amphitheatre plays, though he overstates his case about the different audiences. See R. Ornstein, *The Moral Vision of Jacobean Tragedy* (Madison 1962), p. 12, and *Playgoing in Shakespeare's London*, pp. 153–64.

18 *ES* IV, 332.

19 Valerie Pearl, *London and the Outbreak of the Puritan Revolution* (London 1961), p. 41.

20 *JCS* IV, 555.

21 G. E. Bentley, *The Profession of Dramatist in Shakespeare's Time, 1590–1642* (Princeton 1971), p. 30.

22 Ann Haaker, 'The Plague, the Theater and the Poet', *RD* n.s. 1 (1968), 283–306.

23 Bentley, *The Profession of Dramatist*, p. 131.

24 *Ibid.*, p. 270.

25 Richard Hosley, *Revels History*, p. 207. Hosley's view of the use of hall screens for acting has been challenged, on the grounds that student players at Cambridge colleges did not use them. See p. 23.

26 The two traditions have been studied separately. Glynne Wickham (*EES*) emphasises Court influence on staging, while Robert Weiman (*Shakespeare and the Popular Tradition in the Theater*, ed. and trans. Robert Schwartz, London and Baltimore 1978) emphasises the transfer of popular traditions into the London theatres.

27 Jonson, VII, 735.

28 M. C. Bradbrook, 'Shakespeare and the Multiple Theatres of Jacobean London', *ET* 6 (1978), 94.

29 See Jonson I, 24–31, and David Bevington, *Tudor Drama and Politics* (Cambridge Mass. 1968), pp. 262–88.
30 Jonson, VIII, 601.
31 Marie Axton, *The Queen's Two Bodies* (London 1978), makes a strong case for the Inns-of-Court lawyers using their entertainments as opportunities for political comment in allegorical form. The concept of allegorising, or the 'application' of fictional or historical instances to contemporary events, Jonson said in the dedication to *Volpone* in 1607 had 'grown a trade'.

2. THE COMPANIES (pp. 27–39)

A comprehensive history of the playing companies who kept a foot-hold in London between 1574 and 1642 has not yet been written. J. Leeds Barroll gives a brief general survey of the early conditions in the *Revels History* III. Most of the extant information on each company up to 1616 appears in *ES* II, and for the companies from before that time until 1642 in *JCS* I. The major documents are reprinted in *ES* IV, *Henslowe's Diary* and *Herbert*. The history of the companies is slowly being augmented by the *Records of Early English Drama* volumes giving the recordings of provincial performances for all the major Elizabethan centres. On the players and company membership, *Nungezer* has undergone some supplementation and correction, and work is also being done to correct the work of T. W. Baldwin in *Organisation and Personnel of the Shakespearean Company* (Princeton 1927). The operations of the various Masters of the Revels have been examined, both for their work of censorship and their other functions. These studies are cited in the notes and the Bibliography.

1 *ES* IV, 270.
2 *ES* IV, 324 and 337.
3 See note on playhouse origins, p. 118.
4 *ES* II, 86.
5 *ES* II, 87–8.
6 See Janet S. Leongard, 'An Elizabethan Lawsuit: John Brayne, his Carpenter, and the Building of the Red Lion Theatre', *SQ* 35 (1984), 298–310. For a comprehensive survey of early playhouse building, see John Orrell, *The Human Stage: English Theatre Design 1567–1640* (Cambridge 1988).
7 *ES* IV, 200.
8 *ES* II, 462.
9 *ES* II, 104–5.
10 *ES* IV, 302.
11 *ES* IV, 202.
12 See Michael Shapiro, *Children of the Revels. The Boy Companies of Shakespeare's Time and their Plays* (New York 1977), pp. 10–29.
13 *ES* II, 36.
14 *Dramatic Documents*, p. 19.
15 *ES* II, 123.
16 *Dramatic Documents*, p. 12.
17 *WS* I, 42.
18 For a more detailed account of the changes, see p. 129, and John Orrell and

Andrew Gurr, 'What the Rose can tell us', *Times Literary Supplement*, 9–15 June 1989, pp. 636, 649; reprinted with additions in *Antiquity* 63 (1989), 421–9.

19 *Henslowe Papers*, p. 40.

20 *Dramatic Documents*, p. 47.

21 See above, note 17.

22 See for instance Scott McMillin, 'Casting for Pembroke's Men: the *Henry VI* Quartos and *The Taming of A Shrew*', *SQ* 23 (1972), 141–59; G. M. Pinciss, 'Shakespeare, Her Majesty's Players, and Pembroke's Men', *ShS* 27 (1974), 129–36; David George, 'Shakespeare and Pembroke's Men', *SQ* 32 (1981), 305–23; and Karl P. Wentersdorf, 'The Origin and Personnel of the Pembroke Company', *TRI* 5 (1979), 45–68. The case for Shakespeare having belonged either to the Queen's Men or Pembroke's seems evenly divided.

23 *ES* IV, 311–12.

24 The only comprehensive study of the players' travels is John Tucker Murray's *English Dramatic Companies 1558–1642* (2 vols., London 1910). His work is now being corrected and supplemented by the volumes in the *Records of Early English Drama* series.

25 The appearance of players' names in playtexts does not necessarily mean that they were members of the company for whom the play was originally written. Generally the minor rather than the principal players were named in playscripts, along with any changes made later. Will Kemp must have been added to the second quarto text of *Romeo and Juliet*, for instance. He was in Strange's before the middle of 1594 while the play was being performed by Pembroke's, to judge from the echoes of it that appear in the Pembroke memorial texts. See Pinciss, 'Shakespeare, Her Majesty's Players, and Pembroke's Men', pp. 135–6.

26 Possibly their 'harey the vi' staged in 1594 was Shakespeare's 1 *Henry VI*.

27 In September 1594 the Chamberlain's Men are recorded as asking for leave to play at the Cross Keys Inn in Gracechurch Street in the City. They probably wanted it as a winter house to supplement their outdoor Theatre.

28 See William Ingram, 'The Closing of the Theaters in 1597: A Dissenting View', *MP* 69 (1971–2), 105–15.

29 *ES* II, 152.

30 But see *Henslowe's Diary*, p. xxxix, and Neil Carson, *A Companion to Henslowe's Diary*, pp. 34–9.

31 *ES* II, 158.

32 Baldwin, *Organisation and Personnel*, p. 52.

33 See Andrew Gurr, 'Money or Audiences: The Impact of Shakespeare's Globe'. *TN* 42 (1988), 3–14.

34 *ES* II, 173.

35 *ES* II, 225.

36 *ES* II, 231.

37 Shapiro, *Children of the Revels*, p. 21.

38 Reavley Gair, *The Children of Paul's: The Story of a Theatre Company, 1553–1608* (Cambridge 1982), pp. 118–27.

39 *ES* II, 44, 52.

40 In a letter by Sir Thomas Edmondes, in *Court and Times of James I*, ed. Thomas Birch (2 vols., London 1848), 1.60–1.

41 Mark Eccles, 'Martin Peerson and the Blackfriars', *ShS* 11 (1958), 101.

42 See *Byron*, ed. John Margeson (Manchester 1988), p. 276.

43 *ES* III, 258.

44 A concise account of the war is given in Jonson I, chapter on *Poetaster*.

45 *JCS* I, 151. The loss of their playbooks and apparel in the fire was the first of a series of disasters that eclipsed them by 1625.

46 C. J. Sisson, 'Notes on Early Stuart Stage History', *MLR* 37 (1942), 34. Sisson gives the records of the Red Bull litigation on pp. 30–6. They are also summarised in *ES* II, 236–40.

47 *ES* II, 238.

48 See Andrew Gurr, 'Intertextuality in Henslowe', *SQ* 39 (1988), 394–8.

49 Neil Carson's examination of Henslowe's dealings with his playing companies gives the best detail. See *A Companion to Henslowe's Diary*, Chap. 2.

50 *Herbert*, p. 65.

51 *JCS* I, 201.

52 *JCS* I, 4–5.

53 *JCS* I, 328.

54 *JCS* I, 237.

55 *JCS* II, 684.

56 *JCS* I, 234.

57 G. E. Bentley, 'The Salisbury Court Theater and Its Boy Players', *HLQ* 409 (1977), 137.

58 *Ibid.*, p. 143.

59 *Ibid.*, p. 141.

60 *Herbert*, p. 67.

61 *JCS* I, 332–3. See also Martin Butler, *Theatre and Crisis 1632–1642*, Chap. 5.

62 See Arthur H. Nethercot, *Sir William Davenant* (New York 1938; rev. edn 1967), Chap. 11.

63 *JCS* VI, 104–5.

64 Sisson, 'Early Stuart Stage History', 33.

65 *ES* I, 352; *JCS* I, 43.

66 *ES* II, 256–7.

67 *ES* I, 356n.

68 *ES* I, 372.

69 Burnett, *Cost of Living*, p. 71.

70 Irwin Smith, *Shakespeare's Blackfriars Playhouse* (New York 1964), p. 265; *JCS* I, 32–3.

71 *ES* I, 369.

72 Sisson, 'Early Stuart Stage History', 33.

73 *JCS* VI, 243.

74 *ES* I, 373 and note; Bentley, *The Profession of Dramatist*, p. 131.

75 See *ES* I, 71.

76 *ES* IV, 263.

77 *Herbert*, pp. 5–6.

78 W. R. Streitberger, ed. *Jacobean and Caroline Revels Accounts 1603–1642* (Oxford 1986), pp. x, xviii.

79 *Ibid.*, p. 78.
80 *JCS* i, 178.
81 *Herbert*, pp. 44–5.
82 *ES* iv, 263.
83 *ES* iv, 338–9.
  84 *Herbert*, p. 22.
85 *Ibid.*, pp. 18–19.
86 *Ibid.*, p. 23.
87 *ES* iv, 267.
88 G. E. Bentley, 'Lenten Performances in the Jacobean and Caroline Theaters', in *Essays on Shakespeare and Elizabethan Drama*, ed. R. Hosley (New York 1963), pp. 351–60; and J. Leeds Barroll, 'The Chronology of Shakespeare's Jacobean Plays and the Dating of *Antony and Cleopatra*', in *Essays on Shakespeare*, ed. Gordon Ross Brown (Philadelphia 1965), pp. 122–4.
89 *JCS* ii, 690.

3. THE PLAYERS (pp. 80–114)

The best general account of Elizabethan players is M. C. Bradbrook's *The Rise of the Common Player* (London 1962). Alexander Leggatt has an essay in the *Revels History* that covers the main points. Nungezer's *Dictionary of Actors* is an alphabetical list of all the known English players up to 1642, with the contemporary references to them. *ES* ii contains a list with more cursory details, and *JCS* ii gives the players between 1616 and 1642 in rather more detail. Michael Shapiro supplements Hillebrand's work on the boy actors in Chap. 1 of *Children of the Revels*, and lists the repertories and court performances in appendices. On acting R. A. Foakes has an illuminating article, 'The Player's Passion: Some Notes on Elizabethan Psychology and Acting', in *Essays and Studies* n.s. 7 (1954), 62–77. B. L. Joseph's monograph *Elizabethan Acting* (London 1951; rev. edn 1964) has some information, chiefly about gesture. The argument in 1951 was that acting was formal. The 1964 revision redeploys the evidence and concludes that acting was naturalistic. Lise-Lone Marker has summarised the current view about the relations between the teaching of rhetoric and acting in 'Nature and Decorum in the Theory of Elizabethan Acting', *ET* 2 (1970).

1 The social origins of some players are described in detail by Bradbrook, *Rise of the Common Player*.
2 J. Stephens, *Essayes and Characters* (1615), V6r-X1r. Cocke revised his essay for the second edition of Stephens's collection, which was also printed in 1615. See *ES* iv, 255–7.
3 J. Overbury, *New Characters* (1615), M5v-M6v. See *ES* iv, 258–9.
4 The Dulwich gallery has a painting allegedly done by Burbage. See Nungezer, p.77.
5 Bradbrook, *Rise of the Common Player*, p. 203.
6 Alexandra Mason, 'The Social Status of Theatrical People', *SQ* 18 (1967), 429–30.
7 Nungezer, p. 73.
8 *ES* iv, 319–20.

9 Nungezer, p. 219.

10 *Ibid.*, pp. 347–54.

11 *Ibid.*, p. 360.

12 *Ibid.*, p. 363.

13 *Thalia's Banquet* (1620), quoted in Nungezer, pp. 362–3.

14 Quoted in Nungezer, pp. 356–7.

15 A reference to Wilson by Thomas Lodge in his *Defence of Poetry, Musick, and Stage Plays* (1580) has been taken as a compliment to his learning.

16 See R. C. Bald, 'Will, My Lord of Leicester's Jesting Player', *NQ* 204 (1959), 112; and J. A. Bryant jr, 'Shakespeare's Falstaff and the Mantle of Dick Tarlton', *SP* 51 (1954), 149–62.

17 H. D. Gray, 'The Roles of William Kemp', *MLR* 25 (1930), 261–73.

18 C. S. Felver, *Robert Armin, Shakespeare's Fool*, Kent State University Bulletin Research Series 5 (Kent 1961).

19 Nungezer, p. 8.

20 Bradbrook, *Rise of the Common Player*, p. 196.

21 Nungezer, p. 6. The most up-to-date information about Burbage is collected in Mark Eccles 'Elizabethan Actors I: A–D', *NQ* 236 (1991), 38–49. See especially p. 43

22 Nungezer, p. 11.

23 *Ibid.*, pp 67–8.

24 See above p. 44.

25 Nungezer, p. 70.

26 *Ibid.*, pp. 140–1.

27 *Ibid.*, p. 140.

28 *JCS* ii, 401.

29 *JCS* ii, 541.

30 J. B. Streett, 'The Durability of Boy Actors', *NQ* 218 (1973), 461–5.

31 Nungezer, p. 68.

32 Bradbrook, *Rise of the Common Player*, p. 238; and see Shapiro, *Children of the Revels*, p. 4.

33 *See* Joseph, *Elizabethan Acting* (1964), and Andrew Gurr, 'Elizabethan Action', *SP* 63 (1966), 144–56.

34 For an indication of the pressure put on the boy-company managers to prove their respectability by maintaining the educational and chorister functions, see Bradbrook, *Rise of the Common Player*, p.238.

35 Compare Shakespeare's Latin in 2 and 3 *Henry VI* with the versions transcribed in the pirated texts.

36 Bradbrook, *Rise of the Common Player*, p. 205.

37 We cannot understand the following passage in Chapman's *Gentleman Usher* (1601) unless we have some idea of the niceties of academic theory and the theoretical need for the orator to stir up in himself the actual passion he is to convey. Sarpego, a 'fustian lord', first ventures to display his talents:

> when I in Padua schoolde it,
> I plaid in one of *Plautus* Comedies,
> Namely *Curculo*, where his part I acted,
> Projecting from the poore summe of foure lines,

Forty faire actions . . .
Alp. How like you Lords, this stirring action?
Stro. In a cold morning it were good my Lord . . .
Med. My Lord, away with these scholastique wits,
    Lay the invention of your speech on me,
    And the performance too; ile play my parte,
    That you shall say, Nature yeelds more than Art.
*Alp.*Bee't so resolv'd; unartificiall truth
    An unfaind passion can decipher best.

38 Gurr, 'Elizabethan Action', p. 144.

39 The important development is the noun, which signals the growth of a concept of character-impersonation. There is a reference to 'personated' devils in 1594, but Marston seems to have been the neologist of 'personation'.

40 The following passage, in the anonymous *Nero* of 1623, is typical in its terminology:

Nero. Come Sirs, I faith, how did you like my acting?
    What? wast not as you lookt for?
Epaph. Yes my Lord, and much beyond.
Nero. Did I not doe it to the life?
Epaph. The very doing never was so lively
    As now this counterfeyting.

41 BM. MS. Sloane 3709, fol. 8r.

42 See also Joseph, *Elizabethan Acting*, pp. 47–71.

43 See M. C. Bradbrook, *Themes and Conventions in Elizabethan Tragedy* (Cambridge 1936).

44 See Lawrence Babb, 'Sorrow and Love on the Elizabethan Stage', *ShAB*, 18 (1943), 140.

45 Richard Brome, *The Antipodes* (1638), II.ii, describing what in 1638 was thought of as antiquated.

46 S. L. Bethell, *Shakespeare and the Popular Dramatic Tradition* (London 1944), pp. 87–9.

47 *Shakespeare at the Globe 1599–1609* (New York 1962), p. 130.

48 *Organisation and Personnel.* The most substantial questioning of his theory is in Skiles Howard, 'A Re-examination of Baldwin's Theory of Acting Lines', *ThS* 26 (1985), 1–20.

49 Some of his earlier parts are noted by Baldwin Maxwell, *Studies in Beaumont, Fletcher and Massinger* (Chapel Hill 1939), pp. 74–83.

50 See Skiles Howard, *op. cit.*

51 *ES* IV, 258.

52 Nungezer, p. 367.

53 W. W. Greg, *Two Elizabethan Stage Abridgements* (Oxford 1923).

54 *Ibid.*, pp. 133–4.

55 Harold Jenkins, 'Playhouse Interpolations in the Folio Text of *Hamlet*', *SB* 13 (1960), 31–47.

56 J. H. Walter (ed.), *Henry V*, New Arden Shakespeare.

57 See below, p. 218.
58 Nungezer, p. 32.
   59 Andrew Gurr, 'Who Strutted and Bellowed?', *ShS* 16 (1963), 95–102.
60 Nungezer, p. 74.
61 Jenkins, 'Interpolations in the Folio *Hamlet*', p. 32.

4. THE PLAYHOUSES (pp. 115–171)

The discovery of the foundations of the Rose and the Globe in 1989 came at a time when scholars of theatre design were beginning to recognise the substantial differences that existed, not only between the halls and the amphitheatres but in the structure of individual amphitheatres. The Swan ceased to be the definitive statement about amphitheatre interiors and stages. Long after I. A. Shapiro's discrediting of the early Visscher and Hondius views of the Globe in 1948, John Orrell in *The Quest for Shakespeare's Globe* made a plausible case for the reliability of Hollar's 'Long View'. The case for the scaffoldings being made of polygonal timber frames was well established too, though it surprised everyone to find that the Rose had fourteen sides and the Globe twenty rather than the multiples of eight that make sounder sense in geometrical and surveying terms. Much attention has also been given to the hall playhouses, and Orrell's conjecture that the set of Inigo Jones plans discovered in 1969 was made for Beeston's Cockpit in 1616, though often questioned, has not been seriously shaken. Large sections of the playhouse structures remain conjectural, though, especially the precise designs of the stage areas at both the Globe and the Blackfriars.

 1 John Orrell, *The Human Stage: English Theatre Design 1567–1640*, gives a good short history of the evolution of playhouse design.
 2 See Chap. 2, n. 6.
 3 *JCS* VI, 183.
 4 See *ES* IV, 318.
 5 See O. L. Brownstein, 'A Record of London Inn Playhouses from *c.* 1665–1590', *SQ* 22 (1971), 17–24.
 6 See Herbert Berry, *The Boar's Head Playhouse* (Washington 1986), Chap. 2.
 7 See William Ingram, *A London Life in the Brazen Age* (Cambridge Mass. 1978).
 8 *JCS* VI, 140.
 9 *EES* II.2, 138.
10 *ES* II, 373.
11 *ES* II, 358.
12 *ES* II, 359.
13 The playhouses could not have been perfectly circular structures, unless they were built of brick and stone. Elizabethans did not have the technology to bend large timbers.
14 See Richard Southern, 'Colour in the Elizabethan Theatre', *TN* 6 (1951), 57–8.
15 *ES* II, 529–30, 545–6.
16 See archaeological diagrams, and John Orrell and Andrew Gurr, 'What the Rose can tell us'.

17 Henslowe's *Diary* lists in full the items he purchased for the reconstruction and their costs, and the wages he paid the workers. See pp. 9–13.
18 Peter Thomson, *Shakespeare's Theatre* (London 1985), p. 30.
19 A transcription of the accompanying text is in *TN* 10 (1965–6), 57–8.
20 D. F. Rowan, 'The "Swan" Revisited', *Research Opportunities in Renaissance Drama* 10 (1965), reckoned that the roofing was thatch. Richard Hosley, *Revels History*, p. 150, interprets de Witt's drawing as showing a tiled roof. John Orrell sees them as tiles, but curved pantiles, a Dutch shape not used in England for another fifty years.
21 T. J. King, *Shakespearean Staging*, p. 2.
22 Richard Hosley, 'The Gallery over the Stage in the Public Playhouse of Shakespeare's Time', *SQ* 8 (1957), 31.
23 The plot of *England's Joy* at the Swan promised 'beneath under the Stage set forth with strange fireworkes, divers blacke and damned Soules' (*ES* III, 501).
24 *ES* II, 436–9.
25 'A Reconstruction of the Fortune Playhouse', pp. 15–18.
26 *ES* II, 436.
27 *JCS* VI, 154.
28 Berry quotes them in the appendices of *The Boar's Head Playhouse*.
29 Everard Guilpin, *Skialetheia*, 1598, Satire 5.
30 *The Boar's Head*, p. 31.
31 *Ibid.*, Chap. 3.
32 *ES* II, 393. See also Herbert Berry (ed.) *The First Public Playhouse: The Theatre in Shoreditch 1576–1598* (Montreal 1979).
33 Evidence for Tudor prefabrication can be found in many buildings. For an examination of the technique at Tyrell's End Farm, Bedfordshire, see Nicholas Wood, 'Fifteenth-century Prefab', *Architectural Review* 144 (1968), 140–1.
34 The groundplans for the Rose and the Globe, uncovered by archaeology, only give two of the three dimensions of each building. But that is more tangible than the pictorial evidence available up to 1989.
35 The initial dig which found the Globe remains in October 1989 was only intended to find the exact location and the condition of the remains.
36 See 'What the Rose can tell us'; and Andrew Gurr, 'The Rose Repertory: What the Plays might tell us about the Stage', in Franklin J. Hildy (ed.) *New Issues in the Reconstruction of Shakespeare's Theatre* (New York 1991).
37 Everard Guilpin, *Skialetheia*, Epigram 53, 'Of Cornelius'.
38 Bernard Beckerman, *Shakespeare at the Globe*, p. 92; Richard Hosley, 'The Gallery over the Stage', 27; and T. J. King, *Shakespearean Staging*, p. 2.
39 Beckerman, *Shakespeare at the Globe*, p. 90; Hosley, 'Shakespeare's Use of a Gallery over the Stage', *ShS* 10 (1957), 78.
40 Hosley, *ibid.*, 78, 85.
41 I. A. Shapiro, 'Robert Fludd's Stage-Illustration', *ShStud* 2 (1966), 204.
42 See Richard Hosley, 'Was there a Music-Room in Shakespeare's Globe?', *ShS* 13 (1960), 113.
43 *ES* II, 47.

44 W. T. Jewkes, *Act Division in Elizabethan and Jacobean Plays, 1583–1616* (New York 1958), pp. 100–1.

45 Hosley, 'Was there a Music-Room?', 113–14.

46 *Ibid.*, 115–16.

47 *ES* III, 96.

48 Richard Hosley, 'The Discovery-Space in Shakespeare's Globe', *ShS* 12 (1959), 36.

49 See Beckerman, *Shakespeare at the Globe*, pp. 82–4.

50 See p. 226.

51 Beckerman, *Shakespeare at the Globe*, pp. 85–7; Hosley, 'The Discovery-Space', 36.

52 See John H. Astington, 'The Origins of the *Roxana* and *Messallina* Illustrations', *ShS* 43 (1991), 149–69.

53 G. F. Reynolds, *The Staging of Elizabethan Plays at the Red Bull Theater, 1605–1625* (London 1940), p. 188. Elsewhere (p. 109) Reynolds suggests that the third entry might have been through the hangings concealing the discovery-space.

54 *JCS* VI, 215.

55 King, *Shakespearean Staging*, p. 2.

56 See Lupold von Wedel, quoted in *ES* II, 455.

57 *ES* II, 466–8.

58 *ES* II, 434.

59 *ES* II, 477–81.

60 *ES* II, 503.

61 *ES* IV, 319–20.

62 *JCS* VI, 5.

63 *JCS* VI, 6.

64 *ES* II, 513.

65 John Orrell, 'The Private Theatre Auditorium', *TRI* 9 (1984), 79–94.

66 Herbert Berry, 'The Stage and Boxes at Blackfriars', *SP* 63 (1966), 163–86.

67 See the discussion of this prologue in *Playgoing in Shakespeare's London*, pp. 188–90.

68 *The Dutch Courtesan*, V.iii, and Henry Fitzgeoffery, *Observations at Blackfriars* (1617), G3r.

69 *JCS* VI, 7. The prices quoted are not supported by all the evidence, and there may well have been some variation in the standard charges through the forty or so years of the playhouse's existence. See Smith, *Shakespeare's Blackfriars Playhouse*, pp. 299–301. That stool-sitters reached the stage through the tiring-house and not by clambering over the stage rails is indicated by references in *The Gull's Hornbook* and Fitzgeoffery to gallants emerging through the hangings, and by the difficulty the Citizen's Wife in *The Knight of the Burning Pestle* has climbing onto the stage from the pit. There cannot have been any stairs from pit to stage.

70 *ES* III, 144.

71 John Orrell, *The Theatres of Inigo Jones and John Webb* (Cambridge 1985), Chap. 3.

72 D. F. Rowan, 'The English Playhouse: 1595–1630', *RD* n.s.4 (1971), 43.

73 *JCS* VI, 54.

74 See T. J. King, 'Staging of Plays at the Phoenix in Drury Lane, 1617–42', *TN* 19 (1965), 146–66.
75 Bentley, 'Salisbury Court Theater', pp. 129–49.
76 *JCS* vi, 269.
77 *EES* ii.2.52.
    78 Such information as exists is collected in *JCS* vi, 255–8.
79 *JCS* vi, 264; Per Palme, *Triumph of Peace* (London 1957), p. 143.
80 *JCS* vi, 266–7.
81 *JCS* vi, 285.
82 Reproduced in *JCS* vi, 276.
83 *JCS* vi, 272–3.

5. THE STAGING (pp. 172–211)

Performance criticism has gained force in recent years, and close attention has been paid to details of the original staging, with considerable profit. A collection of essays made in memory of Bernard Beckerman, *Shakespeare and the Sense of Performance*, edd. Marvin and Ruth Thompson (Newark 1989), describes the objectives of this kind of analysis of play-texts and includes some 'state of the art' essays. Glynne Wickham's third volume in *EES* has appeared, examining the staging from 1300 to 1576. But the general art of Shakespearean staging, and more particularly the history of developments and innovation in staging, is still largely unknown territory. A series of books about the original staging, including contributions on the period by Michael Hattaway, Peter Thomson and Keith Sturges, are of mixed quality. Richard Southern's *The Staging of Plays Before Shakespeare* (London 1973), T. W. Craik's *The Tudor Interlude* (Leicester 1958), Michael Hattaway's *Elizabethan Popular Theatre*, and Peter Thomson's *Shakespeare's Theatre* are sound studies of limited periods and specific kinds of venue, but give little sense of any historical change. These works, trying to draw pictures of the general practice in the earlier period, have not been matched by studies of the Stuart period. Most work has gone instead into particular features of staging, and even more to the staging of particular plays, Shakespeare's above all. Studies of staging at particular playhouses by Reynolds (the Red Bull), Beckerman (the Globe) and King (the Cockpit) have not been extended to other playhouses, although the Rose plays are now receiving considerable attention.

1 Kenneth R. Richards, 'Changeable Scenery for Plays on the Caroline Stage', *TN* 23 (1968), 20. See also John Freehafer, 'Perspective Scenery and the Caroline Playhouses', *TN* 27 (1973), 102–4, and T. J. King, *'Hannibal and Scipio* (1637): How "The Places Sometimes Changed"', *TN* 29 (1975), 20–2.
2 King, 'Staging of Plays at the Phoenix', p. 166.
3 Andrew Gurr, 'Hearers and Beholders in Shakespearean Drama', *Essays in Theatre* 3 (1984), 30–45.
4 A more detailed account of the trends in theatre fashion and changing tastes is in *Playgoing in Shakespeare's London*, Chap. 5.
5 Quoted in C. R. Baskervill, *The Elizabethan Jig* (Chicago 1929), p. 102.
6 *Ibid.*, p. 99.

7 *Attewell's Jig* is reprinted in Baskervill, *ibid*. pp. 450–64, and *Singing Simkin* on pp. 444–9.

8 *ES* IV, 340–1.

9 Baskervill, *The Elizabethan Jig*, p. 115.

10 *Turners dish of Lenten stuffe* (1613?), in H. E. Rollins (ed.), *A Pepysian Garland* (Cambridge 1922), p. 35.

11 John Scott Colley, 'Music in the Elizabethan Private Theatres', *Yearbook of English Studies* 4 (1974), 69.

12 *JCS* II, 354.

13 Beaumont's *Knight of the Burning Pestle* has inter-act performances of music with a boy dancing after Acts I and III, music (fiddlers) after Act II, and a burlesque Maylord speech after Act IV.

14 Warren D. Smith, 'New Light on Stage Directions in Shakespeare', *SP* 47 (1950), 173.

15 Rafe's Maylord speech in the last Interact of *The Knight of the Burning Pestle* has thirty-six lines of poulter's rhyme.

16 Jonson, VI, 15. See David Klein, 'Time Allotted for an Elizabethan Performance', *SQ* 18 (1967), 434–8.

17 *ES* III, 126.

18 See n.1. King refutes Freehafer's claim that Nabbes is referring to a physical 'scene'.

19 Hosley, 'Gallery over the Stage', p. 78; King, 'Staging of Plays at the Phoenix', p. 166.

20 For a history of the recognition of the open stage and the slow destruction of the 'inner stage' concept, see George F. Reynolds, 'The Return of the Open Stage', in *Essays on Shakespeare and Elizabethan Drama in Honor of Hardin Craig* (London and New York 1963), pp. 361–8.

21 Quoted in *ES* III, 40–1.

22 Inga-Stina Ewbank, '"The Eloquence of Masques": A Retrospective View of Masque Criticism', *RD* n.s.1 (1968), 322.

23 Quoted in John Orrell, *The Theatres of Inigo Jones and John Webb*, p. 157.

24 W. J. Lawrence, *Pre-Restoration Stage Studies* (Cambridge Mass. 1927), p. 221.

25 *Ibid.*, p. 204.

26 Noted by Reynolds, *The Staging of Elizabethan Plays*, p. 13.

27 Quoted in *ES* III, 72. For a detailed analysis of the Wagner Book, see Andrew Gurr, 'The Rose Repertory: What the Plays might tell us about the Stage', in *New Issues in the Reconstruction of Shakespeare's Theatre*, ed. Franklin J. Hildy (New York 1991), pp. 119–35.

28 John Melton, *Astrologaster* (1620), E4r.

29 *ES* II, 455.

30 *ES* III, 79, n. 3.

31 See *EES* II.1.206–44.

32 King, 'Staging of Plays at the Phoenix', p. 162.

33 See Werner Habicht, 'Tree Properties and Tree Scenes in Elizabethan Theater', *RD* n.s. 4 (1971), 91.

34 *EES* II.1.315.

35 Allardyce Nicoll, 'Passing over the Stage', *ShS* 12 (1959), 47–55. J. L. Simmons, 'Elizabethan Stage Practice and Marlowe's *Jew of Malta*', *RD* n.s. 4

(1971), 93–104, proposes that Barabbas is thrown off the stage in Act V, in a similarly spacious use of the stage environs. I do not find the suggestion plausible.

36 Inter-act IV. There are two other similar dumb-shows in the play.

37 Beckerman, *Shakespeare at the Globe*, p. 106.

38 A comment on the original staging of the opening scene, and the tricks it plays on its Blackfriars audience, is in Andrew Gurr, 'The Tempest's Tempest at Blackfriars', *ShS* 41 (1988), 91–102.

39 Lawrence, *Pre-Restoration Stage Studies*, p. 314; and Andrew Gurr, 'The "State" of Shakespeare's Audiences', in *Shakespeare and the Sense of Performance*, edd. Marvin and Ruth Thompson (Newark 1989), pp. 162–79.

40 *Ibid.*, p. 23. Lawrence cites the second of these passages in a text that provides only one man to carry the scaffold.

41 Magett's activities are regularly noted in *Henslowe's Diary*, pp. 37, 180 and elsewhere.

42 *Thomas Platter's Travels in England, 1599*, trans. Clare Williams (London 1959), p. 167.

43 M. Channing Linthicum, *Costume in the Drama of Shakespeare and his Contemporaries* (Oxford 1936), p. 14.

44 Quoted in Curt Breight, ' "Treason doth never prosper": *The Tempest* and the Discourse of Treason', *SQ* 41 (1990), 13.

45 Eldred D. Jones, 'The Physical Representation of African Characters on the English Stage during the 16th and 17th Centuries', *TN* 17 (1962), 18.

46 Ralph Winwood, *Memorials of Affairs of State*, quoted by Jones, *ibid.* p. 20.

47 Quoted by Richards, 'Changeable Scenery', p. 11.

48 *JCS* vi, 107–9; and see King, 'Staging of Plays at the Phoenix', pp. 147–8.

49 William E. Miller, '*Periaktoi* in the Old Blackfriars', *MLN* 74 (1959), 1–3; and '*Periaktoi*: Around Again', *SQ* 15 (1964), 61–5.

50 *JCS* vi, 283.

51 Quoted in Stephen Orgel and Roy Strong, *Inigo Jones: The Theatre of the Stuart Court* (2 vols., Berkeley 1973), I.281–4.

52 Richards, 'Changeable Scenery', p. 18.

53 Neil Carson, *A Companion to Henslowe's Diary*, p. 56, calculates that between 5 June 1594 and 28 July 1597, the first three years of the Admiral's Company after its separation from Strange's, the company took in fifty-four new plays, an average of seventeen per year.

54 Holinshed, *Chronicles* iii (1578), 760. See also p. 735: 'Where he went abroad, his eies whirled about, his bodie privilie fenced, his hand ever upon his dagger.'

6.   THE AUDIENCES (pp. 212–231)

Studies of Shakespearean audiences have fluctuated in ways that will be familiar to cultural materialists and most students of critical theory. The two most substantial American studies, Alfred Harbage's *Shakespeare's Audience* (New York 1941) and Ann Jennalie Cook's *The Privileged Playgoers of Shakespeare's London, 1576–1642* (Princeton 1981), are each characterised by what they took to be the typical playgoer. Harbage's was the industrious artisan, Cook's the wealthy and privileged. By their nature these studies narrowed the focus so that they lost any sense of historical change. The most recent study, Andrew Gurr's *Playgoing in Shakespeare's London* (Cambridge 1987), adopted the pragmatism that has been called the philosophical disease of the British, and looked at the diversity between different playhouse audiences and across the seventy-five years of commercial playhouses.

1 Quoted in Harbage, *Shakespeare's Audience*, p. 71.

2 *Ibid.*, pp. 22–34.

3 *Ibid.*, p. 30.

4 Irwin Smith, *Shakespeare's Globe Playhouse* (New York 1956), p. 65.

5 Quoted in Harbage, *Shakespeare's Audience*, p. 91.

   6 *Thomas Platter's Travels in England*, pp. 166–7.

7 W. A. Armstrong, 'The Audience of the Elizabethan Private Theatres', *RES* n.s. 10 (1959), 240–1.

8 Harbage, *Shakespeare's Audience*, p. 56. See also his table of comparative prices, p. 59.

9 *JCS* II, 673–81.

10 *Historia Histrionica* (1699), p. 5.

11 Epigrammes 17, 'In Cosmum', *The Poems of Sir John Davies*, ed. Robert Kruger (Oxford 1975), p. 136.

12 John Chamberlain to Dudley Carleton, 21 August 1624, quoted in R. C. Bald (ed.), *A Game at Chesse* (London 1929), pp. 163–4.

13 *C. S. P. Venetian 1617–19*, pp. 67–8.

14 John Earle, *Microcosmographie* (1628), H3r.

15 Verses by Thomas Craford. For a more detailed account of this quarrel, see Andrew Gurr, 'Singing through the Chatter: Ford and Contemporary Theatrical Fashion', in *John Ford: Critical Re-Visions*, ed. Michael Neill (Cambridge 1988), pp. 81–96.

16 *Ibid.*, and *Playgoing in Shakespeare's London*, pp. 170–7.

17 *Shakespeare's Audience*, p. 17.

18 S. P. Zitner, 'Gosson, Ovid, and the Elizabethan Audience', *SQ* 9 (1958), 206–8.

19 See David Klein, *The Elizabethan Dramatists as Critics* (London 1962), pp. 173–84.

20 *ES* I, 264–5.

21 Berry, 'Stage and Boxes', pp. 163–86.

22 *Shakespeare's Audience*, p. 93.

23 William Ingram, '"Neere the Playe House": The Swan Theater and Community Blight', *RD* n.s. 4 (1972), 53.

24 *JCS* VI, 147. For the idea that the play for which Moll sang her song was the play Dekker and Middleton wrote about her, see P. A. Mulholland, 'The Date of *The Roaring Girl*', *RES* n.s. 28 (1977), 18–31.

25 *Pleasant Notes upon Don Quixot* (1654), p. 272.

26 See W. J. Lawrence, *Those Nut-cracking Elizabethans* (London 1926), pp. 1–9.

27 *The Works of Michael Drayton*, ed. J. William Hebel (5 vols., Oxford 1934–41), II, p. 334.

28 Quoted by G. Tillotson, *Times Literary Supplement* (20 July 1933), 494.

29 See p. 102.
30 Jonson, vi, 283.
31 *The Gull's Hornbook* (1609), Chap. 6: 'How a Gallant should behave himself in a Play-house'.
32 Jonson, vi, 527–8.
33 An[thony] Sc[oloker], *Diaphantus* (1604), A2r.

Select Bibliography

Adams, J. Q. (ed.), *The Dramatic Records of Sir Henry Herbert*, New Haven, 1917.
Armstrong, W. A., *The Elizabethan Private Theatres. Facts and Problems*, London, 1958.
    ' "Canopy" in Elizabethan Theatrical Terminology', *NQ* n.s. 4 (1957), 433–4.
    'Shakespeare and the Acting of Edward Alleyn', *ShS* 7 (1954), 82–9.
Ashton Robert, *The City and the Court 1603–1643*, Cambridge, 1979.
Astington, John H., 'Inigo Jones and the Whitehall Cockpit', in *ET* 7, ed. G. R. Hibbard, Port Credit, 1980, 46–64.
    'The Whitehall Cockpit: the Building and the Theater', *ELR* 12 (1982), 301–18.
    'Gallow Scenes on the Elizabethan Stage', *TN* 37 (1983), 3–9.
    'Descent Machinery in the Playhouse', *Medieval and Renaissance Drama in England* II (1985), 119–34.
    'The Red Lion Playhouse: Two Notes', *SQ* 36 (1985), 456–7.
    'The Origins of the *Roxana* and *Messallina* Illustrations' *ShS* 43 (1991), 149–69.
Axton, Marie, *The Queen's Two Bodies*, London, 1977.
Bald, R. C., 'Will, My Lord of Leicester's Jesting Player', *NQ* 204 (1959), 112.
    'The Entrance to the Elizabethan Theatre', *SQ* 3 (1952), 17–20.
Baldwin, T. W., *Organisation and Personnel of the Shakespearean Company*, Princeton, 1927.
Barish, Jonas, *The Anti-Theatrical Prejudice*, Berkeley, 1981.
Barroll, J. Leeds, 'The Chronology of Shakespeare's Jacobean Plays and the Dating of *Antony and Cleopatra*', in *Essays on Shakespeare*, ed. Gordon Ross Brown, Philadelphia, 1965, 115–62.
Barroll, J. Leeds, Leggatt, Alexander, Hosley, Richard, and Kernan, Alvin, *The Revels History of Drama in English*, Vol. III, 1576–1613, London 1975.
Baskervill, C. R., *The Elizabethan Jig*, Chicago, 1929.
Bawcutt, N. W., 'New Revels Documents of Sir George Buc and Sir Henry Herbert, 1619–1662', *RES* 35 (1984), 316–31.
    'Craven Ord Transcripts of Sir Henry Herbert's Office-Book in the Folger Shakespeare Library', *ELR* 14 (1984), 83–94.
Beckerman, Bernard, *Shakespeare at the Globe 1599–1609*, New York, 1962.
    'Theatrical Plots and Elizabethan Stage Practice', in *Shakespeare and Dramatic Tradition. Essays in Honor of S. F. Johnson*, edd. W. R. Elton and William B. Long, Newark, 1989, pp. 109–24.
Beier, A. L., 'Social Problems in Elizabethan London', *Journal of Interdisciplinary History* 9 (1978), 205–18.

Bentley, G. E., *The Jacobean and Caroline Stage*, 7 vols., Oxford, 1941–68.
　'Shakespeare and the Blackfriars Theatre', *ShS* 1 (1948), 38–50.
　The Profession of Dramatist in Shakespeare's Time, 1590–1642, Princeton, 1971.
　'The Salisbury Court Theater and Its Boy Players', *HLQ* 40 (1977), 129–49
　The Profession of Player in Shakespeare's Time, 1590–1642, Princeton, 1984.
Bergeron, David M., *English Civic Pageantry, 1558–1642*, Columbia, 1971.
　(ed.), *Pageantry in the Shakespearean Theater*, Columbia, 1985.
Berry, Herbert, 'The Stage and Boxes at Blackfriars', *SP* 63 (1966), 163–86.
　(ed.), *The First Public Playhouse: The Theatre in Shoreditch 1576–1598*, Montreal, 1979.
　'The Player's Apprentice', *Essays in Theatre* 1 (1983), 73–80.
　The Boar's Head Playhouse, Washington, DC, 1986.
　Shakespeare's Playhouses, New York, 1987.
　'The First Public Playhouses, Especially the Red Lion', *SQ* 40 (1989), 133–45.
Bethell, S. L., *Shakespeare and the Popular Dramatic Tradition*, London, 1944.
Bevington, David, *From 'Mankind' to Marlowe. Growth and Structure in the Popular Drama of Tudor England*, Cambridge, Mass., 1962.
　Tudor Drama and Politics, Cambridge, Mass., 1968.
　Action is Eloquence: Shakespeare's Language of Gesture, Cambridge, Mass., 1984.
Billington, Sandra, *A Social History of the Fool*, Brighton, 1984.
Boswell, Jackson Campbell, 'Seven Actors in Search of a Biographer', *Medieval and Renaissance Drama in England* 2 (1985), 51–6.
Bradbrook, Muriel, *Elizabethan Stage Conditions*, Cambridge, 1932.
　Themes and Conventions in Elizabethan Tragedy, Cambridge, 1936.
　The Rise of the Common Player, London, 1962.
　The Living Monument, London, 1976.
　The Collected Papers, 4 vols., Brighton, 1982–9.
Briley, John, 'Of Stake and Stage', *ShS* 8 (1955), 106–8.
　'Edward Alleyn and Henslowe's Will', *SQ* 9 (1958), 321–30.
Bristol, Michael D., *Carnival and Theater: Plebeian Culture and the Structure of Authority in Renaissance England*, New York, 1985.
Bromberg, Murray, 'Theatrical Wagers: A Sidelight on the Elizabethan Drama', *NQ* 196 (1951), 533–5.
Brownstein, O. L., 'A Record of London Inn Playhouses from *c.* 1565–1590', *SQ* 22 (1971), 17–24.
　'Why didn't Burbage lease the Beargarden? A Conjecture in Comparative Architecture', in *The First Public Playhouse: The Theatre in Shoreditch 1576–1598*, ed. Herbert Berry, 1979, 81-96.
Burkhart, Robert E., *Shakespeare's Bad Quartos: Deliberate Abridgments Designed for Performance by a Reduced Cast*, The Hague, 1975.
Butler, Martin, *Theatre and Crisis 1632–1642*, Cambridge, 1984.
Campbell, Lily B., *Scenes and Machines on the English Stage During the Renaissance*, Cambridge, 1923.
Carson, Neil, 'The Staircases of the Frame: New Light on the Structure of the Globe', *ShS* 29 (1976), 127–31.
　A Companion to Henslowe's Diary, Cambridge, 1988.

Cerasano, S. P., 'Revising Philip Henslowe's Biography', *NQ* n.s. 32 (1985), 66–72.

'New Renaissance Players' Wills', *MP* 82 (1985), 299–304.

'The "Business" of Shareholding, the Fortune Playhouse, and Francis Grace's Will', *Medieval and Renaissance Drama in England* 2 (1985), 231–52.

'Edward Alleyn's Early Years: His Life and Family', *NQ* n.s. 34 (1987), 237–43.

Chambers, E. K., *The Elizabethan Stage*, 4 vols., Oxford, 1923.

Clare, Janet, *'Art made Tongue-tied by Authority': Elizabethan and Jacobean Censorship*, Manchester, 1990.

Cole, Maja Jansson, 'A New Account of the Burning of the Globe', *SQ* 32 (1981), 352.

Colley, John Scott, 'Music in the Elizabethan Private Theatres', *Yearbook of English Studies* 4 (1974), 62–9.

Cook, Ann Jennalie, *The Privileged Playgoers of Shakespeare's London, 1576–1642*, Princeton, 1981.

Cope, Jackson J., 'Tourneur's *Atheist's Tragedy* and the Jig of "Singing Simkin"', *MLN* 70 (1955), 571–3.

Craik, T. W., *The Tudor Interlude*, Leicester, 1958.

'The Reconstruction of Stage Action from Early Dramatic Texts', *ET* 5, ed. G. R. Hibbard, Don Mills, 1975, 76–91.

Darlington, Ida, and Howgego, James L., *Printed Maps of London circa 1553–1850*, London, 1964.

Dessen, Alan C., *Elizabethan Drama and the Viewer's Eye*, Chapel Hill, 1977.

Elizabethan Stage Conventions and Modern Interpreters, Cambridge, 1984.

Donawerth, Jane L., 'Shakespeare and Acting Theory in the English Renaissance', in *Shakespeare and the Arts*, edd. Cecile Williamson Cary and Henry S. Limouze, Dayton, Ohio, 1983, pp. 165–78.

Drew-Bear, Annette, 'Face-Painting in Renaissance Tragedy', *RD* n.s. 12 (1981), 71–93.

Dutton Richard, '*Hamlet, An Apology for Actors*, and The sign of the Globe', *ShS* 41 (1981), 35–43.

Eccles, Mark, 'Martin Peerson and the Blackfriars', *ShS* 11 (1958), 100–6.

'Brief Lives: Tudor and Stuart Authors', *SP* 79 (1982), special numbers.

'Elizabethan Actors I: A–D', *NQ* 236 (1991), 38–49.

Edmond, Mary, 'Pembroke's Men', *RES* n.s. 25 (1974), 129–36.

Rare Sir William Davenant, Manchester, 1987.

Evans, G. Blakemore, 'An Elizabethan Theatrical Stocklist', Harvard Library Bulletin 21 (1973), pp. 254–70.

Ewbank, Inga-Stina, '"The Eloquence of Masques": A Retrospective View of Masque Criticism', *RD* n.s. 1 (1968), 307–27.

'"What words, what looks, what wonders?": Language and Spectacle in the Theatre of George Peele', *ET* 5, ed. G. R. Hibbard, Don Mills, 1975, 124–54.

Feather, John, 'Robert Armin and the Chamberlain's Men', *NQ* 19 (1972), 448–50.

Felver, C. S., *Robert Armin, Shakespeare's Fool*, Kent State University Bulletin Research Series 5, Kent, 1961.

Finkelpearl, Philip J., ' "The Comedians' Liberty": Censorship of the Jacobean Stage Reconsidered', *ELR* 16 (1986), 138–58.

Finlay, Roger, *Population and Metropolis: The Demography of London 1580–1650*, Cambridge, 1982.

Foakes, R. A., 'The Player's Passion: Some Notes on Elizabethan Psychology and Acting', *Essays and Studies* n.s. 7 (1954), 62–77.

    and Rickert, R. T., (eds.), *Henslowe's Diary*, Cambridge, 1961.

    (ed.) *The Henslowe Papers*, 2 vols., London, 1978.

    Illustrations of the London Stage, 1580–1642, London, 1985.

Fotheringham, Richard, 'The Doubling of Roles on the Jacobean Stage', *TR* 10 (1985), 18–32.

Freehafer, John, 'Perspective Scenery and the Caroline Playhouses', *TN* 27 (1973), 102–4.

Gair, W. Reavley, *The Children of Paul's: The Story of a Theatre Company, 1553–1608*, Cambridge, 1982.

Gaw, Allison, 'John Sincklo as one of Shakespeare's Actors', *Anglia* 49 (1925), 289–303.

George, David, 'Another Elizabethan Stage: Further Comment', *TN* 35 (1981) 10–12.

    'Shakespeare and Pembroke's Men', *SQ* 32 (1981), 305–23.

Gerritsen, Johan, 'De Witt, Van Buchell, The Swan and the Globe: Some Notes', in *Essays in Honour of Kristian Smidt*, edd. Peter Bilton and others, Oslo, 1986, 29–46.

Gibson, Colin A., 'Another Shot in the War of the Theatres (1630)', *NQ* n.s. 34 (1987), 308–9.

Gleason, John B., 'The Dutch Humanist Origins of the De Witt Drawing of the Swan Theatre', *SQ* 32 (1981), 324–8.

Goldsmith, R. B., *Wise Fools in Shakespeare*, Liverpool, 1958.

Graves, R. B., 'The Duchess of Malfi at the Globe and Blackfriars', *RD* n.s. 9 (1978), 193–209.

    'Elizabethan Lighting Effects and the Conventions of Indoor and Outdoor Theatrical Illumination', *RD* n.s. 12 (1981), 51–69.

    'Daylight in the Elizabethan Private Theatres', *SQ* 33 (1982), 80–92.

Graves, T. S., 'Some Aspects of Extemporall Acting', *SP* 19 (1922), 317–27.

Gray, H. D., 'The Roles of William Kemp', *MLR* 25 (1930), 261–73.

    'The Chamberlain's Men and the "Poetaster" ', *MLR* 42 (1947), 173–9.

Greg, W. W., (ed.), *The Henslowe Papers*, London, 1907.

    Two Elizabethan Stage Abridgements, Oxford, 1923.

    Dramatic Documents from the Elizabethan Playhouses, 2 vols., Oxford, 1931.

Grivelet, Michel, 'Note sur Thomas Heywood et le théâtre sous Charles 1er', *Études Anglaises* 7 (1954), 101–6.

Gurr, Andrew, 'Who Strutted and Bellowed?', *ShS* 16 (1963), 95–102.

    'Elizabethan Action', *SP* 63 (1966), 144–56.

    Playgoing in Shakespeare's London, Cambridge, 1987.

    'Money or Audiences: The Impact of Shakespeare's Globe', *TN* 42 (1988), 3–14.

    'A First Doorway into the Globe', *SQ* 41 (1990), 97–100.

'The "State" of Shakespeare's Audiences', in *Shakespeare and the Sense of Performance*, edd. Marvin and Ruth Thompson, Newark, 1989, pp. 162–80.

'The Rose Repertory: What the Plays can tell us about the Stage', in *New Issues in the Reconstruction of Shakespeare's Theatre*, ed. Franklin J. Hildy, New York, 1991, pp. 119–35.

Haaker, Ann, 'The Plague, the Theater and the Poet', *RD* n.s. 1 (1968), 283–306.

Habicht, Werner, 'Tree Properties and Tree Scenes in Elizabethan Theater', *RD* n.s. 4 (1971), 69–92.

Harbage, Alfred B., *Annals of English Drama, 975–1700*, Philadelphia, 1940; revised by S. Schoenbaum, 1964, 1970; third edition, ed. Sylvia S. Wagenheim, New York, 1989.

　　Shakespeare's Audience, New York, 1941.

　　Shakespeare and the Rival Traditions, New York, 1952.

Hart, A., 'The Length of Elizabethan and Jacobean Plays', *RES* 8 (1932), 139–54.

　　'The Time Allotted for Representation of Elizabethan and Jacobean Plays', *RES* 8 (1932), 395–413.

Hattaway, Michael, *Elizabethan Popular Theatre*, London, 1982.

Hawkins, Harriet Bloker, '"All the World's a Stage": Some Illustrations of the *Theatrum Mundi*', *SQ* 17 (1966), pp. 174–8.

Heinemann, Margot, *Puritanism and Theatre*, Cambridge, 1980.

Hildy, Franklin J. (ed.) *New Issues in the Reconstruction of Shakespeare's Theatre*, New York, 1991.

Hillebrand, H. N., *The Child Actors: A Chapter in Elizabethan Stage History*, Urbana, 1926.

Hodges, C. Walter, *The Globe Restored*, London, 1953; 2nd edn 1968.

　　Shakespeare's Second Globe: The Missing Monument, London, 1973.

　　and Schoenbaum, S., and Leone, Leonard (eds.), *The Third Globe: Symposium for the Reconstruction of the Globe Playhouse*, Detroit, 1981.

Holmes, Martin, 'An Unrecorded Portrait of Edward Alleyn', *TN* 5 (1950), 11–13.

Holzknecht, K. J., *The Backgrounds of Shakespeare's Plays*, New York, 1950.

Homan, Sidney (ed.), *Shakespeare's 'More than Words Can Witness': Essays on Visual and Nonverbal Enactment in the Plays*, Lewisburg, 1980.

Hosking, G. L., *The Life and Times of Edward Alleyn*, London, 1952.

Hosley, Richard, 'The Gallery over the Stage in the Public Playhouse of Shakespeare's Time', *SQ* 8 (1957), 16–31.

　　'Shakespeare's Use of a Gallery over the Stage', *ShS* 10 (1957), 77–89.

　　'The Discovery-Space in Shakespeare's Globe', *ShS* 12 (1959), 35–46.

　　'Was there a Music-Room in Shakespeare's Globe?', *ShS* 13 (1960), 113–23.

　　'Elizabethan Theatres and Audiences', *RORD* 10 (1967), 9–15.

　　'A Reconstruction of the Second Blackfriars', *ET* [1], ed. David Galloway, Toronto, 1969, 74–88.

　　'Three Renaissance English Indoor Playhouses', *ELR* 3 (1973), 166–82.

　　'The Second Globe', *TN* 29 (1975), 140–5.

　　'The Playhouses', in *Revels History* III, 122–226.

　　'A Reconstruction of the Fortune Playhouse: Part I', *ET* 6, ed. G. R. Hibbard, Don Mills, 1978, 1–20.

'A Reconstruction of the Fortune Playhouse: Part II', *ET* 7, ed. G. R. Hibbard, Don Mills, 1980, 1–20.

Howard, Jean E., *Shakespeare's Art of Orchestration*, Urbana, 1984.

Howard, Skiles, 'A Re-Examination of Baldwin's Theory of Acting Lines', *ThS* 26 (1985), 1–20.

Howgego, James L., *Printed Maps of London circa 1553–1850*, Folkestone, 1978.

Hunter, G. K., 'Flatcaps and Bluecoats: Visual Signals on the Elizabethan Stage', *Essays and Studies* 33 (1980), 16–47.

Ichikawa, Mariko, "A Note on Shakespeare's Stage Direction', *ShStud* 22 (1983), 31–56.

Ingram, William, 'The Theatre at Newington Butts', *SQ* 21 (1970), 385–98.

'The Closing of the Theatres in 1597: A Dissenting View', *MP* 69 (1971–2), 105–15.

A London Life in the Brazen Age, Cambridge, Mass., 1978.

'Henry Laneman', *TN* 36 (1982), 118–19.

'The Playhouse as an Investment, 1607–1614; Thomas Woodford and Whitefriars', *Medieval and Renaissance Drama in England* 2 (1985), 209–30.

'Robert Keysar, Playhouse Speculator', *SQ* 37 (1986), 476–85.

'The Early Career of James Burbage', in *ET* 10, ed. C. E. McGee, Port Credit, 1988, 18–36.

Jackson, MacDonald P., '*Edward III*, Shakespeare, and Pembroke's Men', *NQ* n.s. 41 (1965), 329–31.

Jensen, Ejner J., 'A New Allusion to the Sign of the Globe Theater', *SQ* 21 (1970), 95–7.

Jewkes, W. T., *Act Division in Elizabethan and Jacobean Plays, 1583–1616*, New York, 1958.

Johnston, Alexandra, and others (eds.), *Records of Early English Drama*, Toronto, 1978-, (in progress).

Jones, Eldred Durosimi, *Othello's Countrymen*, London, 1965.

Joseph, B. L., *Elizabethan Acting*, London, 1951; rev. edn 1964.

Kennedy, Edward D., 'James I and Chapman's Byron Plays', *JEGP* 64 (1965), 677–90.

King, T. J., 'Staging of Plays at the Phoenix in Drury Lane, 1617–42', *TN* 19 (1965), 146–66.

Shakespearean Staging 1599–1642, Cambridge, Mass., 1971.

'Hannibal and Scipio (1637): How "The Places Sometimes Changed"', *TN* 29 (1975), 20–2.

'The King's Men on Stage: Actors and Their Parts, 1611–32', *ET* 9, ed. George Hibbard, Port Credit, 1986, 21–40.

Klein, David, 'Did Shakespeare Produce his own Plays?' *MLR* 57 (1962), 556–60.

'Time Allotted for an Elizabethan Performance', *SQ* 18 (1967), 434–8.

Lancaster, Marjorie S., 'Middleton's Use of the Upper Stage in *Women Beware Women*', *Tulane Studies in English* 22 (1977), 69–85.

Lavin, J. A., 'Shakespeare and the Second Blackfriars', *ET* 3, ed. David Galloway, Toronto, 1973, 66–81.

Lawrence, W. J., 'John Kirke, the Caroline Actor-Dramatist', *SP* 21 (1924), 586–93.

Pre-Restoration Stage Studies, Cambridge, Mass., 1927.

   Speeding Up Shakespeare, London, 1937.
Leech, Clifford, *Shakespeare's Tragedies, and other Studies in Seventeenth-Century Drama*, London, 1950.
   and Craik, T. W., (eds.) *The Revels History of Drama in English*, 8 vols., London, 1975–81; Vol. 2, 1500–1576; Vol. 3, 1576–1613; Vol. 4, 1613–1660.
Levin, Richard, 'Women in the Renaissance Theatre Audience', *SQ* 40 (1989), 165–74.
Linthicum, M. Channing, *Costume in the Drama of Shakespeare and his Contemporaries*, Oxford, 1936.
Leongard, Janet, 'An Elizabethan Lawsuit: John Brayne, his Carpenter, and the Building of the Red Lion Theatre', *SQ* 35 (1984), 298–310.
Long, John H., *Shakespeare's Use of Music: A Study . . . of Seven Comedies*, Miami, 1955.
   Shakespeare's Use of Music: The Histories and Tragedies, Miami, 1972.
   'The Music in Percy's Play Manuscripts', *Renaissance Papers* 1980, 39–44.
Long, William B., '"A Bed / for Woodstock": A Warning for the Unwary', *Medieval and Renaissance Drama in England* 2 (1985), 91–118.
   '*John a Kent and John a Cumber*. An Elizabethan Playbook and Its Implications', in *Shakespeare and Dramatic Tradition. Essays in Honor of S. F. Johnson*, edd. W. R. Elton and William B. Long, Newark, 1989, pp. 125–43.
McManaway, James G., 'A New Shakespeare Document', *SQ* 2 (1951), 119–22.
McMillin, Scott, 'Casting for Pembroke's Men: The *Henry VI* Quartos and *The Taming of A Shrew*', *SQ* 23 (1972), 141–59.
   'Simon Jewell and the Queen's Men', *RES* 27 (1976), 174–7.
   The Elizabethan Theatre and the Book of Sir Thomas More, Ithaca, New York, 1987.
McPherson, David, 'Three Charges against Sixteenth and Seventeenth Century Playwrights: Libel, Bawdy, and Blasphemy', *Medieval and Renaissance Drama in England* 2 (1985), 269–82.
Marker, Lise–Lone, 'Nature and Decorum in the Theory of Elizabethan Acting', *ET* 2, ed. David Galloway, Toronto, 1970, 87–107.
Mehl, Dieter, *The Elizabethan Dumb Show*, London, 1965.
Merchant, W. Moelwyn, 'Classical Costume in Shakespearean Productions', *ShS* 10 (1957), 71–6.
Metz, G. Harold, 'The Early Staging of *Titus Andronicus*', *ShStud* 14 (1981), 99–109.
Miller, William E., '*Periaktoi* in the Old Blackfriars', *MLN* 74 (1959), 1–3.
   '*Periaktoi*: Around Again', *SQ* 15 (1964), 61–5.
Mossberger, Robert E., *Swordplay on the Elizabethan and Jacobean Stage*, Salzburg, 1974.
Mowat, Barbara A., '"The Getting up of the Spectacle": The Role of the Visual on the Elizabethan Stage, 1576–1600', *ET* 9, ed. George Hibbard, Toronto, 1983, 60–76.
Murray, John Tucker, *English Dramatic Companies 1558–1642*, 2 vols., London, 1910.
Nagler, A. M., *Shakespeare's Stage*, New Haven, 1958.
Neill, Michael, '"Wits most accomplished Senate": The Audience of the Caroline Private Theaters', *SEL* 18 (1978), 341–60.

Nethercot, Arthur H., *Sir William Davenant*, New York, 1938; rev. edn 1967.

Newton, Stella Mary, *Renaissance Theatre Costume and the Sense of the Historic Past*, London, 1975.

Nicoll, Allardyce, *Stuart Masques and the Renaissance Stage*, London, 1938.

'A Note on the Swan Theatre Drawing', *ShS* 1 (1948), 23–4.

'Passing over the Stage', *ShS* 12 (1959), 47–55.

Nosworthy, J. M., '*Macbeth* at the Globe', *Library* 2 (1947), 108–18.

'A Note on John Heminge', *Library* 3 (1948), 287–8.

Nungezer, E., *A Dictionary of Actors and Other Persons Associated with the Public Representation of Plays in England before 1642*, New Haven, 1929.

Orgel, Stephen, and Strong, Roy, *Inigo Jones: The Theatre of the Stuart Court*, Berkeley, 1973.

Orrell, John, *The Quest for Shakespeare's Globe*, Cambridge, 1982.

'The Private Theatre Auditorium', *TRI* 9 (1984), 79–94.

'Sunlight at the Globe', *TN* 38 (1984), 69–76.

The Theatres of Inigo Jones and John Webb, Cambridge, 1985.

The Human Stage: English Theatre Design, 1567–1640, Cambridge, 1988.

(with Andrew Gurr) 'What the Rose can tell us', *Antiquity* 63 (1989), 421–9.

Palme, Per, *Triumph of Peace*, London, 1957.

Parry, Graham, 'A New View of Bankside', *ShS* 31 (1978), 139–40.

Patterson, Annabel, '"The Very Age and Body of the Time His Form and Pressure": Rehistoricising Shakespeare's Theater', *New Literary History* 20 (1988), 83–104.

Peat, Derek, 'Looking Back to Front: the View from the Lords' Room', in *Shakespeare and the Sense of Performance*, edd. Marvin and Ruth Thompson, Newark, 1989, pp. 180–94.

Pilkinton, Mark C., 'The Playhouse in Wine Street, Bristol', *TN* 37 (1983), 14–21.

Pinciss, G. M., 'The Queen's Men, 1583–1592', *ThS* 11 (1970), 50–65.

'Thomas Creede and the Repertory of the Queen's Men', *MP* 67 (1970), 321–30.

'Shakespeare, Her Majesty's Players, and Pembroke's Men', *ShS* 27 (1974), 129–36.

Rappaport, Steve, *Worlds within Worlds: Structures of Life in Sixteenth-Century London*, Cambridge, 1989.

Reynolds, George F., *The Staging of Elizabethan Plays at the Red Bull Theater, 1605–1625*, London, 1940.

'Was there a "Tarras" in Shakespeare's Globe?' *ShS* 4 (1951), 97–100.

'*Hamlet* at the Globe', *ShS* 9 (1956), 49–53.

Richards, Kenneth R., 'Changeable Scenery for Plays on the Caroline Stage', *TN* 23 (1968), 7–20.

Riewald, J. G., 'Some Late Elizabethan and Early Stuart Actors and Musicians', *English Studies* 40 (1959), 33–41.

Righter, Anne, *Shakespeare and the Idea of the Play*, London, 1962.

Ringler, William A., jr, 'The Number of Actors in Shakespeare's Early Plays', in *The Seventeenth-Century Stage*, ed. G. E. Bentley, Toronto, 1968.

Roach, Joseph R., *The Player's Passion, Studies in the Science of Acting*, Newark, 1985.

Rosenberg, Marvin, 'Elizabethan Actors, Men or Marionettes', *PMLA* 69 (1954), 915–27.

Rowan, D. F., 'The Cockpit-in-Court', *ET* [1], ed. David Galloway, Toronto, 1969, 89–102.

'A Neglected Jones/Webb Theatre Project, Part II: A Theatrical Missing Link', *ET* 2, ed. David Galloway, Toronto, 1970, 60–73.

'The Staging of *the Spanish Tragedy*', *ET* 5, ed. G. R. Hibbard, Don Mills, 1976, 112–23.

Rutter, Carol Chillington, (ed.), *Documents of the Rose Playhouse*, Manchester, 1984.

Salomon, Brownell, 'Visual and Aural Signs in the Performed English Renaissance Play', *RD* n.s. 5 (1972), 143–69.

Saunders, J. W., 'Vaulting the Rails', *ShS* 7 (1954), 69–81.

'Staging at the Globe, 1599–1613', *SQ* 11 (1960), 401–25.

Schanzer, Ernest, 'Hercules and his Load', *RES* n.s. 19 (1968), 51–3.

Schrick, Willem, *Foreign Envoys and Travelling Players in the Age of Shakespeare and Jonson*, Wetteren, 1986.

Schoenbaum, Samuel, *William Shakespeare. A Compact Documentary Life*, Oxford, 1977.

Scouten, Arthur H., 'The Anti-Evolutionary Development of the London Theatres', in *British Theatre and the Other Arts*, ed. S. S. Kenny, Washington, DC, 1984, 171–81.

Seltzer, Daniel, 'Elizabethan Acting in *Othello*', *SQ* 10 (1959), 201–10.

'The Staging of the Last Plays', in *Later Shakespeare*, edd. J. R. Brown and Bernard Harris, London, 1966, 127–65.

Shapiro, I. A., 'The Bankside Theatres: Early Engravings', *ShS* 1 (1948), 25–37.

'An Original Drawing of the Globe Theatre', *ShS* 2 (1949), 21–3.

Shapiro, Michael, *Children of the Revels. The Boy Companies of Shakespeare's Time and their Plays*, New York, 1977.

'Annotated Bibliography on Original Staging in Elizabethan Plays', *RORD* 24 (1981), 23–49.

Shirley, Frances Ann, *Shakespeare's Use of Off-Stage Sounds*, Lincoln, Nebraska, 1963.

Simmons, J. L., 'Elizabethan Stage Practice and Marlowe's *The Jew of Malta*', *RD* n.s. 4 (1971), 93–104.

Sisson, C. J., 'Notes on Early Stuart Stage History', *MLR* 37 (1942), 25–36.

'The Red Bull Company and the Importunate Widow', *ShS* 7 (1954), 57–68.

Smith, Hal H., 'Some Principles of Elizabethan Stage Costume', *Journal of the Warburg and Courtauld Institutes* 25 (1962), 240–57.

Smith, Irwin, 'Theatre into Globe', *SQ* 3 (1952), 113–20.

'"Gates" on Shakespeare's Stage', *SQ* 7 (1956), 159–76.

Shakespeare's Blackfriars Playhouse, New York, 1964.

'Their Exits and Reentrances', *SQ* 18 (1967), 7–16.

Smith, Warren D., 'Evidence of Scaffolding on Shakespeare's Stage', *RES* n.s. 2 (1951), 22–9.

Shakespeare's Playhouse Practice: A Handbook, Hanover, New Hampshire, 1975.

Southern, Richard, 'Colour in the Elizabethan Theatre', *TN* 6 (1951), 57–8.

Changeable Scenery: Its Origin and Development in the British Theatre, London, 1952.

The Staging of Plays Before Shakespeare, London, 1973.

Sternfeld, F. W., *Music in Shakespearean Tragedy*, London, 1963.

Stevens, David, 'The Staging of Plays at the Salisbury Court Theatre, 1630–1642', *Theatre Journal* 31 (1979), 511–25.

English Renaissance Theatre History: A Reference Guide, Boston, 1982.

Streett, J. B., 'The Durability of Boy Actors', *NQ* 218 (1973), 461–5.

Streitberger, W. R., (ed.) *Jacobean and Caroline Revels Accounts, 1603–1642*, Malone Society Collections XIII, Oxford, 1986.

Teague, Frances, 'Ben Jonson's Stagecraft in *Epicoene*', *RD* n.s. 9 (1978), 175–92.

Thompson, Marvin and Ruth (edd.) *Shakespeare and the Sense of Performance*, Newark, 1989.

Thomson, Peter, *Shakespeare's Theatre*, London, 1985.

Venezky, Alice, *Pageantry on the Shakespearean Stage*, New York, 1951.

Weimann, Robert, *Shakespeare and the Popular Tradition in the Theater*, ed. and trans. Robert Schwartz, London, 1978.

Welsford, Enid, *The Fool*, London, 1935.

Wentersdorf, Karl P., 'The Origin and Personnel of the Pembroke Company', *TRI* 5 (1979), 45–68.

White, Beatrice, *An Index to 'The Elizabethan Stage' and 'William Shakespeare: A Study of the Facts and Problems' by Sir Edmund Chambers*, Oxford, 1934.

Wickham, Glynne, *Early English Stages, 1300–1660*, 4 vols., London, 1959–.

Shakespeare's Dramatic Heritage, London, 1969.

'"Heavens", Machinery, and Pillars in the Theatre and Other Early Playhouses', in *The First Public Playhouse: The Theatre in Shoreditch 1576–1598*, ed. Herbert Berry, Montreal, 1979, 1–15.

Wiles, David, *Shakespeare's Clown. Actor and Text in the Elizabethan Playhouse*, Cambridge, 1987.

Wilson, F. P., *Elizabethan and Jacobean*, Oxford, 1948.

'The Elizabethan Theatre', *Neophilologus* 39 (1955), 40–58.

Wilson, J. Dover, '*Titus Andronicus* on the Stage in 1595', *ShS* 1 (1948), 17–22.

Wren, Robert M., 'Salisbury and the Blackfriars Theatre', *TN* 23 (1968), 103–9.

Wright, W. S., 'Edward Alleyn, Actor and Benefactor, 1566–1626', *TN* 20 (1965), 155–60.

Wrightson, Keith, *English Society 1580–1680*, London, 1981.

Zitner, Sheldon P., 'Gosson, Ovid, and the Elizabethan Audience'. *SQ* 9 (1958), 206–8.

Index

𝓎𝓈𝓎